A TEXT BOOK OF

PHARMACEUTICS

FOR

FIRST YEAR BACHELOR OF PHARMACY

RAJIV GANDHI UNIVERSITY OF HEALTH SCIENCES, KARNATAKA

By

Dr. R. S. GAUD
M. Pharm. Ph. D., F.I.C. F. I. P. A.
Ex- Advisor- I
AICTE , **NEW DELHI**
Dean of Pharma Sciences,
NMIMS University Vlle Parle (west),
MUMBAI - 400 056.

Dr. P. V. KASTURE
M. Pharm. Ph. D.
Professor of Pharmaceutics,
D. Y. Patil College of Pharmacy,
Pimpri - **PUNE - 411 018.**

Dr. S. G. GATTANI
M. Pharm. Ph. D.
Professor and Head of Pharmaceutics-Dept.,
R. C. Patel College of Pharmacy,
SHIRPUR - 425 405.

S. B. GOKHALE
M. Pharm. A.I.C.
Principal,
SVKM's College of Diploma in Pharmacy,
V. M. Road, Vile Parle (W), **MUMBAI - 400 056.**

NIRALI PRAKASHAN

PHARMACEUTICS (Rajiv Gandhi University of Health Sciences, Karnataka)

ISBN NO. : 978-81-85790-56-5
Fourth Edition : June 2010
© : Authors

The test of this publication, or any part thereof, should not be reproduced or transmitted in any form or stored in any computer storage system or device for distribution including photocopy, recording, taping or information retrieved system or reproduced on any disc, tape, perforated media or other information storage device etc. Without the written permission of Author wit6h whom the rights are reserved. Breach of this condition is liable for legal action.

Every effort has been made to avoid errors or omissions in this publication. In spite of this, errors may creep in. Any mistake, error or discrepancy noted may be brought to out notice which shall be taken care of in the next edition. It is notified that neither the publisher nor the author or seller will be responsible for any damage or loss of action to any one, of any kind, in any manner, therefrom.

Published By :
PRAGATI BOOKS PVT. LTD.
Abhyudaya Pragati, 1312, Shivaji Nagar,
Off J.M. Road, Bank of Baroda Lane,
PUNE – 411005
Tel - (020) 25512336/37/39, Fax - (020) 25511379

Printed By :
Repro Knowledgecast Limited,
Thane

DISTRIBUTION CENTRES

PUNE
Nirali Prakashan
119, Budhwar Peth, Jogeshwari Mandir Lane
Pune 411002, Maharashtra
Tel : (020) 2445 2044, 66022708 Fax : (020) 2445 1538
Email : niralipune@pragationline.com

MUMBAI
Nirali Prakashan
385, S.V.P. Road, Rasdhara Co-op. Hsg. Society Ltd.,
Girgaum, Mumbai 400004, Maharashtra
Tel : (022) 2385 6339 / 2386 9976, Fax : (022) 2386 9976
Email : niralimumbai@pragationline.com

DISTRIBUTION BRANCHES

NAGPUR
Pratibha Book Distributors
Above Maratha Mandir, Shop No. 3, First Floor,
Rani Jhanshi Square, Sitabuldi, Nagpur 440012,
Maharashtra, Tel : (0712) 254 7129, Mob : 98222 01952

NASIK
Nirali Prakashan
741, Gaydhani Sankul, First Floor, Raviwar Karanja,
Nasik 422001, Maharashtra
Tel : (0253) 250 6438, Mob : 94222 53538

HYDERABAD
Nirali Book House
22, Shyam Enclave, 4-5-947, Badi Chowdi
Hyderabad 500095, Andhra Pradesh
Tel : (040) 6554 5313, Mob : 94400 30608
Email : niralibooks@yahoo.com

JALGAON
Nirali Prakashan
34, V. V. Golani Market, Navi Peth, Jalgaon 425001,
Maharashtra, Tel : (0257) 222 0395
Mob : 94234 91860

KOLHAPUR
Nirali Prakashan
Ganesh Krupa, 2430-A, Gandhi Maidan Road,
Near Gulmohar Book Depot, Shivaji Peth,
Kolhapur 416 012, Maharashtra. Mob : 9860183678

BANGALORE
Pragati Book House
House No. 1, Sanjeevappa Lane, Avenue Road Cross,
Opp. Rice Church, Bangalore – 560002.
Tel : (080) 64513344, 64513355,
Mob : 9880582331, 9845021552
Email:bharatsavla@yahoo.com

CHENNAI
Pragati Books
9/1, Montieth Road, Behind Taas Mahal, Egmore, Chennai 600008 Tamil Nadu
Tel : (044) 6518 3535, Mob : 94440 01782 / 98450 21552 / 98805 82331
Email : bharatsavla@yahoo.com

RETAIL OUTLETS

PUNE

Pragati Book Centre
157, Budhwar Peth, Opp. Ratan Talkies,
Pune 411002, Maharashtra
Tel : (020) 2445 8887 / 6602 2707, Fax : (020) 2445 8887

Pragati Book Centre
152, Budhwar Peth, Pune 411002, Maharashtra
Tel : (020) 2445 2254 / 6609 2463

Pragati Book Centre
676/B, Budhwar Peth, Opp. Jogeshwari Mandir,
Pune 411002, Maharashtra
Tel : (020) 6601 7784 / 6602 0855

Pragati Book Centre
917/22, Sai Complex, F.C. Road, Opp. Hotel Roopali,
Shivajinagar, Pune 411004, Maharashtra
Tel : (020) 2566 3372 / 6602 2728

Pragati Book Centre
Amber Chamber, 28/A, Budhwar Peth, Appa Balwant Chowk,
Pune : 411002, Maharashtra, Tel : (020) 20240335 / 66281669
Email : pbcpune@pragationline.com

MUMBAI
Pragati Book Corner
Indira Niwas, 111 - A, Bhavani Shankar Road, Dadar (W), Mumbai 400028, Maharashtra
Tel : (022) 2422 3526 / 6662 5254
Email : pbcmumbai@pragationline.com

www.pragationline.com   info@pragationline.com

PREFACE TO FOURTH EDITION

We are pleased to release the revised Fourth Edition of **Pharmaceutics** for First Year Bachelor of Pharmacy (B. Pharm) of RGUHS, Karnataka State.

In addition to the contents to few chapters, figures and few recipes have also been added, where so ever they were essential. The chapter 'Dispensing of Medication' has been enriched by adding two types of classification of dosage forms suitably. We hope to receive the some overwhelming response from the students and colleagues as future, on received in the past.

July 2010

GAUD R. S.
KASTURE P. V.
GATTANI S. G.
GOKHALE S. B.

PREFACE TO FIRST EDITION

Rajiv Gandhi University of Health Sciences, Karnataka has revised the syllabii of Bachelor of Pharmacy recently.

Taking into consideration the course contents, due care has been taken to provide the desired information in lucid language along with neat diagrams in this package. Specifically the chapters Development of profession of pharmacy, Monophasic dosage forms, Biphasic dosage forms have been written with exhaustive information.

We are thankful to Shri. Dineshbhai Furia, Mr. Jignesh Furia, and staff of Nirali Prakashan for their sincere efforts in bringing out the book in the shortest period.

December 2007

GAUD R. S.
KASTURE P. V.
GATTANI S. G.
GOKHALE S. B.

SYLLABUS

PHARMACEUTICS (THEORY : 50 HOURS)

1. Historical background and development of profession of pharmacy and pharmaceutical industry in brief. (2)

2. Development of Indian Pharmacopoeia and introduction to other pharmacopoeias such as B.P., U.S.P., European Pharmacopoeia, Extra Pharmacopoeia and Indian National Formulary. (3)

3. (a) Introduction to dosage forms, classification and definitions.
   (b) Prescription : Definition, parts of prescription and handling
   (c) Posology : Definition, factors affecting dose selection, calculation of children and infant doses. (6)

4. Different types of weights and measures, calculations involving percentages of solutions, allegation, proof spirit, isotonic solutions etc. (3)

5. Heat processes : Introduction to different types like fusion, desiccation, sublimation, exciccation, ignition, evaporation, distillation, drying, various types of baths. (3)

6. Galenicals : Definition, equipments for different extraction process like infusion, decoction, maceration and percolation, method of preparation of spirits, tinctures and extracts. (6)

7. Surgical aids : Surgical dressings, absorbable gelatin sponge, sutures, ligatures and medicated bandages. (3)

8. Powders and granules : Classification, advantages and disadvantages, preparation of simple, compound powders, insufflations, dusting powders, Eutectic and explosive powders, tooth powders and effervescent granules. (5)

9. Monophasic dosage forms : Theoretical aspects including commonly used vehicles, essential adjuvants like stabilisers, colorants, flavours with examples, study of following monophasic liquids like gargles, mouth washes, throat paints, ear drops, nasal drops, liniments and lotions, enemas, collodions. (5)

10. Biphasic dosage forms : Suspensions and emulsions, definition, advantages and disadvantages, classification, tests for the type of emulsion, formulation, stability and evaluation. (6)

11. Suppositories and pessaries : Definition, advantages and disadvantages, types of bases, method of preparation, displacement value, evaluation. (4)

12. Incompatibilities : Introduction, classification and methods to overcome the same. (4)

PRACTICALS (75 HOURS)

1. Syrups :
   - (a) Simple syrup IP*
   - (b) Syrup of ephedrine hydrochloride NF*
   - (c) Syrup vasaka IP*
   - (d) Syrup of ferrous phosphate IP*
   - (e) Orange syrup*

2. Elixirs :
   - (a) Piperazine citrate elixir BP*
   - (b) Cascara elixir BPC*
   - (c) Paracetamol elixir (Paediatric)*

3. Linctus :
   - (a) Simple linctus BPC*
   - (b) Paediatric simple linctus BPC*

4. Solutions :
   - (a) Solution of cresol with soap IP**
   - (b) Strong solution of ferric chloride BPC**
   - (c) Aqueous iodine solution IP*
   - (d) Strong solution of iodine IP*
   - (e) Strong solution of ammonium acetate IP**

5. Liniments :
   - (a) Liniment of turpentine IP**
   - (b) Liniment of Camphor IP*

6. Suspensions :
   - (a) Calamine lotion IP**
   - (b) Magnesium hydroxide mixture BP**

7. Emulsions :
   - (a) Liquid paraffin**
   - (b) Cod liver oil emulsion**

8. Powders :
   - (a) Eutectic powder*
   - (b) Explosive powder*
   - (c) Dusting powder*
   - (d) Insufflations*

9. Suppositories :
   - (a) Boric acid**
   - (b) Chloral hydrate**

10. Incompatibilities : Mixtures containing incompatibilities (Physical and Chemical)*

●●●

SCHEME OF EXAMINATION

Q. 1 Synopsis	... 15 Marks
Q. 2 Major Experiments (Experiments indicated by**)	... 35 Marks
Q. 3 Minor Experiments (Experiments indicated by*)	... 20 Marks
Q. 4 Viva voce	... 10 Marks

●●●

CONTENTS

1.	History and Development of "Profession of Pharmacy" in India	1 – 4
2.	Introduction to Pharmacopoeias	5 – 15
3.	Dispensing of Medication	17 – 42
4.	Weights and Measures	43 – 53
5.	Heat Processes	55 – 69
6.	Galenicals	71 – 78
7.	Surgical Aids	79 – 82
8.	Powders and Granules	83 – 92
9.	Monophasic Dosage Forms	93 – 104
10.	Biphasic Dosage Forms	105 – 125
11.	Suppositories and Pessaries	127 – 133
12.	Incompatibilities	135 – 140
•	Bibliography	141 – 143
•	Index	145 – 146

CHAPTER 1: HISTORY AND DEVELOPMENT OF "PROFESSION OF PHARMACY" IN INDIA

Introduction

Plants and animals are used as food since antiquity. Few of them were then differentiated for therapeutic purposes to treat disorders. Thus the use of herbal medicine is as old as human civilization.

'Ayurveda' the oldest, most holistic, comprehensive system of Indian medicine traced back to more than 5000 years has described many herbs for medicinal use. Ayurveda is a combination of two sanskrit words *Ayu* (life) and *veda* (knowledge), thus Ayurveda is a science of life. Like medical pypari of ancient Egypt such as Smith pypyrus and Ebers papyrus, Indians do not have any written documents from pre-Arian civilization of Indus valley. In Vedic medicines such as *Osadhisukta* of Rigveda has described many medicinal plants, while Atharvaveda has mentioned several ailments.

To achieve the main aims of human-life, long and healthy life is necessary and Ayurveda has described the ways to achieve it.

According to Indian mythology Lord **Brahma** perceived Ayurveda, who taught it to his son **Daksha Prajapati** and in turn to **Indra**. It was transmitted to **Bhardwaj**. One of the sages **Atreya** got it from Bhardwaj and got it written in the form of samhita as Agnivesa-samhita from **Agnivesa**. Acharya charaka redacted this text and later on named as **Charaka-samhita.** Thus charaka-samhita is not an original writing but is a continuation and renewal of ancient knowledge.

Sushrutha, the disciple of vedic sage **vishwamitra** was born in sixth century BC and learnt surgery and medicine from **Dhanvantari**. His encyclopaedia known as **sushrutha-sanhita** is known through out the world and is translated in many important languages. Sushrutha is known as father of plastic-surgery.

Archaeological survey discovered the material related to the historical part of drugs or medicines, one of which is Papyrus-Ebers of 16th Century BC, which contains important information on vegetable drugs and the formulations made from them. The drugs described in this document are still being used today ! Then came the era of individuals by virtue of their involvement in the profession, contributed for development in science, which in turn has affected pharmacy profession.

Hippocrates, Aristotle, Dioscorides, and **Claudius Galen** were the authorities responsible for such advancement in the medical profession.

Hippocrates (466-377 BC) systematised the knowledge available and linked it with ethics. His concepts were then accepted worldwide and still utilized by health professional.

Dioscorides (040 – 80 AD) a Greek physician linked botany to this field and wrote *materia medica*, which included various drugs of vegetable origin. He described opium, hyoscyamus and other naturally occurring drugs and provided the basic information regarding its identification, cultivation, collection and storage.

Galen (131 – 200 AD) who was a physician known for his medical literature carrying description of number of drugs, their formulae and method of preparations. His work is still known as **Galenical Pharmacy**. Untill 1240 AD, pharmacy remained linked with medicine, but when it became difficult to be handled simultaneously due to increase in number of drugs pouring in, it was separated. German Emperor **Frederick II** felt that field of pharmacy is altogether different than the medicine and hence he implemented this separation.

Further the involvement of botany as a base for pharmacy was changed to chemistry by **Paraselsus** (1493 – 1541) a Swiss physician. He is responsible for developing the basic thinking of using individual chemical moiety for the treatment of diseases. Then further contribution was made by number of scientists by developing new drugs from different sources. In India, however the Ayurvedic medicines were used as per the ancient books written by **Charaka**, a physician, which was gradually replaced by allopathic medicines in the regime of British rule.

To maintain the uniformity and to control the standards of drugs and devices available in the market, each government has to make some rules and the standards are to be specified so as to avoid the availability of substandard or adulterated drugs. Each country has its own book of standards which includes the list of the drugs along with related substances their complete protocols viz. descriptions, tests formulae for its preparations, storage, use, dose and all other information which is essential for its proper manufacturing and safe use. Thus, the book which mentions, all these standards and norms is known as pharmacopoeia. Most of the countries have their own pharmacopoeia as the stability and efficacy of drug is affected by environment in which it is used, geographical location, source and many other factors. Every country has its own procedure to involve scientists in preparation of these standards as per its requirement, which is ammended from time to time depending upon the changes in the drug list (deletion and addition) as per the need.

Development of Profession of Pharmacy :

After independence due to liberalisation policies procedures in granting the licences and also encouragement given by central and several state governments many small scale and large scale industries, either with foreign collaboration or Indian have been set up. In the first half of the twentieth century pharmaceutical industries in India were located in West Bengal only, then to (Bombay) Mumbai and later on to Ahmedabad in Gujrat but as on today North India is also not far behind and good number of industries are located in states like UP and Delhi.

According to the recent survey in the year 2000-2001, there are about 24000 units in India producing bulk drugs and formulation. Covering the range of allopathic, Ayurvedic, herbal, small scale and large scale units too !

Hundred years before, i.e. in 1901 Bengal chemical and pharmaceutical works (Calcutta) Kolkata was established by Dr. P. C. Roy. Due to British rule most of the drugs used to get imported from England (U.K.), France and Germany and India was fully dependant on them. Due to two world wars there was no progress in pharmaceutical industry. After independence in 1947, due to five-year plans India marched ahead. Requirement of most of the life saving drugs was met by import only. In 1950 first antibiotic, (Penicillin) producing unit was set up near Pune, while streptomycin unit at Rishikesh and Indian drugs and pharmaceuticals Ltd. Hyderabad in 1960. Industrial revolution has made tremendous developments in medical and life sciences, and as a result it is possible to control many diseases now. As on today India is one of the largest and most advanced among the developing countries. All types of bulk-drug manufacturing and various types of formulations like oral-liquids, tablets, capsules, parenterals are being manufactured in India. The achievement is not only quantitative, but qualitywise also it is not far behind. About 80 % of bulk drug requirement and almost all requirement of formulations is met here and here only.

Following table shows the investment and production of pharmaceuticals in India for the last five decades.

Table 1.1 : Investment and production value

Year	Investment (Rs. in crores)	Production value (bulk-drugs and formulations together) (Rs. in crores)
1951	024	011
1971	150	300
1981	575	1500
1985	650	2150
1990	850	4060
1995	1380	10500
2000	2800	19750

India has all types of climatic conditions and hence drugs from various botanical sources are available abundantly. By imposing heavy restrictions on import of foreign goods, several industries have been given every assistance to produce the import substitutes.

Thus alkaloids like caffeine, Strychnine, morphine, quinine are produced now in India on a commercial scale, along with many biological products like, vaccines, sera, liver extracts. Good number of plants like, senna, Isapgoal, Ipecacunha, cinchona, poppy, papita rauwolfia are being cultivated on commercial scale. With that, we have not only become self sufficient but we are also exporting all these to various developed countries.

As on today, the basic-drugs like sulpha-drugs aspirin, antibiotics, vitamines, essential oils are being produced here on very large scale. Research and development activities have also been increased to a great extent to meet the Indian requirement. Following table shows the amount invested in India in the last decade by pharmaceutical industries for R and D activities.

Table 1.2 : Amount invested in research and development

Year	Expenditure incurred (Rs. in crores)
1990 - 91	070.00
1994 - 95	140.00
1997 - 98	220.00
1999 - 00	320.00
2000 - 01	370.00

Pharmaceutical industry in India is the most important foreign exchange earner for the nation, since our exports in pharmaceuticals are more than imports. In the year 1966 India use to export drugs of worth Rs. 3.05 crores only and was importing drugs of Rs. 8.20 crores. But due to continuous research and development we could turn the picture, our imports were restricted to only Rs. 1840 - crores where as Rs. 4090 crores were earned by way of exports in 1996 - 1997. The following table gives the stepwise progress of exports of drugs from India.

Table 1.3 : Imports and exports of drugs from India

Year	Total imports (Rs. in crores)	Total exports (Bulk drugs and formulations) Rs. in crores
1980 - 81	0112.5	046.40
1984 - 85	0215.5	128.75
1990 - 91	0652.0	665.00
1994 - 95	1369.0	2265.50
1999 - 2000	3341.0	6631.00

With all odds India is developing like any thing, though India covers 16 percent of world population. Our rates of literacy, life-expectancy have also been increased. Life expectancy during 1945 - 1951 was 27.5 years but has gone upto 58.5 years in 1990 - 1991 and more than 65 in 2000.

Developed medical facilities have brought down the mortality rate per thousand from 146 in 1950 to only 95 in 1987.

Due to Continuous development in the process technology, the cost of many life saving drugs have been reduced. We have successfully eradicated diseases like small pox and plague. Whereas malaria, polio-myletis, cholera, typhoid, leprosy and tuberculosis have been controlled.

Several newly developed sophisticated instruments have changed the methods of analysis or methods of identification of several much complicated medicinal substances, which has resulted not only in reducing the cost but also standards of analysis.

Radio-immuno assay, NMR, HPTLC are few of techniques which have made revolutionary changes and needs to be quoted.

Computer aided drug design, recombinant DNA technology, DNA finger printing are the new tools at the disposal of pharmaceutical research scientists.

Developments in the field of biotechnology like genetic engineering has given us new impetus in the manufacture of biologically active rare medicines, like insulin or vaccines. Now-a-days insulin an antidiabetic harmone is manufactured by gene-splicing which was produced earlier from animal pancreas, where as Hepatitis B is being produced by using transgenic plants. About 30 medicines using biotechnological methods have been approved by Food and Drug Administration officials in United States.

Pharmaceutical education in India : In India first degree college in pharmacy started in 1934 at Banaras Hindu University, Banaras while second in 1937 in Andhra University.

At present there are about 380 Diploma and 190 degree pharmacy colleges in India, with an intake of 22500 and 12250 respectively. Besides we have about 50 post graduate institutes with an intake of over 1000.

●●●

CHAPTER 2: INTRODUCTION TO PHARMACOPOEIAS

INTRODUCTION

The word pharmacopoeia has its origin in Greek language i. e. *pharmakon* : a drug and *poieo* : I make, thus it is the list of medicinal substances, crude drugs and formulae for making preparations from them.

Number of attempts have been made in the past and numerous books have been written for the guidance of persons in the practice of medicine, but until seventeenth century no book was published by any official body.

" **Pharmacopoeia Angustana** " was probably the first official book which appeared in 1601 and was official pharmacopoeia of Augsburg in Bavaria. **Pharmacopoeia Londinensis,** published in 1918 by college of physicians written entirely in Latin was the next attempt in the series. Thirteen subsequent editions of Pharmacopoeia Londinensis appeared upto 1851, with several alkaloids and formulae.

College of physicians Edinburgh in 1699 published as first **Edinburgh Pharmacopoeia** and continued to publish the same upto 1841 subsequently. It was written in Latin. **Dublin-pharmacopoeia** published by college of physicians, Dublin, appeared for the first time in 1809, continued to get published in latin upto 1926, but the last edition of the same published in 1850 was in English. Supplement to Dublin Pharmacopoeia was published in 1856 and was containing the use of different types of glass bottles and vessels for external and internal use.

BRITISH PHARMACOPOEIA (BP)

In the mean while it was felt that a pharmacopoeia which will meet the needs of Scotland. England and Ireland should be materialised, but the unification work did not finalise. In 1855 college of physicians undertook the work of publication of revised edition of London pharmacopoeia and sought the help of pharmaceutical society for the first time The Medical Act of 1858 brought the drastic changes in the medical professions. In this act only the provision to publish a book containing a list of medicines, method of their preparation along with weights and measures has been made. Under Section of this act General Council of Medical Education and Registration enacted and was given this work. The book was named as **British Pharmacopoeia.**

Thus General Council of Medical Education and Registration was empowered to alter, amend and republish as often as necessary. Thus college of physicians was relieved of this duties. The Pharmacopoeial committee and Pharmaceutical Society served as foundation of First British Pharmacopoeia which was published in 1864. More useful and successful reprint was published in 1874 with the alphabetical arrangement of monographs. 1885 and 1898 editions with number of changes including various grades of alcohol. chemistry of the drugs, uniformity in the doses of tinctures and extracts were taken out. While doing so recommendations from India were also taken into consideration.

A sub-committee of Committee of Civil Research in 1926, recommended, that Pharmacopoeia commission be formed and it should be entrusted the work of new editions. Committee of Civil Research also recommended that British Pharmacopoeia be revised and reissued at an interval of ten years only. Thus Pharmacopoeia was eventually published on 30th Sept. 1932. Subsequent editions have been prepared similarly. medicines Act of 1968 fixed up the responsibility of preparing the British Pharmacopoeia with the medicines commission. Medicines commission in accordance with the same act reconstituted the British Pharmacopoeia Commission, and Under Section 99 (1) of the Medicines Act. Preparation of the British Pharmacopoeia is the responsibility of British Pharmacopoeial Committee. The thirteenth edition of BP was published in 1980, 14th in 1988 and fifteenth in 1993.

BP - 1988, edition contains 2100 monographs. It is divided in two volumes. Vol. I contains monographs on medicinal and pharmaceutical substances along with Infrared reference spectra, while Vol. II contains formulated preparations, blood products, immunological products, radio pharmaceutical preparations, BP is the source of standards of drugs in United Kingdom and other parts of Common Wealth.

Latest 15th edition of BP was published in 1993. It comprises of main volume and four addendum viz. 1994, 1995, 1996 and 1997. Addendum 1997 adds new drugs and preparations to amend the BP 1993. Major change includes the replacement of all the edited texts of the monographs of European Pharmacopoeia by entries in the form of cross references to the monographs published in the third edition of the European Pharma-copoeia. BP has provided authorative standards for the quality of substances, preparations and articles used in medicines and pharmacy for about 130 years. There are two volumes. The first volume deals with medicinal and pharmaceutical substances. It also includes IR reference spectra needed for the identification of drugs. While Vol. II contains section on formulated preparations blood products, immunological products, radio pharmaceutical preparations and surgical materials. This 15th edition contains 2040 monographs for substances and articles used in practice of pharmacy. 800 monographs of the second edition of European pharmacopoeia also have been included in this edition. The side headings, definition and production have been introduced where appropriate throughout the pharmacopoeia to provide clarity and consistence of approach. This is specifically useful for biological products.

BP 2002 : It contains 2800 monographs.

It includes 14 new monographs of national origin and 46 new monographs reproduced from the supplements 4.1 and 4.2 of the E.P.

Volume - I contains monographs of medicinal and pharmaceutical substances.

Volume - II contains IR spectra and appendices, formulated preparation, blood products, immunological product, radio pharmaceutical preparations, surgical materials.

BP 2004 : It contains 3000 monographs.

The new edition comprises 6 volumes as follows :

Volume I and II	Medicinal substances.
Volume III	Formulated preparations, Immunological products, radio pharmaceutical preparation, and surgical materials.
Volume IV	Appendices, IR spectra and Index
volume V	B.P. (Veterinary) 2003
Volume VI	CD ROM version of the BP 2003 and BP (veterinary) 2003 incorporating British approved names 2002.

It includes 5 new monographs of national origin and 60 new monographs reproduced from supplements 4.6, 4.7 and 4.8 of EP.

BRITISH PHARMACEUTICAL CODEX (BPC)

With an intention to provide authoritative guidance to the persons engaged in the medical practice (physicians) and pharmacists in the British Empire, the Council of Pharmaceutical Society, 1903 proposed to produce a reference book.

This reference book was published for the first time in 1907 under the title **British Pharmaceutical Codex.** Since then, subsequent revised editions in 1911, 1923, 1934, 1949, 1959, 1963, 1968 and 1973 were published. British Pharmaceutical Codex

(BPC) use to serve as supplement for the information in British Pharmacopoeia in several respects like actions of drugs, undesirable effects, standard uses etc. Codex also furnished valuable information of medicaments and formulations not included in the BP. From 1963, BP and BPC use to get published simultaneously for the convenience of users. However, in 1972 **Medicines commission** stated that there should be only one book of standards for all medicines in UK, the provision of codex standards have been discontinued. 1973 edition of the codex was 10th edition and 1979 edition revised with the desired changes in the 11th edition and is known as "**The Pharmaceutical Codex**" only.

The book is going to be an encyclopaedia of drug information for medical practitioners, pharmacists, in hospitals and in pharmaceutical industry. This also gives references to the published literature including information on bioavailability.

BRITISH NATIONAL FORMULARY

This is a ready source of essential information on the drugs and medicinal preparations in common use. It is prepared and published by Pharmaceutical Society of Great Britain and British Medical Association. It has arranged the preparations as per pharmaceutical norms and is of importance to Pharmacist. Pharmacological classification is given for the convenience of medical practitioners. It gives valuable information about actions, uses, dosage of drugs, and adverse reactions of drugs are also given. National Formulary also gives the vital information of the new drugs as they are included in the formulary before the achieve the status for incorporation either in Pharmacopoeia or codex. British national formulary does not give any standards for drugs or their preparations.

UNITED STATES PHARMACOPOEIA (USP)

First United States Pharmacopoeia was published on 15th December 1820 by United States Pharmacopoeia convention in English and Latin. The Pharmacopoeia consisted of total 217 drugs and was having 272 pages. Further the constitution and bylaws of the convention made provision for subsequent meetings and to revise Pharmacopoeia after every 10 years. In the meeting of 1940, convention directed that Pharmacopoeia be revised after every five years. Upto 1960 fourteen convention meetings were held from 1820.

The First National Formulary of United States was published in 1868 by American Pharmaceutical Association. The books of standards for drugs like Pharmacopoeia, codex, formulary are prepared and published by some recognised authorities in most of the countries but USP and USNF are published by private organization. In 1906, American Congress passed the first Food and Drug Act, and with this act only USP originally published in 1820 and national Formulary published received legal recognition by the US govt. In 1974 United States Pharma-copoeial Convention purchased the national formulary, and from supplement to 1975 edition of NF, United States Pharmacopoeial Convention accepted the responsibility of publication. Upto 1980 separate issues (i.e. 20th revision of USP in 1980 and 15th edition of NF in 1980) were published, but at present the combined issue (i.e. USP and NF together) are being published.

In the 20th USP emphasis was given to GMP and bioavailability and also tools for content uniformly, microbial limits, dissolution rates, container standards were set.

The USP 21st and NF 16th whereas USP 23 and NF 18th were published in 1985 and 1995 respectively.

United State Pharmacopoeia (USP) and National Formulary (NF) standards and specifications relate to the quality and strength, packaging and labelling of medicines and related articles.

The USP 24-NF19 contains 3777 monographs and 164 general chapters. There are 543 new monographs, 504 in the USP and 39 in the NF. 3941 individual revisions were processed through Pharmacopoeial forum (PF) during the 5 year cycle. Obsolete material deleted during the preparation of this volume included 130 USP and 12 NF monograph and 4 general chapters.

USP now represents 25th revision of USP and 20th revision of NF (USP - 25 - NF 20), which became official on January 2002. Starting with this edition, USP-NF will be published annually.

USP contains over 3,400 monographs for drug sub and products, together with over

160 general chapters that describe specific procedures to support monograph tests and other informations as well. USP also contains 16 monographs and 9 general chapters pertaining specifically to nutritional supplements. NF contains over 380 monographs for excipients and dietary supplements.

Unlike all other pharmacopoeias, the USP and NF are not produced by government. The USP and NF are published by the U. S. Pharmacopoeial Convention, Inc., a voluntary not for profit institution that holds the public trust.

The mission of the USP to promote the public health through establishing and disseminating legally recognized standards of quality and information for the use of medicine and related articles by healthcare professionals, patients and consumers.

INTERNATIONAL PHARMACOPOEIA

Since the pharmacopoeias are generally national in origin, a need to establish International uniformity and methods of standardization of drugs was felt in 1874, but until 1906 no progress was made to materialize the idea. In 1906, International agreement for unification of formulae for potent drugs and preparations was made. Health Organisation of League of Nations also tried to publish the International Pharmacopoeia. However, by virtue of resolution of the Third World Health Assembly (WHA), World Health Organisation (WHO) Geneva, Switzerland, published **first edition of Pharmacopoeia Internationalis** in two volumes. Volume first in 1951, volume second in 1955, followed by supplement in 1959. These volumes were in English, French and Spanish. German and Japanese translations were also published.

Second edition in English, French, Russian and Spanish was published in 1967 and supplements in 1971.

Third edition is proposed in five volumes of which volume I. General methods of analysis in 1979 and volume II quality specifications in 1981 have already been published. Rest of the volumes are yet to come.

EUROPEAN PHARMACOPOEIA

Since the World Health Organisation (WHO) publishing authority of the International Pharmacopoeia, does not have official jurisdiction in any of the countries there still remains a need for a documents, which is legal and binding authority. Thus Council of Europe consisting of seven countries in 1964, started the work of preparing European Pharmacopoeia, Switzerland joined latter. European Pharmacopoeia, being legal and binding to members of Council of Europe consisted to Belgium, France, United Kingdom, Italy, Luxemburg, Federal Republic of Germany, Netherlands and Switzerland.

European Pharmacopoeia, Volume I was published in 1969, Volume II in 1971. In 1973 a supplement was issued to it. In 1975 volume III of the European Pharmacopoeia was released.

Second edition of European Pharmacopoeia 80-82 part I was published in 1980 by Maisonneuve, S. A. France.

The **third edition** supplement of 1999 has been recently launched, which has added 105 new European monographs and 124 revised monographs. It is effective from 1st January 1999, to all member statics throughout the European Economic Area, as well as 10 other European countries superseding national standards on the same subject.

Following is the list of the Pharma-copoeias of various countries available at present in market.

1. Argentine Pharmacopoeia.
2. Austrian Pharmacopoeia.
3. Belgian Pharmacopoeia.
4. Brazilian Pharmacopoeia.
5. Chinese Pharmacopoeia.
6. Czechoslovakian Pharmacopoeia.
7. French Pharmacopoeia.
8. German Pharmacopoeia.
9. Hungerian Pharmacopoeia.
10. Indian Pharmacopoeia.
11. Italian Pharmacopoeia.
12. Japanese Pharmacopoeia.

13. Yugoslavian Pharmacopoeia.
14. Mexican Pharmacopoeia.
15. Netherlands Pharmacopoeia.
16. Nordic Pharmacopoeia.
17. Polish Pharmacopoeias.
18. Portuguese Pharmacopoeia.
19. Romanian Pharmacopoeia.
20. Russian Pharmacopoeia.
21. Spanish Pharmacopoeia.
22. Swiss Pharmacopoeia.
23. Turkish Pharmacopoeia.
24. United States Pharmacopoeia.

INDIAN PHARMACOPOEIA

The **first edition** of Indian Pharma-copoeia was published in 1955, but actually the process of which started as early as 1944. In 1944, Government of India asked the Drugs Technical Advisory Board to prepare the list of drugs in use, in India, having sufficient medicinal value to justify their inclusion in official pharmacopoeia.

The list of drugs which were not included in the British pharmacopoeia along with standards to secure their usefulness, tests for identity and purity was prepared by the committee and was published by the Government of India under the name **The Indian Pharmacopoeial List 1946.**

The committee constituted under the chairmanship of **Lt. Col. Sir R. N. Chopra** along with other nine members, prepared the list of drugs with the following details.

1. Substances included in the British Pharmacopoeia, 48 monographs for crude drugs, chemicals and their preparations.

2. Substances not included in the British Pharmacopoeia:

(a)	Drugs of plant origin	: 90
(b)	Drugs of animal origin	: 10
(c)	Biological products	: 05
(d)	Insecticides	: 07
(e)	Colouring agents	: 03
(f)	Synthetics	: 05
(g)	Miscellaneous	: 15
(h)	Drugs for veterinary use	: 02

The Indian Pharmacopoeial List 1946, was prepared by department of Health, Government of India. Delhi in 1946 and having a price of Rs. 5 - 8 or 8s 7d. It was reprinted in 1950.

Most of the crude-drugs included in this list, are still official in the Indian pharmacopoeia.

INDIAN PHARMACOPOEIA 1955

After the publication of Indian Pharmacopoeial List 1946 and in order to undertake the preparation of the Indian Pharma-copoeia on the lines of Pharmacopoeias existing in other countries, a permanent Indian Pharmacopoeia Committee was constituted by Government of India on 23rd November 1948, under the Ex-officio Chairmanship of Director General of Health Services, Ministry of Health, New Delhi. Chairman of Drugs and Pharmaceuticals committee, CSIR Delhi, was ex-officio member along with other nine renowned scientists. The tenure of the committee was five years. Several other sub-committees were appointed to assist the Pharmacopoeial Committee.

Clinical sub-committee, Pharmacology sub-committee, Biological sub-committee, Pharmacognosy sub-committee, Pharmacy sub-committee and Pharmaceutical sub-committee were important amongst the committees helped in compilation of draft-monographs of the pharmocopoeia. Subsequently, the durations of the Pharmacopoeia committee was extended by one year and Dr. B. N. Ghosh was appointed as chairman of the committee. Thus, first edition of Pharmacopoeia of India was published in 1955 and is written in English. The official titles of the monographs are given in Latin and covered total 986 monographs. It includes crude-drugs, chemicals, biologicals and several formulae derived from them. It costs Rs. 21 or 31 sh.

Supplement to first edition of Indian Pharmacopoeia 1955 - Since many new drugs were introduced to the market, it was felt necessary to provide standards for these drugs and as such the first supplement to first edition of Indian Pharmacopoeia was published in **1960.**

After the death of Dr. B. N. Ghosh, chairman 2nd pharmacopoeias committee in 1958, Dr. B. Mukherji was appointed as chairman, who completed the compilation work and 2nd edition was published in 1966.

In **second edition,** 93 new monographs have been added, while 274 monographs from the first edition and also the supplement have been deleted. The 2nd edition of Indian pharmacopoeia contains 890 monographs and 41 appendices. Several changes have been made in the 2nd edition. The tities of monographs are written in English (and not in Latin) and style of naming the monographs has also been changed. Titles contain the name of the drug first, category of the drug has been indicated at the end and doses given in metric system. Preparations of the drugs are followed immediately after the parent monograph of the drug. For tablets and injections "Usual Strength" has been given. Non-aqueous titrimetry, column chromatography, compleximetry have been included under new analytical technique, pills, pellets and lamellae have been deleted from the pharmacopoeia.

INDIAN PHARMACOPOEIA SECOND EDITION 1966

Indian pharmacopoeias committee reconstituted in 1954 took up the work of compilation of 2nd edition of Indian pharmacopoeia. Supplement to the first edition was published in 1960, because many new drugs were put to use in medical practice after the publication of 1st edition. It was also very essential to provide the official standards of these drugs.

After the death of Dr. B. N. Ghosh, the chairman of 2nd pharmacopoeias committee in 1958, Dr. B. Mukharji was appointed as chairman and who expedited the revision process. 274 monographs from IP '55 and its supplement of 1960, were deleted from the 2nd edition of Indian pharmacopoeia. Where as 93 new monographs neither official in IP '55 nor in its supplement of 1960 were added to 2nd edition.

Addition of monographs consists of vegetable drugs like Jatamansi, Rasna and Vidang, while antibiotics like Bacitracin, Neomycin were also added. Amongst the chemicals and pharmaceuticals of importance are Amylobarbitone, Bemegride Tolbutamidc, Tolazoline HCl and others. Doses were expressed on Metric system only. Column chromatography, non-aqueous titrimetry and complexometry are the new analytical techniques that were adapted. Usual strength for the preparations like tablets and injections was given, when no specific strength is mentioned by prescriber.

PHARMACOPOEIA OF INDIA SUPPLEMENT 1975

This is the supplement of Indian Pharmacopoeia second edition 1966. Since many new drugs were introduced in the medical practice after the publication of second edition of IP, it was very essential to provide them the official standards and also to amend IP 1966, where so ever necessary.

Thus in the supplement 126 new monographs have been included and also 250 monographs of 2nd edition have been amended. Only one monograph Cholera vaccine formalized has been deleted.

Many appendices giving the detailed analytical procedures have been rewritten and some appendices have been added. Monographs on capsules and eye ointments have been rewritten and sterility test for eye ointments has been incorporated for the first time. TLC, GLC and IR spectro photometry have been adopted as new analytical techniques every where applicable.

INDIAN PHARMACOPOEIA III EDITION 1985

After the publication of second edition of Indian Pharmacopoeia 1966 and its supplements in 1975, Indian pharmacopoeia committee for the preparation of third edition was reconstituted under the chairmanship of Dr. Nitya Nand, Director of Central Drug Research Institute, Lucknow in June, 1978. Third Indian pharmacopoeial committee consisted of 13 members along with member secretary and assistant secretary. The committee was assisted by 10 subcommittees in the compilation work.

Third edition of Indian Pharmacopoeia has been published in 1985 in two volumes along with nine appendices. 261 new monographs have been added to this edition, which were not included in second edition. 450 monographs included in second edition have been deleted from this edition. Following are the important salient features of this edition –

1. As far as possible IUPAC system of nomenclature of organic chemical drugs has been used.
2. Analytical techniques like electrophoresis, fluorometry, flame photometry, photometric haemoglobinometry have been given the official recognition for first time.
3. Instrumental techniques i.e. IR and UV spectroscopy, gas liquid chromatography, fluorescence and atomic absorption spectrophotometry have been used where so ever applicable.
4. To ensure the dissolution of contents, dissolution test has been made applicable to six tablets.
5. Limit test for microbial contamination has been mentioned for few frequently used pharmaceutical aids and some oral liquid preparations.
6. The appendices for pharmaceutical containers, water for pharmaceutical use, design and analysis of biological assays have been annexed.

(a) Addendum (I) to Indian Pharmacopoeia 1985 third edition : This is a supplement to Indian pharmacopoeia third edition 1985, published in 1989.

This provides the official standards for several new drugs introduced in medical profession. It has added 46 new monographs and amended 126 monographs of third edition.

(b) Addendum (II) to Indian Pharmacopoeia 1985 third edition : Addendum II to IP third edition was published in 1991 and is effective from 1st Jan. 1992.

It provides the official standards to the new drugs which came into use after the publication of first addendum to third edition. Addendum II covers 62 new drugs and amendments to 110 monographs of the third edition. An appendix on high performance liquid chromatography (HPLC) and determination of water by azotropic distillation have been added.

INDIAN - PHARMACOPOEIA FOURTH EDITION 1996

4th edition of Indian Pharmacopoeia i.e. Indian Pharmacopoeia 1996, has been made effective from 1st Dec. 1996. It supersedes the 1985 edition and its addenda.

Fourth edition has 1149 monographs and 123 appendices. This edition includes 294 new monographs not included in third edition while 110 monographs have been deleted.

A Good number of general monographs like creams, eye drop, gels, nasal preparations, oral liquids, pesseries, suppositories, have been incorporated.

Important among the new appendices added to the 4th edition are the Biological Indicators, jelly-strength, osmolarity, particulate matter, contents of packaged dosage forms etc.

Method of preparation and in-process control for many biological products, IR and UV absorption tests for identity have been added to many drug substances.

Test for bacterial endotoxins as a substitute test for the pyrogens, and the extensive use of HPLC for analysis of drug-substances are few of the salient features of 4th edition of IP 96.

Addendum (I) to Indian Pharmacopoeia 1996 Fourth Edition :

Later on addendum (I) to I. P. fourth edition was published which is effective from 31st December 2000.

It provides the official standards for several new drugs introduced in medical profession. Addendum I covers 44 new monographs and amendments to 285 monographs of the fourth edition. An appendix on Bacterial

version which include quantitative tests in addition to the conventional gel clot test. This test replaces the pyrogen test for a number of substances and their preparations. Supplement to the Indian pharmacopoeia under the name of veterinary supplement 2000 is also being issued almost simultaneously with this addendum.

A list of few important monographs added to the I. P. 1996 through this addendum is as under :

Acetic acid, Glacial
Acetic acid, Ear drops
Aciclovir
Amiodarone hydrochloride
Cinnarizine
Minoxidil
Oxazepam
Pindolol
Warfarin sodium clathrate.

IP 1996, Addendum 2000 :

In view in compliance of the WTO, IP committee decided that there is a need for normalising and integrating the pharmacopoeial standards in India so as to bring it, on par with other pharmacopoeias. Thus number of tests and standards for may monographs have been amended.

42 new monographs have been added to IP 1996 through this addendum. The carbamazine monograph have undergone major changes while, bacterial endotoxin test for pyrogens has been replaced by extensively revised version to the earlier gel clot test. This has come into force from 31st December 2000.

IP 1996, Addendum 2002 :

This has came into effect from **30th June** 2003, New 19 monographs have been added through this addendum to IP 1996. Due to the rapid developments in the field of practical sciences, it was essential to update the official compendium. A new appendix on residual solvents has been added to monitor the content of organic volatile impurities which are used to produce in the manufacture of active pharmaceutic substance, excipients or medicinal products. The appendix for HPLC has also been replaced by revised version covering ion chromatography.

The Extra Pharmacopoela :

Over the last 110 years the extra pharmacopoeia has developed through 30 editions.

The first edition of the extra pharmacopoeia was published in July - 1883. The Twenty-ninth edition was published in January 1989. The **thirtieth edition** was published in April 1993 and **reprinted** in September 1993.

As with previous edition the monographs for all the drugs and substances have been completely revised. In all there are 5132 monographs describing individual compounds or groups of related compounds. About 280 monographs were deleted from the last edition and about 620 have been added. The extra pharmacopoeia is divided into three parts :

(1) Monographs on drugs and auxiliary substances
(2) Supplementary drugs and other substances
(3) Preparations.

Martindale is widely used to identify proprietary medicines. In the last edition preparations containing more than one active ingredient and their proprietary names were listed under each monograph describing the relevant active ingredient. For this edition coverage of mixed preparation has been widened and the detail information on each preparation has been presented, it also includes description of 46000 preparations or group of preparation from 14 countries.

Another important aspect of this edition is increased clinical emphasis.

Present **31st edition** has been published in 1996. It contains 283 new monographs in addition to previous 30th edition whereas 173 monographs have been deleted. It has also included description of those diseases, which are treated by drugs along with a review of the choice of treatment in such cases. The book has been divided in three parts. Part I contains 4458 monograph. Part II contains a series of 784 short monographs of new drugs, toxic substances and drugs not used clinically but still of interest. Part III contains proprietory preparation from a range of countries as well as official preparations from the current edition of the BP, USP, NF and BPC. It also includes list of 4800 manufacturers and distributors in it. It covers information from various pharmacopoeias viz. Austrian, Belgian, British, Chinese, Czecks, Italian, Japanese, Netherland, Portugese, Swiss and USNF.

This edition also contains 11600 abstracts or reviews based on information in an ever widening range of publication. Over the last 110 years Extra Pharmacopoeia has developed through 31 editions from William Martindale's small pocket book to this large volume.

Contents of Martindales Extra Pharmacopoeia are based on published information. It is not a book of standards.

The Ayurvedic Pharmacopoeia of India :

In 1946, a committee was constituted under the chairmanship of Lt. Col. R. N. Chopra by the Government of India. It was the Chopra committee that had first gone into the question of need for proper identification of Ayurvedic medicinal plants, control over collection and distribution of crude drugs and made positive recommendations for compilation of Ayurvedic Pharmacopoeia, to the government.

The Government of Bombay appointed a committee for standard and Genuine Ayurvedic herbs and drug in 1955 and subsequently appointed second committee called committee for standard Ayurvedic Herbs and Drugs in 1957 both under the Chairmainship of Vaidya Bapalal Shah. The Bapalal Committee has elaborately recommended the compilation of the Ayurvedic Pharmacopoeia as an urgent prerequisite for effective control of Ayurvedic Drugs to ensure quality assurance. Finally, Government of India appointed the "Ayurvedic Research Evaluation Committee", under the Chairmanship of Dr. K. N. Udupa (1958) which had strongly highlighed urgency of the compilation of an Ayurvedic Pharmacopoeia.

In the compliance in some of these recommendations, the Government of Bombay State established its board of Ayurveda, Bombay in 1951, which was subsequently reconstituted in 1955 and 1958. The Government of India established CCRIMH in 1969 for research in all aspects including drug standardization in Indian Medicine and Homeopathy. This council was divided into 4 research councils in 1978. The First Ayurvedic Pharmacopoeia committee was constituted in 1966 under the Chairmanship of Col. Sir Ram Nath Chopra. The committee was reconstituted in 1972 under the Chairmanship of Prof. A. N. Namjoshi which took over the work of compilation of the Ayurvedic formulary of India as a pre-requisite for undertaking, the work of Ayurvedic Pharmacopoeia of India.

After publication of the first and the second part of the Ayurvedic Formulary of India, part III of the formulary is under preparation.

The first and second part of the Ayurvedic Formulary of India comprising of some 444 and 191 formulations respectively cover more than 351 single drugs of plant origin. This take up about 500 priority drugs of plant origin to come within the ambit of the Ayurvedic pharmacopoeia of India.

The Union Government have brought the Ayurvedic drugs under the preview of Drug and Cosmetic Act 1940 from 15-9-1964. The publication of the Ayurvedic formulary of India and Ayurvedic Pharmacopoeia of India would give Government a base for fuller enforcement of the Act in respect of standards.

The Ayurvedic Pharmacopoeia of India **part-I, Vol-I (1990)** comprises of 80 monographs of Ayurvedic single drugs of plant origin, which go into one or more formulations enlisted in the Ayurvedic Formulary of India part-I. In compiling the monographs, the title of each drug has been given in Sanskrit. Then comes definition of drug giving its identity in scientific nomenclature and very brief information about its source, occurrence, distribution and precautions in collection etc.

This is followed by a list of synonyms in Sanskrit and also in the other Indian regional languages. The monograph then records the detailed microscopic discription of the drug. The norms and limits under "Identity, purity and strength like tolerance of foreign organic matter, total ash, acid insoluble ash, alcohol soluble extractive, water soluble extractive, volatile oil. Constituents, properties and action, important formulations, therapeutic uses and dose, are also described towards the end of the monograph.

Part–I, Vol–II 1996 of Ayurvedic pharmacopoeia of India comprising of 78 single drugs of vegetable origin. The Ayurvedic Pharmacopoeia of India, **Part–I, Vol –III 1998** may also be notified by Government as a book of reference for implementation of the drug and Cosmetic Act, 1940 all over India as Ayurvedic Pharmacopoeia of India Vol–I is already included in the first schedule of drug and Cosmetic Act, 1940.

INDIAN PHARMACEUTICAL CODEX 1953 (IPC, 53)

The Pharmaceuticals and Drugs Research Committee of the Council of Scientific and Industrial Research, New Delhi, in February, 1947 passed a resolution that a book containing detailed information on Indigenous Drugs of India be compiled.

The work was entrusted to two important personalities Dr. S. Siddiqui, Director, Chemical Laboratories, Delhi and Dr. B. Mukarji, Director Central Drugs Laboratory, Calcutta. Dr. Siddqui left for Pakistan and Dr. B. Mukarji was asked to complete it when he was Director of Central Drug Research Laboratory, Lucknow.

The work of this volume I was divided in two parts. Part I dealing with general monographs and Part II with formulary of galenicals and other preparations of vegetable and animal origin.

The work was undertaken with an intention.

1. To focus the attention on the need for intensive research on indigenous drugs, and

2. To serve as a guide for research on indigenous drugs.

The indigenous drugs were not prescribed by medical practitioners as no standards were laid down for them.

Since the **Indian Pharmaceutical Codex-volume-I** got published in **1953** along with standards, methods of preparation, dosage and other details, it has served the purpose to a great extent.

NATIONAL FORMULARY OF INDIA

Multiplicity of drugs, their several preparations and continuous flow of new drugs in the medical practice has made it difficult even for a qualified and experienced physician to discriminate the choice of drugs. Drug interaction, resistance, cumulative effects are the other factors, which the physician has to take into consideration while treating the patients. Thus, for the guidance of medical practitioners, medical students and pharmacists in hospitals and in sales departments, National Formulary of India has been formulated.

The **First Edition** of National Formulary was published in 1960 by Government of India, Ministry of Health.

Since many new drugs had come into use, after the publication of first edition, it became essential to revise the formulary and bring it up-to-date. Thus, the second National formulary committee under the Chairmanship of Dr. B. B. Yodh, consulting physician, was constituted and **second edition** was published in 1966.

206 formulations of first edition have been detected and 219 formulations of new drugs have been added to second edition. Separate pediatric section and a chapter on diet has been added to formulary. Methods of treatment or poisons, list of diagnostic agents, list of proprietary and trade names are the other features of second edition.

While compiling the valuable information BP, USP, British National Formulary, NF of United States, BPC, several renowned teachers in the profession, consulting physicians have been consulted.

Revised **Third Edition** of the National Formulary has been brought up in 1979, under the Chairmanship of Dr. Wig K. L. which has deleted 255 formulations of second edition, while added 342 new formulations.

Separate chapters on drug-interactions, drug -dependence, prescription writing are the special features of this edition .

QUESTIONS

1. Answer the following :
   (a) What is Pharmacopoeia ?
   (b) When was first pharmacopoeia of India published ?
   (c) Which pharmacopoeia we were following before independence ? Why ?
   (d) Which is the current edition of I.P. ?
2. Write history of Indian Pharmacopoeia.
3. Differentiate between Indian Pharmacopoeia, Indian Pharmacopoeial Codex and Indian National Formulary. Write a note on I.P.C.
4. What you know about the history of BP. ?
5. What is current edition of BP and USP ? When it was published ? How it differs from its earlier editions ?
6. Why European Pharmacopoeia has been formulated though there is International Pharmacopoeia ?
7. Write short note on European Pharmacopoeia and International Pharmacopoeia.
8. Why USP and USNF are being published together ? Since when ?
9. What is addendum ? Why it is published for IP/BP/USP regularly ?
10. What is Ayurvedic Pharmacopoeia of India ? How it differs from Indian Pharmacopoeia ?

CHAPTER 3: DISPENSING OF MEDICATION

(A) INTRODUCTION TO DOSAGE FORMS

Nature has provided all that is needed for the mankind. Perhaps God created man after creating every thing necessary for his survival. The entire universe bears the testimony to the same.

The human species has been gifted with the sense of taste, sound, sight, touch and smell with an instinct to admire the best around him. He is observed with a wisdom to exploit the nature to his welfare and to achieve perfection in all walks of life.

Human disease and the man's desire to survive lead him to the discovery of drugs which already existed in the form of vegetation and minerals. Thus, the science of pharmacy (medicine) was born. Osler once wrote " the desire to take medicine is perhaps the greatest feature which distinguishes man from the animals."The primitive man started taking the drugs in the form they existed in the nature. Such as the barks, the roots and the leaves of certain trees. May be that he chewed and masticated them at first. Then powdered them and perhaps extracted them with water.

It may not be an exaggeration if we mention that the basic dosage forms of drugs i. e. solid, liquid and semisolid already existed in nature. To illustrate solid in the form of vegetative drugs and minerals, liquid in the form of latices juices and honey semisolid in the form of animal fats and bees wax. Science as a matter of fact mimicks nature. It may improvise it. This applies to all branches of science.

Thus, an attempt in the science and art of pharmacy is continuously being made to provide the drug in the best suited form to a "diseased" person to put him at ease on all accounts. The varied dosage forms, different formulations and number of routes of administration are the outcome of achieving the above set goal.

Any form in which a drug is administered in a prescribed quantity is referred as a dosage form of drugs although in case of preparations for external use, the dose is not prescribed.

A pharmacist has to make lot of considerations before giving a form to the drug. Important ones being its stability, acceptibility bioavailability, biotransformation, its physical and chemical nature, dissolution, disintegration availability, onset of action, duration of action absorption degradation and excretion. He has to meet the requirements of a physician, look to the patients convenience and the acceptability of the product by the consumer. Efficacy of the product is also to be assured from the date of manufacture till it is consumed.

The different dosage forms of the drugs may be broadly classified as under on the basis of their physical nature. These categories include both external and, internal use preparations that have been formulated with the help of best suited adjuvants (pharmaceutical aids), many a time depending on the individual requirements of the product.

A broad based classification of dosage forms may be as under :

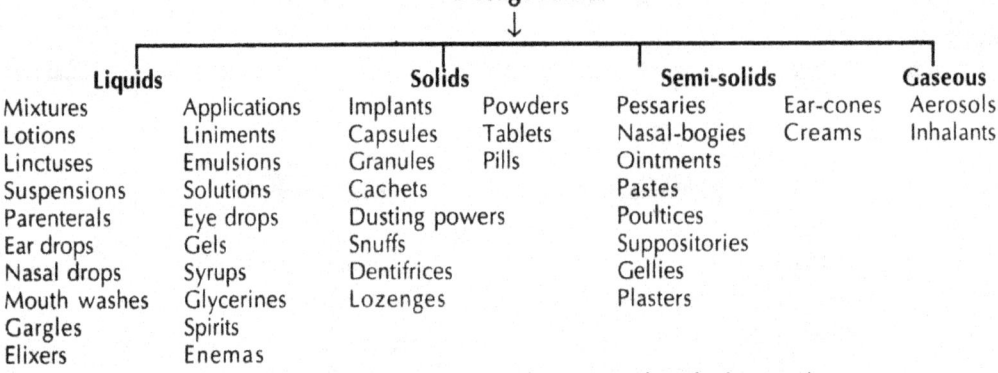

Depending upon the sterility, nature dosage forms are classified as under.

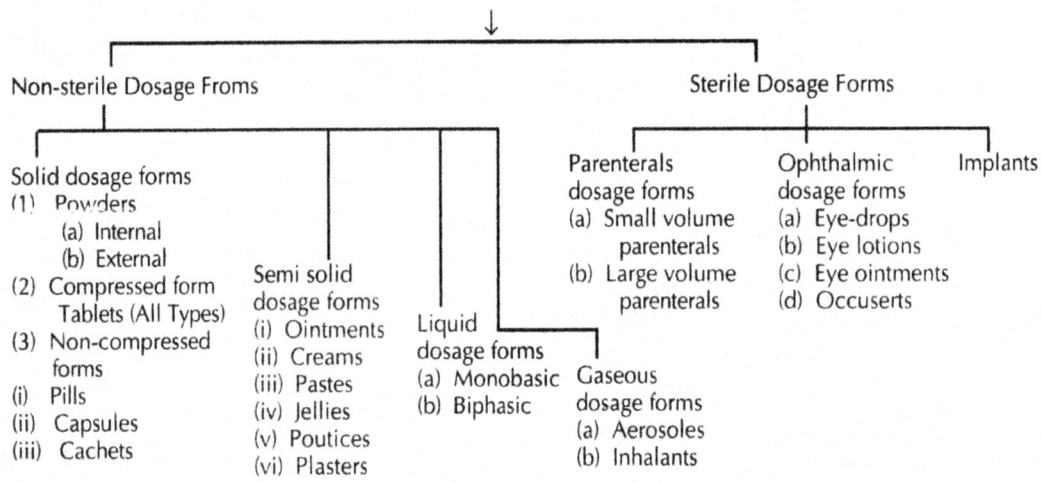

Liquids :

1. Elixirs : Elixirs are clear, liquid hydroalcoholic oral preparation of potent or nauseous drugs. They are pleasantly flavoured and attractively coloured.

e.g. Piprazine citrate elixir, Paracetamol elixirs.

2. Mixtures : Mixtures are the most common form of liquid oral preparation in which vehicle is usually aqueous and the medicaments may be in solution or suspension. Generally they are not formulated for a long life and should be used quickly within a month.

e.g. Kaolin mixture, magnesium sulphate mixtures.

3. Suspensions : Suspensions are biphasic liquid dosage form of medicament in which finely divided solid particles ranging from 0.5 to 5 micron are dispersed in a liquid or a semi-solid vehicle.

e.g. Chalk mixture, paediatric, Kaolin mixture paediatric.

4. Emulsions : Emulsions are biphasic liquid preparations in which two immisible liquids are made miscible with help of third agent i.e. emulsifying agent.

e.g. Cod liver oil emulsion, Castor oil emulsion.

5. Mouth washes : Mouth washes are usually aqueous solution in concentrated form with pleasant taste and flavour used for rinsing, deodorant, refreshing or antiseptic action. Medicated mouth wash may contain astringent, anti bacterial agent, protein precipitant or other agent.

e.g. Zinc sulphate and zinc chloride mouth wash.

6. Throat paints : Throat paints are viscous liquid preparations used for mouth and throat infections.

e.g. Mandle's paint.

7. Parentals : Parental preparations or injectables are the sterile solution or suspensions of drugs in aqueous or oily vehicles meant for introduction into the body by means of an injection under mucous membrane.

e.g. Terramycin injection, Aminophylline injection, Calcium gluconate injection.

8. Eye drops : Eye drops are sterile aqueous or oily solutions or suspensions for instillation into the eye. They are usually applied into the space between eyeball and eyelids or on to corneal surface.

e.g. Betnisol eye drop, Chloramphenicol eye drop.

9. Ear drops : Ear drops are solutions of drugs that are instilled into the ear with a dropper.

e.g. Chloramphenicol ear drop.

10. Nasal drops : Nasal drops are usually aqueous solution intended for instillation into nostrils by means of drops.

e.g. Xylometazoline hydrochloride nasal drop.

11. Lotions : Lotions are fluid preparations for external application without friction. They are either rubbed on skin or applied on suitable dressings and covered with water proof material to reduce evaporation.

e.g. Calamine lotion, Salicylic acid lotion.

12. Liniments : Liniments are fluid, semi-fluid or occasionally, semi-solid preparation which may be alcoholic or oily solutions or emulsions intended for application to skin which are to be massaged into the skin and not to be applied to broken skin.

e.g. White liniment, Turpentine liniment.

13. Gargles : Gargles are aqueous solution used to prevent or treat throat infections. Usually obtained in concentrated form.

e.g. Sodium chloride gargles, Potassium chlorate and phenol gargles.

Solids :

1. Powders : Powders are solid dosage form which are intended for internal as well as for external use.

e.g. Dextrose oral powder, Talc dusting powder.

2. Tablets : Tablets are extensively used spherical, flat or biconvex solid unit dosage forms which are administered orally.

e.g. Paracetamol tablets, Aspirin tablets.

3. Capsules : Capsule is solid-unit dosage form in which the empty-gelatin shell can contain any solid, liquid or semisolid preparation.

e.g. Phenytoin sodium hard capsules.

4. Granules : Granules are comparatively unusual means of administrating drugs that possess an unpleasant taste. The small irregular particles, ranging from 2 to 4 mm in diameter are often supplied in single - dose sachets, the contents of which are stirred in water before taking.

e.g. Effervescent granules, Methyl cellulose granules.

5. Pills : Pills are oral dosage form that have largely been replaced by tablets and capsules. They are spherical or less often, ovoid, and usually sugar coated.

e.g. Phenolphthalein pills compound, B. P. C.

6. Cachets : Cachets are solid unit dosage form of medicament in which nauseous or disagreeable powder are enclosed in tasteless sheet made by pouring a mixture of rice floor in between two hot, polish, revolving cylinders.

e.g. Wet seal cachets.

7. Snuffs : Snuffs are finely divided solid dosage form of medicament which are inhaled into nostril for their antiseptic, decongestant or bronchodialator action.

8. Tooth powders : Tooth powders are powders applied to the teeth to remove foreign particles, food substances plaque and clean the teeth.

e.g. Calcium carbonate tooth powders.

9. Dusting powders : Dusting powders are meant for external application to skin, for antiseptic, astringent, antiperspirant, absorbent, protective and lubricant purpose.

e.g. Starch and talc dusting powder.

10. Implants : Implants are sterile small tablets meant for insertion under skin by giving small act into skin which it stiches afterward.

e.g. Steroidal harmones like testosterone, stillbesterol etc.

Semi-solids :

1. Ointments : Ointments are semi-solid greasy preparations for application to skin, and nasal mucosa. The base is usually anhydrous and contains medicaments in solution or suspension.

e.g. Calamine ointment, Benzoic acid ointment.

2. Creams : Creams are semi-solid emulsions for external use. There are two-types, aqueous and oily creams, in which emulsions are oil in water and water in oil respectively. The o/w type is non-greasy. Creams are very popular form of external medications.

e.g. Centrimide cream, Hydrocortisone cream.

3. Jellies : Jellies are transparent or translucent, non-greasy, semi-solid preparation mainly used externally. The jelling agent may be starch, gelatin, cellulose, etc.

e.g. Proflavin jelly, Ichthammol jelly.

4. Ear cones : Semisolid dosage form meant for introduction into ear cavity.

5. Nasal bougies : They are also known as nasal suppositories or buginaria and are meant for introduction into the nasal cavity.

6. Pessaries : Pessaries are solid medicated preparations for introduction into vagina, where they melt or dissolve and exert a local action.

e.g. Lactic acid pessaries, Nystatin pessaries.

7. Suppositories : Suppositories are conical or ovoid, solid preparation for insertion into rectum where they melt, dissolve or disperse and exert a local or a systemic effect.

e.g. Betadine vaginal pessaries, Alum suppositories.

8. Pastes : Pastes are semi-solid preparation for external application that differ from similar product in containing a high proportion ot finely powdered medicaments. The base may be anhydrous (liquid or soft paraffin) or water soluble (glycerol or a mucilage). Their application as a protective coating is due to their stiffness.

e.g. Magnesium sulphate paste, Zinc and coal tar paste.

9. Plasters : Plasters are solid or semi-solid self-adhesive substances applied to the skin for protection, mechanical support or enhance intimate contact between drug and skin.

e.g. Belladonna plaster, corn plaster, back plaster, etc.

Liquid dosage form consists of internal, external and parenteral preparations. They are either monophasic or biphasic. Monophasic preparations include true solutions, colloidal solutions and solubilised preparations whereas biphasic preparations are exemplified by emulsions and suspensions. Emulsions consist of two immiscible liquids whereas in suspension one of the phase is a solid in a finely divided form.

Solid dosage forms are represented by powders; capsules, tablets etc. Normally, they are unit dose systems to be taken internally. However, powders comprise of both external and internal use preparations and may also be supplied in bulk e.g. dusting powders, tooth powders for external use and effervescent powders for internal use.

Semisolid dosage forms comprise of ointments creams, pastes, plasters suppositories and are meant for topical applications, mostly having a focalised action.

However, the topical route of administration has only recently been employed to deliver drugs to the body for systemic effects with two classes of marketed products nitroglycerin for the treatment of angina and scopolamine for the treatment of motion sickness.

These dosage forms of drugs have relative merits and demerits, a few to illustrate.

LIQUIDS :

Merits :
1. Onset of action is quick as compared to pills, tablets and capsules.
2. Certain medicinal substances can only be given in liquid form such as liquid paraffin, castor oil etc.
3. Certain drugs are to be in suspended or diffused form to produce maximum surface area viz., kaolin.
4. Few drugs if taken in dry form may cause pain and irritation for e.g. potassium bromide and aspirin.
5. Psychological satisfaction to a patient of some thing in the bottle.

Demerits :
1. Dose has to be measured.
2. Stability and preservation presents a problem.
3. Storage and transportation hazards.

SOLIDS :

Merits :
1. Unit dose system.
2. Physical, chemical and physiological stability, long shelf life.
3. Economic.
4. Ease of transportation.
5. Ease of administration.
6. Tastelessness and elegance.

Demerits :
1. Swallowing difficulty by some adults and children.
2. Onset of action is slow and depends on disintegration and dissolution.

Injectables :

Merits :
1. Onset of action is quick. This can also be controlled by way of changing the routes of administration and modification of the formula.
2. The therapeutic effect of the drug is ensured as compared to the uncontrolled absorption from the intestine when the drug is given by oral route.
3. The drugs which are inactivated by the gastric or intestinal fluids can be safely given by this route.
4. Unconscious patients or the patients who are vomitting and or purging can be given the medicine by this dosage form.

Demerits :
1. Injections cause pain.
2. Need trained persons having a knowledge of aseptic technique for administration.
3. Since the onset of action is quick any untoward action after giving the drug by this route is rather difficult to be corrected.

SEMISOLIDS :

Merits :
1. Ointments are applied to the skin for therapeutic or protective action or cosmetic function.
2. Lubricating and emollients.
3. Able to efficiently release medicament.
4. Rate of absorption is fast.
5. Ease of application.
6. Elegant in appearance.
7. Retained for prolonged period at site of application.
8. Compatible with skin secretions.
9. It avoids pre-systemic metabolism of drug.

Demerits :
1. Hot water washable leaves stain at site of application.
2. Greasiness.
3. Microbial contamination due to fatty acids.
4. Sometimes it causes irritation, sensetization.
5. No specification about amount, how much quantity to apply, at one time.

(B) PRESCRIPTIONS

(a) READING AND UNDERSTANDING OF PRESCRIPTIONS

Definition : *A prescription is a written order from a registered physician, a dentist, or a veterinarian or a surgeon or any-other person licensed by law to prescribe drugs, containing instructions for preparation and dispensing to the pharmacist along with mode of administration for the patient.*

Pharmacist may accept a prescription on telephone in emergency and it needs to be followed by a regular written prescription.

Importance : In the modern era of potent drugs, if a wrong prescription is delivered a patient is likely to suffer from the serious consequences.

While considering the safety of the patient, a prescription

1. Should be written in ink.
2. Should not have over writing.
3. Should be legible.
4. Should have only official abbreviations of weights and measures.
5. As far as possible only generic names of the drugs be used in the prescription.
6. Full names of medicaments be used and no abbreviations.

Parts of a prescription :

An ideal prescription consists of the following parts :

(a) Superscription (b) Inscription (c) Subscription (d) Signature.

(a) Superscription : It consists of name, qualification and address of the physician, date, name, age and address of the patient. The physician's name qualification and address are essential for the identity of the prescriber, particularly for a narcotic prescription.

Date helps in judging the interval between the issue of prescription and that of dispensing it. It is important to know the date of prescription particularly when the drugs like narcotics and cummulative drugs like digitalis, santonin, arsenic etc., are prescribed.

The name, sex and address of the patient are important to facilitate proper handling. It helps to avoid confusion among prescriptions meant for some other patient. These are especially required for prescriptions of drugs like narcotics. The age of the patient is important particularly in case of children. From the age, the pharmacist can recheck the correctness of the dose.

It consists of the symbol R_x · R stands for Latin word Recipe meaning, *'take thou of,* the oblique dash after R is considered as an ancient invocation of physician to Jupiter.

(b) Inscription : It is the body of the prescription and contains the official English name and the amount of each ingredient. Abbreviations should be avoided since they are likely to result in errors. The name of each drug is placed on a separate line directly under the preceding one. First letter of the name of the drug should be in capital. If there are more than one ingredients, their ideal order should be as follows :

(i) Basis : It is the principal active drug and gives the prescription its chief action.

(ii) Adjuvant : It aids or increases the action of the base;

(iii) Corrective : It modifies or corrects any undesirable effect of the basis or adjuvant. It may be a flavouring, colouring or a sweetening agent.

(iv) Vehicle : It is an inert agent used to distribute the above ingredients. It may serve either as a solvent or to increase the bulk or both. In the case of a liquid, if it is intended merely to dilute the active drug, it is called a **diluent.** In powders, an inert powder may serve as a diluent. The inert substance added to medicine to give it a proper consistency, as in pills, is known as an **excipient.** In ointments, the soft or greasy substance in which a more active drug is incorporated is usually called the **ointment base.**

The inscription also consists of doses of drugs in metric system.

(c) Subscription : It contains directions to the pharmacist, which is usually only *'Mix'* or *'Send.such ... tablets or capsules, etc.".*

(d) Signature : The word signature is derived from the Latin *'signatur'* meaning 'write', 'make' or 'label'. It consists of directions to the patient regarding the use of medicine. The directions should be simple, complete, and clear to the patient. It also contains the signature of the physician with his registration number, which is especially necessary when any narcotic drug is prescribed. Occasionally this part of prescription is called **transcription** and the term signature is then reserved for **physician's name.**

Refill information : The prescription is never to be repeated unless the physician so desires, particularly in case of dangerous drugs and narcotics.

The Prescriber's signature : A prescription is never complete without the signature of the prescriber. In case the prescription is through a telephonic message, pharmacist must obtain the signature later on.

After dispensing, the pharmacist should prepare a label to be attached to the container. This label includes :

(a) Type of preparation e.g. mixture, lotion, ointment, etc.

(b) Special directions e.g.*'Shake well before use,'* or *'For external use only,',* *'Poison'; to be diluted before use,* etc.

(c) Name of the patient in full.

(d) Directions to the patient, signature of pharmacist, date, and place of dispensing.

(e) Quantity of the medicament.

Deshpande Accident Hospital
Tagore Nagar   Kolhapur.

Date : 12/10/2001

Phone : (0234) 22 55 50
Dr. Sunil Deshpande
M. S.
Reg. No. 23456

Shri. Shamkant Sane
14/4 Pratap Nagar
Satara.

Male - 43 years

Δ   Compound fracture tibia febula R

R$_x$

Tab. Ciprofloxacin 600 mg 1 BD
Tab. Paracetamol 500 mg 1 T D S.

Tab. B-plex c̄ Vit C 1 BD
For 7 days

- Elevation on pillow
- Not to walk
- Care of plaster
- Dressing.

Sd –

If the directions are lengthy they should be written on a separate sheet of paper and handed over to the patient. When the directions are embarassing for the patient they should not be written on the label but given to the patient in private.

Nature of bottles used for liquid preparations :

White, round and small bottle should be used for draughts, gargles mouthwashes, etc. Fig. 3.1.

Round, blue or amber coloured and ribbed bottles should be used for preparations for external use such as lotions and liniments, in order to prevent reaction of light and to make identifiable from a distance.

Vertically fluted bottles with bakelite caps and attachments should be used for eyedrops, ear drops and nasal preparations.

Graduated, flat, blue or amber coloured bottles with uniform internal diameter should be used for mixtures. It is not ideal, if graduation marks are incorrect, hence a dose marking slip is necessary.

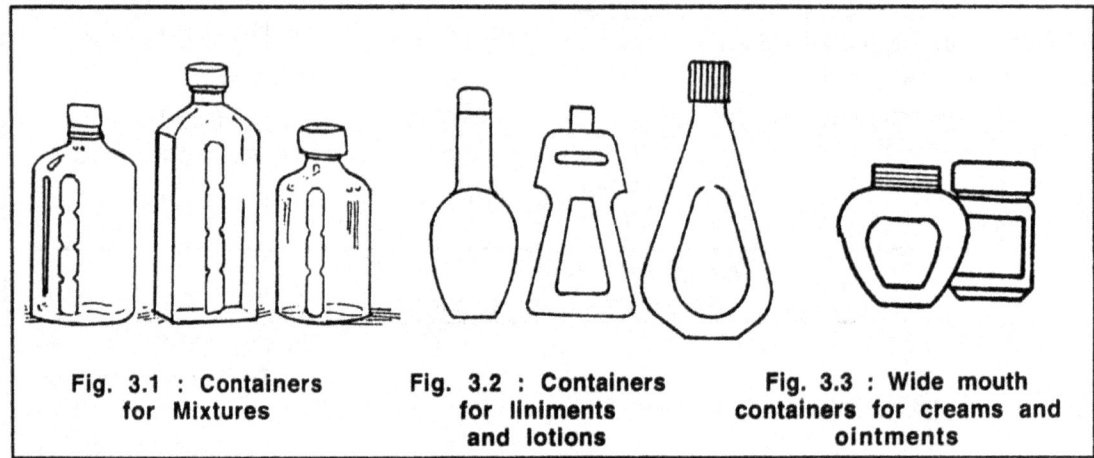

Fig. 3.1 : Containers for Mixtures

Fig. 3.2 : Containers for liniments and lotions

Fig. 3.3 : Wide mouth containers for creams and ointments

Examples of a prescription :

				Dr. A. B. C.	
Superscription		For		Address :	
		Mr. XYZ		Date :	
		Age : 27 Years			
		Address :			
	I	R̥			
	n				
	s				
(Basis)	c	Liquor ammonium acetate fortis		9	g
(Adjuvant)	r	Potassium acetate		3	g
	i				
(Adjuvant)	p	Spiritus aetheris nitrosi		3	g
	t				
(Corrective)	i	Orange syrup		6	g
	o				
(Vehicle)	n	Water upto		90	ml

Subscription : Mix and prepare a mixture. Divide into 3 doses.
Signature : *Direction :* One dose to be taken 3 times a day

ABC
Regd. No. xxxx

Handling of Prescription :

Receiving, checking the prescription, finishing and delivering of medicaments to the patient is part and parcel of the duty of a pharmacist. While receiving a prescription, never show carelessness. In an hospital, it is wise to have a method at hand to see that the prescription goes to the right person. A suitable method would be to give prescription number on three slips. One slip is given to the patient, the second is attached to the prescription and the third is fixed to the final container. This will ensure identification.

Checking the Prescription :

Never depend on guess work. When in doubt about the ingredients or their quantities, always fall back and contact the prescriber and confirm the authenticity of your own interpretation.

Compounding the Prescription :

When handling the prescription for compounding, always check for the picking up of correct drug from the shelf, and again recheck from the label when returning the container of medicine to the shelf.

Compounding accuracy :

Choose a balance which gives a good accuracy.

A balance, shown in Fig. 3.4 is a typical Dispensing balance used for the purpose.

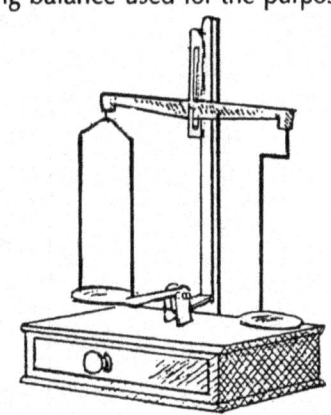

Fig. 3.4 : Dispensing balance

When the product is finished, choose a suitable container label it, see that it is presentable and then deliver it to the patient.

(b) LATIN TERMS USED IN PRESCRIPTIONS

Physicians still use abbreviations, which on writing at length are, latin terms. A short but useful english translation appears on the next page.

Table 3.1 : Abbrevations and Translation of Latin terms

Abbreviation	Latin	English
a	Ante	Before
aa	Ana	Of each
a.c	Cibos	Before meals
ad	–	Sufficient to produce
add	Addature	Let it be added
aq	Aqua	Water
b.i.d.	Bis in die	Twice a day
sig	Signetur	Let it be labelled
coach	Cochleare	Spoonful
	Amplum	Following the word
	Magnum	Cochleare means
	Maximum	One table spoonful
	Plenum	

Abbreviation	Latin	English
	Medium	Following the word Cochleare means one dessert spoonful.
	Modicium	
	Minimum	Following the word cochleare means one teaspoonful
	Parvum	
t.i.d.	Ter in die	Thrice a day
	Post cibos	after meals
	Ante cibos	before meals
	Sumendum	To be taken
	Capiendum	
mitt	Mitte	Send
	Semi hora	Half an hour
	Ante Jentaculum	Before breakfast
	Secundis horis	Every two hours
	Ex Lacte	With milk
	Dolore urgente	When the pain is severe
	Fiat Mistura	Let a rnixture be made.
	Fiat haustus	Let a draught be made
	Statim	At once
	More dicto danda	Let it be given
	Utenda	To be used
	Quotidie	Daily
	Secundum artem	in pharmaceutical manner.
	Hora sommi	At bed time.
	Collunarium	A nasal douch
	Guttae	Drops
	Haustus	A draught
	Insufflation	An insufflation
	Nebula	A spray solution
past	Pasta	A paste
ung	Unguentum	An ointment
pil	Pilula	A pill
pulv	Pulvis	A powder
	Pulvis conspersus	A dusting powder
troch	Trochiscus	A lozenge
n.p.	Nomen Proprium	Label with name of article.
chart	Charta	A powder

Abbreviation	Latin	English
	In phiala	In a bottle
p.p.a	Phiala pirus agitata	The bottle being Shaken first
tal	Talis, Tales Talia	Such
dimid	Dimidium	The half
reliq	Reliquum	The remainder
infricand.	Infricandus	To be rubbed in
sugatur	Sugatur	Let it be sucked
	Sumat	Let him take
d.	Da	Give
	ut antea	As before
ad lib	Ad libtum	As much as you please
dos	Dosis	A dose
–	Pro	For
	Prodosi	As a dose
Terquot	Teraotidie	Three times daily
prim luc.	Prima luce	Early in the morning.
	Primo mane	
	Mane	In the morning
	Nocte	At night
	Nocte et mane	Night and morning
	Hac nocte	Tonight
	Cras vespere	Tomorrow evening
q.i.d.	Quarter in die	Four times a day
m.d.	More dicto	As directed
	Lente	Slowly
p.r.n.	Pro re nata	Occasionally
quot. o. s.	Quoties opus sit	As often as necessary
s. o. s.	Si opus sit	When necessary
tuss urg	Tussi urgente	When the cough is troublesome.
cyath	Cyathus	A glass
	Ex	With
ligament	Ligamentum	Bandage
gutt	Guturi	To the throat
ocul	Oculis	For the eyes
	Prococulo lacvo	For the left eye
	In oculum dextrum	Into the right eye

Table 3.2 : Numerals

unus	1	undecim	11
duo	2	duodecim	12
tria	3	tredicim	13
quartor	4	quatturodecium	14
quinque	5	quindecium	15
six	6	sedecim	16
Septum	7	septemdecim	17
octo	8	duodeviginti	18
novem	9	undeviginiti	19
decem	10	viginti	20

(C) MODERN METHODS OF PRESCRIBING

Apart from the general prescription which we have discussed, there are prescriptions which are commonly encountered. In general the prescriptions are classified as follows :

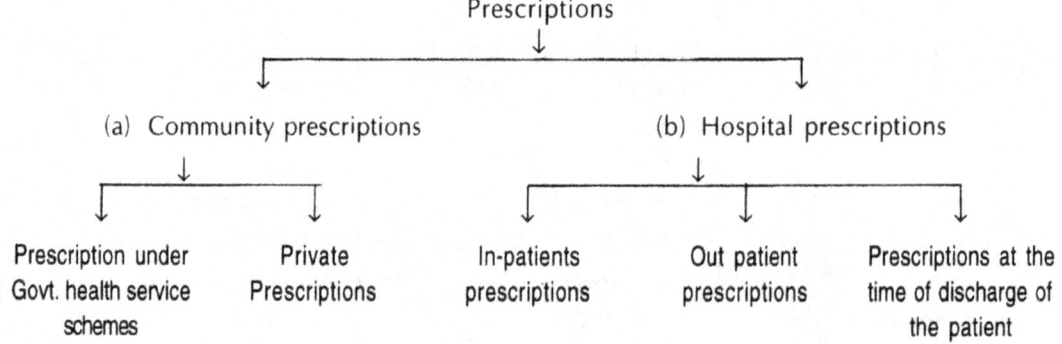

(a) Community Prescriptions : The physicians and dentists who are approved by the Government (may be State or Central under Health service schemes may prescribe the drugs, medicines or other appliances in a special prescription form.

In this form alongwith the general parts of the prescription there is an endorsement section for completion by the pharmacist. The pharmacist should enter the details of the medicaments supplied and date in the endorsement section. At one corner there will be the stamp of the name and address of the pharmacy with date of dispensing.

For such prescriptions remuneration will be paid only if the prescription is in the specific format. The remuneration will be paid to the pharmacist every month after endorsement and submitted to the pricing authority. Thus, such prescriptions are to be retained for a month then they are sent for pricing.

In private prescriptions now-a-days the physicians prescribe the ready made dosage forms which do not need any compounding instructions for the pharmacist.

In private prescription apart from general prescription, veterinary prescriptions are increasing in number in recent time. A typical veterinary prescription is given below :

```
Date : 12/9/2001                          Dr. THAKALE  S. M.
                                                    M. V. Sc.
                                                 Petcare clinic
                                            Paud road, Pune 38.

          This prescription is for an animal under my care.

Mr. S. S. Joshi (for Tommy)
3/4 Kailash Apts; Paud road.
Pune - 411 038.

     Age: 2 Years

                        Rx
                             30 Tabs. Oxytetracycline 50 mg
                             1 Tab. Three times daily

     10 ml. Gentamicin eye drops
     Use four times daily

                                                          Sd
```

On the private prescriptions received, prescriptions containing only medicine or controlled drug are to be retained for two years. After dispensing the medicines the prescription is stamped, dated and given the reference number.

(b) **Hospital Prescriptions :**

1. In-patient Prescription : In most of the hospitals the physician writes the prescription on a patient's record sheet. This prescription contains patient identification; name of the drug; route of administration, dose, time of the administration and the prescriber's signature.

In these prescriptions, for drugs which are taken only on one occasion are written as 'once only', for drugs which are to be taken prior to surgery 'pre-medication drugs'. Some drugs prescribed which are to be taken after regular intervals or on requests. Such drugs include laxatives, post operative analgesics, sedatives etc.

In hospitals pharmacist may receive a parenteral prescription or intravenous admixture prescription. The prescription may be as follows :

```
        MAHATMA GANDHI GENERAL
             HOSPITAL, PUNE

For                              Date : 06/11/98
Mr. Pravin More
Age :26 yrs.
Ward No. 10
     Rx
              NSS    1000 ml
              125 ml/hr.


                         Physician's Signature
```

In the above prescription of the patient's record will be sent to the pharmacist. The above prescription means sodium chloride injection (Normal saline solution) 1000 ml, is to be administered at the flow rate of 125 ml per hr.

There may be *prescriptions for total parenteral nutrition (TPN) mixture* as :

MUNICIPAL HOSPITAL, BELGAUM

For   Date : 10/10/2001

Roy P. N.

Age : 38 years

Male Ward

R_x

1000 Hyperal + 10 Nacl

+ 10 KCl + 5 $MgSO_4$ + 10 Insulin

Physician's Signature

This is a prescription for preparation of one litre of the hospital's basic TPN solution which is to be provided with the addition of 10 m Eq sodium chloride, 10 m Eq. potassium chloride, 5 m Eq. magnesium sulphate and 10 units of insulin.

These prescriptions should be checked for proper dose, in compatibility, drug allergies, drug-interaction and stability. Expiration period for such preparations is usually 24 hours from the time of preparation.

2. Out patient prescriptions : The out patient dispensing prescriptions are given in the form where identification of patient, name, address, age and hospital registration number are mentioned. Generally, the medicines prescribed are sufficient to last until the next out patient appointment.

3. Prescriptions for patients at the time of discharge : These are similar to out patient prescription or may be written on the patients chart. Depending on the hospital's policies the quantity prescribed may be for one or two weeks period.

There can be following types of prescription depending upon the conditions under which they have been prescribed.

(1) Preventive prescriptions
(2) Pathological prescriptions
(3) Drug-induced prescriptions
(4) Etiological prescriptions
(5) Miasmatic prescriptions
(6) Constitutional prescriptions
(7) Prescriptions on totality of symptoms
(8) Prescriptions on key-note symptoms

(C) POSOLOGY

Posology deals with doses of drug. The Greek term *posos* means how much; and *logos* means science. So it is a science of how much (dose) drug is to be given for its expected effect. Doses of different medicines are different. They are dependent on the state of patient, sex, age and severity of the disorder. It is also dependent on she factors such as :

1. Route of administration : Effectiveness of drug formulation is controlled by the route of administration. Injection gives quick effect in small dose whereas comparatively large doses are required when administered orally.

2. Rate of elimination : If the rate of drug elimination from the body is increased due to some reason or the other, the same drug shows a prolonged effect.

3. Formulation : Type of formulation also affects the dose size. Same drug in repeated single dosage form requires more quantity than does the prolong drug formulation.

4. Drug Interaction : Simultaneous administration of drugs may give synergistic effect reducing the dose of one or both the drugs.

5. Idiosyncrasy : Sometimes one comes across a patient or person, who, on administration of a minimum dose of certain drug, suffers unpleasant symptoms of temporary nature, or individual intolerance. Such a person is said to be suffering from idiosyncrasy arising from that particular drug. ex. quinine, aspirin etc. Remedy is to discontinue the drug.

Natural and Acquired Tolerance

Some individuals tolerate comparatively large doses, while others may get an adverse effect. Similarly, repeated doses of a drug for a prolonged period affects the individual in such a way that the dose is required to be increased in order to produce therapeutic effect. Normally the quantity of drug or dose decreases in the following order.

Oral → Subcutaneous → intramuscular → intravenous

Frequency

Generally, a dose is repeated three or four times a day. The frequency depends on the effective blood concentration of the drug, rate of metabolism and excretion.

Paediatric dose

Pharmacopoeia gives range of quantities for adult dose for 24 hours by oral route and by any other specified route. Adult dose and paediatric doses are different. In order to calculate paediatric dose the following formulae are used :

1. Young's Rule

$$\frac{\text{Age in Years}}{\text{Age in Years} + 12}$$

= Proportion of adult dose

Example : For a child of 6 years.

$$\frac{6}{6+12} = \frac{6}{18} = 3 \text{ of adult dose.}$$

If adult dose is 150 mg then child dose is 50 mg.

2. Dilling's Rule

$$\frac{\text{Age in Years}}{20} = \text{Part of adult dose}$$

Example : For a child of 6 years

$$\frac{6}{20} = \frac{3}{10} \text{ parts of adult dose}$$

If adult dose is 150 mg then child dose is 45 mg.

3. Fried's Rule for Infants

[Below the age of 2 years]

$$\frac{\text{Age in months} \times \text{Adult dose}}{150}$$

If the age is 6 months and Adult dose is 600 mg

then $\frac{6 \times 600}{150}$ = 24 mg dose of child.

4. Clark's Rule for infants

$$\frac{\text{Weight in pounds} \times \text{adults dose}}{150}$$

If adult dose is 300 mg and weight is 20 pounds

$$\frac{20 \times 300}{150} = 40 \text{ mg dose of a child}$$

5. Cowling's Rule

$$\frac{\text{Age at next birthday (In years)} \times \text{Adult dose}}{24}$$

If the adult dose is 240 mg and age is 6 years

$$\frac{6 \times 240}{24} = 60 \text{ mg}$$

Sometimes, dose is calculated on the basis of body weight. This is essential because quantity of drug at site is dependent on the size of the patient and hence heavily built person should receive more drug than does a normal person. Therefore, for some drugs, doses are prescribed on the basis of body weight. For example, propanidid dose is 10 mg per kg of body weight. For a person weighing 60 kg, the dose becomes :

60 × 10 = 600 mg by intravenous route.

Surface Area:

In 1966, **Catzel** devised a method for calculating doses based on surface area of body. Some of the formulae are given below. Tables according to weight and age are also available to find out surface area of the body. Although this method is a good for calculation of dose, it is tedious for calculating the surface area.

1. $\dfrac{\text{Surface area of patient in m}^2}{\text{Average adult surface area}}$

   × Adult dose = dose for patient

2. Surface area of patient in m^2

   × dose of drug per m^2 = dose of patient

Dose Table:

Following is a dose table for commonly used drugs. Maximum dose and route of administration is also specified:

Unless and otherwise mentioned, doses are suitable for adults. In the range of doses, lower dose applies at the lower age and higher dose at the higher age limit. Although the doses are based on the opinions of medical experts and are for general guidance they are not binding on the prescriber. A pharmacist must ensure the intention of the prescriber before he advises. Unless specifically mentioned dose is to be administered by oral route.

Name of the Drug	Maximum dose
Acetazolamide	500 mg initial dose, 250 mg subsequently every six hours
Acetyl salicylic acid	1 g for headache, 8 g daily in divided doses in rheumatism.
Acetomenaphone	5 - 10 mg daily, one week before delivery.
Adrenaline acid tartarate	1 mg by subcutaneous injection as single dose.
Adrenaline injection	0.5 ml by subcutaneous injection
Allopurinol	200 - 400 mg daily 1.8 g daily in divided doses. 8 mg as emetic 100 mg by intravenous 200 mg daily maintenance dose.
Aloes	300 mg.
Alpha amylase	0.2 to 5 g
Aluminium hydroxide gel	7.5 -15 ml
Amantadine HCl	200 mg daily
Amino caproic acid	5 g followed by 1 - 1.25 g every hour.
Aminophylline	250 - 500 mg by slow I/M injection 300 mg oral
Amitriptyline HCl	75 - 150 mg daily
Ammonium chloride	3 - 6 g daily in divided doses
Amodiaquine	before the administration of mersalyl injection.
Amoxycillin trihydrate	400 mg suppresive dose,
Amphetamine sulphate	0.75 to 4.5 g daily
Ampicillin trihydrate	10 mg morning and mid day.
Amylobarbitone	2 to 6 g daily
Amylobarbitone sodium	100 - 200 g oral sedative
Analgin	100 - 200 mg sedative
Aneurine hydro chloride	0.5 to 3.0 g daily 50 mg oral. prophylactic dose, 100 mg daily therapeutic oral dose.

Name of the Drug	Maximum dose
Antazoline hydrochloride	100 mg oral antihistaminic
Anise oil	0.2 ml oral
Ascorbic acid injection	1 g intramuscular
Ascorbic acid	Oral 75 mg daily prophylactic, 500 mg therapeutic
Atropine sulphate	2 mg orally, 0.2 by intra muscular injection.
B. C. G vaccine	0.1 ml by intra-cutaneous injection as prophylactic.
Bacitracin	For amoebasis 80000 to 120000 IU. orally.
Barbitone sodium	600 mg orally, sedative
Bel liquid extract	8 ml orally as digestive and astringent
Belladonna dry extract	60 mg orally
Belladonna tincture	2 ml orally
Bemegride	1 g total. 50 mg at intervals of ten minutes by intravenous injection in the treatment of barbiturate poisoning
Bendrofluazide	5 - 20 mg daily
Benzathine penicillin	0.9 g prophylactic by intramuscular injection every two or three weeks.
Benzyl penicillin.	500 mg every four hours orally. 600 mg by I/NI injection 2 to 12 times daily.
Bephenium hydroxyna	5.0 g single dose
Betamethazone	0.5 - 5 mg daily
Bethanidine sulphate	10 - 20 mg daily
Bisacodyl	5 to 10 mg daily
Bismuth sodium subcarbonate	200 mg by I/M injection antisyphilic, Antacid 2 g daily.
Busulphan	2 - 4 mg daily
Caffeine	600 mg daily C. N. S stimulant
Caffeine citrate	600 mg daily.
Calciferol	Prophylactic (antiricketic) 400 to 1000 units, 5 mg or 200,000 units in the treatment of hypothyroidism
Calcium levulinate	1.0 g daily
Calcium aminosalicylate	10 - 20 g daily ;
Calcium gluconate	1 to 5 g daily
Calcium lactate	5 g orally
Calcium pentothenate	10 - 100 mg

Name of the Drug	Maximum dose
Carbamazepine	0.2 to 1.2 g daily
Carbenicillin disodium	10 to 30 g daily
Carbimazole	30 - 60 mg daily
Castor oil	20 ml single dose as purgative
Cephalexin	1 - 4 g daily
Cephaloridine	1 - 4 g daily
Chloral hydrate	0.5-2g
Chloramphenical	1.5 - 3 g daily, children dose 500 mg per kg of body weight
Chlorcyclizine HCl	50 - 200 mg daily
Chloroquine phosphate	Antimalerial suppressive 0.5 g weekly, therapeutic initial 1 g 0.5 g daily
Chloroquine sulphate	400 mg - 1.2 g
Chlorpheniramine maleate	4 - 16 mg daily
Chlorpopamide	100 - 500 mg daily
Chlorpromazine HCl	75 - 800 mg daily
Chlortetracycline	3 g in divided doses daily, children 30 mg per kg body weight
Chlorthalidone	100 - 200 mg daily
Cholera vaccine	0.5 ml
Chordiazepoxide	10 - 100 mg daily
Cloxacillin sodium	1.5 - 3.0 g
Cimetidine	200 - 400 mg
Clofazimine	100 mg six times weekly
Clofibrate	2 g daily
Clonidine HCl	100 - 300 mg daily
Cod liver oil	10 ml daily
Codeine phosphate	60 mg
Corticotrophin	40 - 80 mg daily
Cortisone acetate	50 - 400 mg daily
Cyanocobalamine	1 - 2 mg by I/M injection in divided doses
Cyclizine HCl	25 - 50 mg daily
Cyclophosphamide	100 - 200 mg daily
Cycloserine	250 - 750 mg daily
Cypraheptadine HCl	4 - 20 mg daily

Name of the Drug	Maximum dose
D-panthenol	0.25 - 0.5 g
Dapsone	25 - 50 mg, twice weekly
Dehydro-emetine HCl	60 - 90 mg by I/M injection
Deslanoside	0.8 - 1.2 mg by I/M injection
Dexamethazone	0.5 - 10 mg
Di-iodohydroxy quinoline	2g daily for 20 days in amoebasis
Diazepam	5 mg for inducing sleep
Diethylcarbamazine	100 - 500 mg daily
Digitalis prepared	1.5 g initial dose in divided doses for rapid digitilisation
Digitoxin	0.05 - 0.2 mg daily
Digoxin	1 - 1.5 mg daily
Dil. hydrochloric acid	10 ml
Diloxamide furoate	1.5 g daily
Dimenhydrinate	25 - 100 mg
Dimercaprol	2 - 3 mg daily
Diphenhydramine HCl	50 - 200 mg daily
Diphenoxylate HCl	5 - 30 mg daily
Diphtheria antitoxin	50 - 2000 IU
Doxycyclin	100 mg daily, antibiotic
Emetine HCl	30 - 60 mg daily
Ephedrine HCl	15 - 60 mg daily
Ergometrin maleate	1 mg
Ergotomine tartarate	1 - 2 mg daily
Erythromycin	1 - 2 g daily
Ethambutol	15 - 25 mg/kg
Ethionamide	0.5 - 1 g daily
Ethopropazine HCl	50 - 100 mg daily
Ferric ammonium citrate	3 g daily
Ferrous fumarate	0.2 - 0.6 g daily
Ferrous gluconate	1.2 - 1.8 g daily
Ferrous gluconate	Prophylactic 300 mg daily
Ferrous sulphate	Prophylactic 300 mg daily

Name of the Drug	Maximum dose
Fludrocortisone acetate	1 - 2 mg daily
Fluorouracil	3 mg/kg of body weight
Fluphenazine HCl	1 - 2 mg daily
Folic acid	5 - 20 mg daily
Frusemide	40 - 120 mg daily
Furazolidone	400 mg daily
Gentamycin sulphate	80 - 120 mg by i/m injection
Glibenclamide	2.5 - 20 mg daily
Griseofulvin	0.5-1 g daily
Guanethidine sulphate	10 - 20 mg daily
Heparin sodium	20000 - 50000 units
Hyaluronidase	500 - 1000 units by i/v injection.
Hydrochlor thiazide hydrochloride	25-100 mg weekly or once every two weeks in malaria.
Hydrocortisone	50 mg by intravenous route
Hyoscine hydrobromide	600 microgram sc-injection,
Hyoscyamus dry extract	60 mg
Hyoscyamus liquid extract	0.5 ml
Hyoscyamus tincture	5ml
Ibuprofen	0.6 - 1.2 g daily
Imipramine	50 - 150 mg. daily
Indomethacin	75 - 100 mg daily
Insulin	According to requirement of patient
Ipecac liquid extract	0.1 ml
Ipecac. tincture	1 ml
Isocarboxazid	10 - 20 mg daily.
Isoniazid	600 mg in divided doses
Isoprenaline sulphate	5 - 20 mg daily
Kanamycin sulphate	0.5 - 1 g by i/m injection
Lanatoside C	1 - 1.5 mg
Leptazol	50 - 100 mg
Levodopa	250 mg daily
Light kaolin	75g

Name of the Drug	Maximum dose
Light magnesium carbonate	0.3 - 0.6 g antacid
Lincomycin	1.5 g daily
Liquid paraffin	30 ml oral
Liquorice liquid extract	5 ml
Magnesium hydroxide mixture	10 ml as antacid and 50 ml as laxative
Magnesium trisilicate	0.5 - 2 g
Mebendazole	100 mg single dose
Meclizine HCl	25 - 50 mg
Mephenesin	0.1 - 1 mg
Meprobamate	0.4 - 1.2 g daily
Metformin HCl	0.5 - 2 g daily
Methdilazine HCl	8 mg daily
Methotrexate	50 - 100 mg
Methyl dope	0.5 - 3.0 g
Metronidazole	200 mg 3 times daily for seven days
Morphine hydrochloride	5 - 10 mg
Morphine sulphate	10 - 20 mg
Neomycin sulphate	0.7 - 2 g
Nikethamide	2 g by i/v injection
Noscapine	15 - 30 mg
Nuxvomica tincture	2 ml
Nystatin	1 - 2 million units daily
Opium tincture	2 ml
Oxprenolol HCl	40 mg - 2 g daily
Oxyphenbutazone	200 - 400 mg daily
Oxytetracycline	1 - 2 g
Oxytocin	1.5 unit by i/v injection
Paracetamol	0.5 - 1 g every four hours
Paraldehyde	8 ml orally or rectal injection
Pentazocine HCl	25 - 100 mg after food
Pethidine hydrochloride	100 mg, 25 - 100 mg by i/m or i/v inj.
Phenobarbitone	120 mg
Phalcodeine	60 mg daily
Phenobarbitone sodium	120 mg

Name of the Drug	Maximum dose
Phenyl butazone	400 mg daily
Piperazine citrate	2 g daily
Phenytoin sodium	50 mg daily
Potassium citrate	2 g
Potassium iodide	500 mg as expectorant
Prednisolone	5 - 60 mg daily
Prednisone	5 - 60 mg
Prepared belladonna herb	200 mg orally
Primaquine phosphate	15 mg daily
Probenecid	2 g daily
Procaine penicillin	As penicillin 900 mg by intramuscular daily
Proguanil HCl	0.1 to 0.3 g daily
Promethazine HCl	20 - 50 mg daily
Propranolol HCl	3 - 10 mg i/vinjection.
Pyridoxin HCl	10 - 150 mg daily
Quinidine	200 mg three to four times a day in the prophylaxis of cardiac arrythmia.
Quinine hydrochloride	300 - 600 mg in malaria
Quinine sulphate	300 - 600 mg in malaria
Reserpine	5 mg daily in divided doses in psychiatric state
Rhubarb powder	1 g
Rifampicin	450 - 600 mg
Senna leaf powder	2 g
Small pox vaccine	0.02 ml prophylactic
Sodium bicarbonate	5 g as an antacid
Sodium citrate	4 g
Sodium iodide	500 mg as an expectorant
Sodium salicylate	10 gm daily in divided doses for acuterheumatism
Streptomycin sulphate	1 g daily
Sulpha methoxazole	2 g daily
Sulphadiazine	3 g initial dose subsequently 4 gm daily in divided doses.
Sulphafurazole	3 g daily
Sulphadimidine	3 g initial dose. Afterwards 6 gm daily in divided doses
Streptomycin sulphate	1 g daily
Tolbutamide	0.5 - 1.5 g daily
Trimethoprim	100 - 200 mg
Thyroid	250 mg daily
Testosterone	60 mg
Tolu syrup	10 ml

VETERINARY DOSES

It is mentioned eariler that doses depend upon the type of formulation, age of the patient, sex of the patient, idiocyncracy, drug interaction, body weight, surface area and the severity of the disorder. Thus, as compared to human beings the doses required for animals are more or on the higher side, obviously becasue the weight and surface area of animals is normally more than the human beings, except very, few small animals.

Doses for animals are normally mentioned on body weights. Morever unless otherwise mentioned specifically, doses are applicable to 'all-species'.

The term 'all species' as referred in British Pharmacopoeia Veterinary 1977 First Edition is restricted to

Horse and cattle	500 kg
Pigs	150 kg
Sheeps, goats, calves, and foals	50 kg
Dogs	10 kg
Cats	05 kg

For heavier animals, the daily doses may vary. The word daily means once in twenty four hours.

Doses mentioned are per kg of, body weight of animals.

Veterinary doses of some important medicaments are as below :

Table 3.4 : Veterinary doses

Name of the Drug	Maximum dose
Adrenaline acid tartrate	10 microgram/kg
Ampicillin	4 - 12 mg/kg
Apomorphine hydrochloride	0.3 to 0.6 mg/kg
Arsanillic acid	100 - 250 g /tonne of feed
Ascorbic acid	50 - 300 mg/kg
Acetyl salicylic acid	30 - 100 mg/kg
Atropine sulphate	20 - 60 microgram/kg subcutaneously
Azaperone	0.5 - 2 mg/kg
Benzyl penicillin	3 - 6 mg by i/m injection
Beta metha zone	20 microgram/kg
Calciferol	12 - 100 microgram/25 - 50 mg/tonne of feed
Calcium gluconate	100 - 300 mg/kg i/m or i/v injection
Calcium lactate	50 -100 mg/kg of body weight
Carbon tetrachloride	1 to 3 ml
Castor oil	1 to 2 ml/kg
Catechu	10 - 20 mg/ kg
Chalk	0.3 - 0.5 g /kg
Chloral hydrate	60 - 100 mg/kg
Chloramphenicol	50 mg/kg
Chlorpropamide	5 - 15 mg/kg
Chlortetracycline HCl	130 mg/litre of drinking water
Cloxacillin benzathine	500 mg as a single dose
Cod-liver oil	0.2 ml/kg

Name of the Drug	Maximum dose
Danthrone	20 - 50 mg/kg
Dapsone	4 g daily by i/m injection
Decoqu)nate	40 g/tonne of feed
Dexamethasone	25 - 100 microram/kg
Dextrose	1 g/kg
Diamphenethide	100 mg/k);
Diaveridine	15 g /tonne of feed
Dienostml	20 mg/kg
Dihydro streptomycin sulphate	20 mg/kg daily by i/m injection
Dimercaprol	2.5 - 3 mg / kg by i/m injection
Dinitolmide	200 g/tonne of feed.
Erythromycin	2 - 20 mg/kg daily
Ethopabate	5 - 8 g /tonne of feed
Ferrous sulphate	10 - 30 mg/kg
Fluanisone	5 mg/kg
Framycetine sulphate	7000 units / kg daily
Frusemide	5mg/kg daily
Furazol id one	400 g / tonne feed for ten days
Griseofulvin	15 - 20mg/kg daily
Haloxon	50 mg/kg
Hexachlorophene	10 - 15 mg/kg
Hexoestrol	15 - 45 mg by implantation, in non-edible part of the body of animal.
Hydrochlorothiazide	0.2 to 5 mg/kg daily
Hydroxy-cobalmin	5 - 10 microgram/kg
Hyoscine hydrobromide	30 - 60 microgram/kg
Lincomycin HCl	20 mg/kg daily
Magnesium carbonate	15 - 30 mg/kg
Magnesium sulphate	0.5 - 1 g/kg
Mepyramine maleate	5 -10 mg/kg
Methandienone	500 mg/kg daily
Methyl prednisolone acetate	400-1000 microgram/kg once a week
Methyl testosterone	0.25 mg/kg daily
Metronidazole	20 mg/kg
Neomycin sulphate	4000 - 8000 units / kg daily
Nicotinamide	3 - 5 mg/kg
Nitrofurazone	500 g / tonne of feed

Name of the Drug	Maximum dose
Nitroxynil	10 mg/kg
Nystatin	1,00,000 units daily
Oxyclozanide	10 - 15 mg/kg
Oxytetracycline	10 - 55 mg/kg upto
Oxytocin	50 milliunits/kg
Paracetamol	20 mg/kg
Liquid paraffin	1 - 2 ml /kg
Pentobarbitone sodium	20 - 35 mg/kg
Pethidine HCl	1 to 5 mg/kg by i/m injection
Phenobarbitone	6 - 12 mg/kg
Phenoxylmethyl penicillin	16 mg/kg daily
Phenyl butazone	2 - 20 mg/kg
Phenytoin sodium	10 to 20 mg/kg
Piperazine adipate	100 - 300 mg/kg
Prednisolone	0.25 to 0.5 mg/kg
Procain penicillin	20 - 40 mg/kg by i/m injection
Progesterone	200 500 microgramme/kg
Promethazine HCl	2.5 - 10 mg/kg
Reserpine	0.1 kg/tonne of feed
Serum gonadotrophin	5 - 15 units/kg by i/m injection
Sodium acid phosphate	10 - 30 mg/kg daily
Sodium bicarbonate	50 - 100mg/ kg
Sodium salicylate	50 - 200 mg/kg
Stilbesterol	50 mg by implantation, in non edible part of the animal
Streptomycin sulphate	10 mg/kg
Sulfamerazine	upto 100 mg/kg
Sulfadiazine	200 mg/kg
Sulfadimidine	100 mg/kg daily
Sulphamethoxypyridazine	22 mg/kg
Testosterone	0.5 - 2 mg/kg
Thiabendazole	50 - 100 mg/kg
Thiamine HCl	5 - 10 mg/kg
Thyroxine sodium	100 microgram/kg daily
Tolbutamide	10 - 30 mg/kg
Trimepraxine tartrate	2 - 4 mg/kg
Turpentine oil	15 - 60 ml as a single dose

QUESTIONS

1. Define the following :
   (1) Prescription, (2) Inscription, (3) Superscription, (4) Vehicle, (5) Subscription, (6) Signature.

2. Define the following dosage forms :
   (1) Tablets, (2) Capsules, (3) Pessaries, (4) Cachets, (5) Creams, (6) Implants, (7) Gargles, (8) Emulsions.

3. Give the maximum dose and route of administration of
   (a) Sulphaguanidine, (b) Chloramphenicol, (c) Magnesium sulphate
   (d) Cod-liver oil   (e) Testosterone   (f) Piperizine citrate.

4. What is a dose of a drug ? What are different factors which control the dose of a drug, describe them in short.

5. How the paediatric dose is worked out. Name and describe at least three formulae for fixing the doses of drugs.

6. What is Posology ? Give the min and max doses of Reserpine.

CHAPTER 4
WEIGHTS AND MEASURES

INTRODUCTION

In pharmacy two unit systems viz. the metric and the imperial system are in use. The leaning is more towards the metric system. Yet, it is felt that a working pharmacist must be familiar with both. With this view in mind the imperial system is included in this chapter.

THE IMPERIAL SYSTEM

Measures of Weight (Mass):

The standard is the imperial standard pound. This is defined as a cylindrical block made up of platinum and having a diameter 1.15 inch and 1.35 inch in thickness, with an encircling groove into which fits an ivory fork to lift the cylinder. The weight of this cylinder in vacuum is the imperial standard pound.

1. Avoirdupoise System:

(Avoirdupoise : Fr *Avoir* : to have + du : of the + *pois* : weight)

All other measures of mass are derived from the imperial standard pound.

1 ounce (oz) Avoirdupoise
     = 16th part of 1 pound
     = 537.5 grains

1 grain (gr) = 7000th part of 1 pound

2. Apothecaries System:

Apothecary (G *Apotheke* : Storing place)

It includes a set of special weights, known as Apothecaries or Troy weights. The details together with their symbols are given below:

Troy-weight	Symbol
20 grains = 1 scruple	∋
60 grains = 1 drachm	ʒ
480 grains = 1 Apothecaries or Troy ounce	℥

12 Apothecaries or Troy ounces = 1 Troy pound or 5760 grains. 1b

Arabic numbers are used in conjunction with the English words. Examples are:

2 grains, 4 drachms, 3 oz (Troy) etc. Hence 2, 4, 3 are Arabic numbers which precede the English words grain, scruple, etc.

The avoirdupoise ounce is indicated by the abbreviation 'oz'.

The Apothecaries ounce is indicated either by the symbol, '℥' or is written out as ounce (Troy or Apothecaries).

If symbols are used (which is generally the case when a prescription is given), the roman numerals follow the symbol.

For example:

One scruple is written as   ∋ i
Two drachms are written as   ʒ ii
Six ounces Troy are written as   ℥ vi

i, ii, iii, iv, v etc. are roman numericals.

The letters, 'SS' or 'fs' following a symbol means 'half' i.e.

ʒ SS means half a drachm
∋ fs means half a scruple

The symbol for imperial standard pound is 'lb'

43

Measures of Capacity (Volume) :

The standard in the imperial system is the imperial Standard Gallon and this is a secondary standard related to the imperial standard pound. Therefore, it is called *derived* standard.

The Gallon is defined as the volume occupied by ten imperial Standard pounds weight of distilled water weighed in air at 62° F at 30 inches pressure. All other weights are called *derived* weights.

Derived Weights :

1 pint (o)	=	8th part of a gallon
1 fluid ounce (fl. oz.)	=	20th part of a pint
1 fluid drachm (fl. dr.)	=	8th part of 1 fluid ounce
1 fluid drachm	=	60 minims
	=	60th part of a fluid drachm
1 Gallon (c)	=	160 fluid ounces
1 Fluid ounce	=	8 fluid drachms or 480 minims
1 fluid drachm	=	60 minims

Units	Symbols
Minims	m
Gutta (drop)	gtt
Fluid drachm	ʒ
Fluid ounce	fl ʒ
Pint	O
Gallon	C

1. Solids are weighed and liquids measured. Hence, confusion cannot occur even if the symbol viz ... '3' is the same in measures for mass as well as capacity.

2. Similarly as before, Arabic numerals are placed before the English words, and roman numerals follow the symbols.

THE METRIC SYSTEM

The metric units system was legalised in India from 1st April, 1957.

In order, to establish standards of weights and measures and to regulate trade or commerce in weights and measures, the standards of Weights and Measures Act, 1976 has been passed by the Government of India.

Measures of Weight (Mass)

The standard for weight is a *Kilogramme*. A kilogram is defined as *the weight of a piece of platinum iridium whose weight is equal to 1000.027 C.C.* of pure water at 4° C and 760 mm Hg pressure.

All other measures of mass are derived from kilogramme.

1 kilogram	=	1000 grams
1 Gram	=	1000 milligrams i.e. 10^{-3} kg
1 milligram	=	1000 micrograms i.e. 10^{-6} kg
1 microgram	=	10^{-9} kg

Measures of Capacity (Volume)

The litre, is a secondary standard measurement of volume. The standard is a litre. The litre is defined as the volume of 1 kg of pure water at 4° C and 760 mm Hg pressure.

Symbols of weight		Symbols for capacity
kilogram	(kg)	Litre *l*
Gram	(g)	
Milligram	(mg)	Millilitre ml 10^{-3} *l*
Microgram	(µg)	Micro litre µ*l* 10^{-6} *l*

The cubic centimetre (c.c.) is less than one ml.

$$1 \text{ ml} = 1.000027 \text{ c.c.}$$

Relations of capacity to weight

1 minim	=	0.9114 grain of water at 62° F
1 fluid drachm	=	54.688 grains of water at 62°F
1 fluid ounce	=	437.5 grains of water at 62° F
	=	1 ounce (avoirdupoise)
110 minims	=	100 grains of water.

Imperial equivalents of Metric weights and measures

1 microgram (µg)	=	15.432×10^{-6} grain
1 milligram (mg)	=	0.015432 grain
1 gram (g)	=	15.432 grains
	=	0.03215 ounce (apothecaries)
	=	0.03527 ounce (Avoirdupoise)
1 kilogram (kg)	=	2.2046 pounds
1 millilitre (ml)	=	16.894 minims
1 litre (l)	=	0.21997 gallon
	=	1.7598 gallon
	=	35.196 fluid ounces

Metric equivalents of Imperial weights and measures

1 grain (gr)	=	0.064799 g
1 ounce (avoirdupoise) (oz) i. e. 437.5 grains	=	28.350 g
1 ounce (apothecaries) (480 grains)	=	31.104 g
1 pound (lb.)	=	453.59 g
1 minim (min)	=	0.05919 g
1 fluid drachm (fl. dr)	=	3.3515 mls
1 fluid ounce (fl. oz)	=	28.412 mls
1 pint (pt)	=	568.25 mls
1 gallon (gal)	=	4.546 litres

Approximate Equivalents

30 ml	=	1 fluid ounce
30 G	=	1 oz Avoir
1 G	=	15 grains
1 ml	=	15 minims
1 Teaspoonful	=	4 ml
1 Desert spoonful	=	8 ml
1 Table spoonful	=	15 ml

Recently SI units (Systeme International / Unites) have been adopted every where. However, it will have very little effect on dispensing of medication.

As compared to Metric system which has many units including Calorie, horse power etc. the S. I. system has only seven primary units.

Kilogramme primary unit of mass in metric system is available in S. I. system, while the unit of capacity (volume) litre is secondary unit.

CALCULATIONS INVOLVED IN DISPENSING

(I) Alligation

It is a method used in Pharmacy to bind quantities together through lines drawn and in order to arrive at solutions to simple problems.

Example 1

In what proportion should 10 per cent salicylic acid ointment be mixed with white soft paraffin in order to obtain a mixture of 2 per cent salicylic acid ointment ?

Solution :

1. Put the-known strengths on left corner of a rectangle.
2. Place the required strength at a point where the diagonals meet.
3. Subtract the smaller figure from the bigger one on the same diagonal and place the figure on the other end of a diagonal.
4. The figures so obtained represent the number of parts of strength of the solution to be mixed.

Solution :

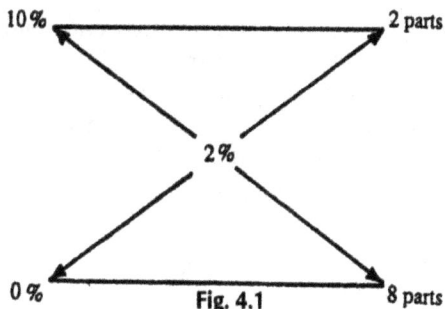

Fig. 4.1

Take 8 parts of soft paraffin and mix with 2 parts of ten per cent of salicylic acid ointment. The 10 parts of mixture will contain 2 per cent salicylic acid.

Example 2

In what proportion should 10 per cent, 8 per cent and 2 per cent sulphur ointments be mixed in order to obtain a mixture of 4 per cent sulphur ointment ?

Solution

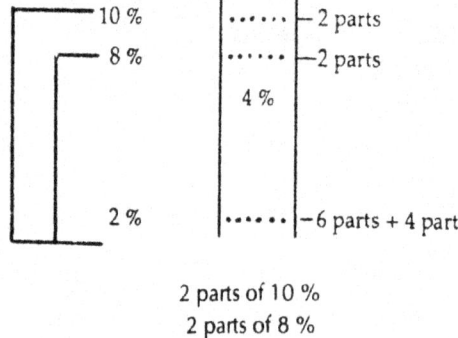

2 parts of 10 %
2 parts of 8 %
10 parts of 2 %
―――
14

1. Link the 10, 8 and 2 per cent ointments as shown. Put the required percentage in the centre of two vertical lines.

2. Subtract the lowest from the required and put the result across the two higher values.

3. Subtract the required percentage from the highest and second highest and put the results against the lowest.

Thus 14 parts of the above mixture will contain 4 per cent of sulphur.

Example 3

A pharmacist has three lots of ichthammol ointment containing 40 per cent, 20 per cent and 10 per cent of ichthammol respectively. In what proportions these be mixed in order to obtain an ointment containing 15 per cent of ichthammol ?

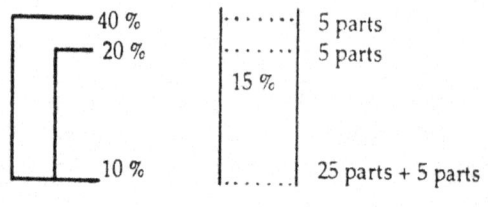

5 parts of 40 %
5 parts of 20 %
30 parts of 10 %
―――
40

Thus 40 parts of the above mixture will contain 15 per cent of ichthammol in the ointment.

Example 4

How many parts of 90 per cent 80 %, 60 per cent and 40 per cent alcohols be mixed so as to obtain alcohol of 70 per cent strength ?

Solution :

1. Pair of a higher strength and lower strength alcohol. Make such two pairs and link them together as shown below.

2. Place the required strength in between two vertically drawn lines.

3. Subtract the required strength from the higher values. Place the result against the lower strengths horizontally.

4. Subtract the lower percentage from the required percentage and place the result across and horizontal to the higher strengths.

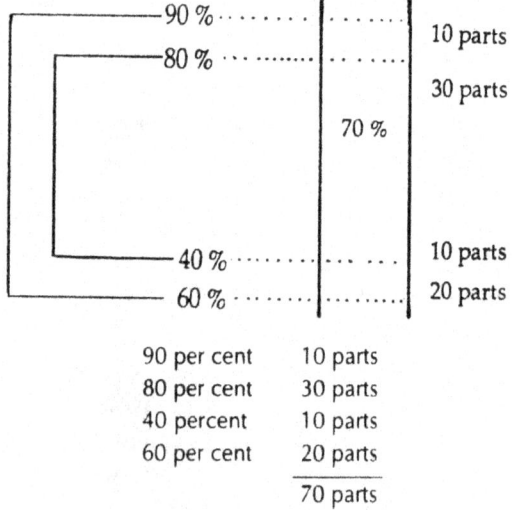

90 per cent	10 parts
80 per cent	30 parts
40 percent	10 parts
60 per cent	20 parts
	70 parts

The mixture of 70 parts will contain 70 per cent of alcohol.

(II) To find out the percentage strength of a mixture

Example 5

20 gallons of 40 per cent, 30 gallons of 60 per cent and 40 gallons of 80 per cent alcohols are mixed. What is the percentage strength of the mixture ?

Solution :

1. Multiply the volume by percentage

    $20 \times 90 = 1800$

    $30 \times 60 = 1800$

2. Divide the product by total volume

    $$\frac{40 \times 80 = 3200}{90 \quad\quad 5800}$$

    $\therefore \quad \dfrac{5800}{90} = 64.44$ per cent

(III) To find out the specific gravity of a mixture of liquids with different dilutions.

Observe the following rules :

1. Multiply the volume with corresponding specific gravity of individual solution.

2. Add the volume of all liquids.

3. Add all the products of multiplication.

4. Then use the following formula.

Specific gravity

$$= \frac{\text{Sum of the product of multiplication}}{\text{sum of the volumes}}$$

Example 6

What is the resultant specific gravity, if the following solutions are mixed ?

    100 ml solution of 0.9 sp. gr.

    200 ml of distilled water of 1 sp. gr.

    300 ml of solution with 1.1 sp. gr.

Solutions :

$100 \times 0.9 = 090.0$

$200 \times 1.0 = 200.0$

$300 \times 1.1 = 330.0$

Total volume $\overline{600 \text{ ml}}$ $\overline{620}$ sum of products

Specific gravity $= \dfrac{620}{600}$

Specific gravity $= 1.03$ of resultant mixture

ISOTONIC SOLUTIONS

Isotonic solutions are related to **colligative properties** of solutions. The colligative properties depend upon the number of molecules of solute present in the solution. Osmotic pressure, vapour pressure, boiling point and freezing point are colligative properties of solutions.

When two solutions are separated by a semipermeable membrane, the solvent passes from a dilute solution into a more concentrated solution and the process continues until the concentration of the solutions on each side becomes equal. This phenomenon is known as *osmosis* and the pressure responsible for this phenomenon is called *osmotic pressure* (O.P.). The osmotic pressure varies with the concentration of the solute. If the solute is a non-electrolyte the osmotic pressure will vary with the concentration of the molecules of solute. On the other hand, if the solute is an electrolyte, the osmotic pressure will vary with the concentration of ions. It therefore follows, that the osmotic-pressure will be greater with ionisable solutes rather than non-ionisable solutes.

Two solutions are said to be iso-osmotic if they exert the same osmotic pressure. In Pharmacy, a solution is said to be isotonic if it has the same osmotic pressure as blood plasma. Those with higher osmotic-pressure are called *hypertonic* and those with lower osmotic-pressure than plasma are called *hypotonic solutions*. However, the term paratonic includes both, hyper and hypotonic solutions.

Solutions intended to be injected into the body fluids should have the same osmotic-pressure as plasma for comfort and safety of patients. It is necessary to calculate quantities of solutes, so that the injectable preparation is isotonic with plasma. It is easier and convenient to prepare isotonic solutions by determining the freezing point, rather than from data collected through other colligative properties. The freezing point of plasma is – 0.52. It therefore follows, that any other solution having –0.52°C as its freezing point must be isotonic with plasma. Lachrymal fluid also has the same (– 0.52°C) freezing point.

All hypotonic solutions have a freezing point higher than that of plasma. All hypotonic solutions must be more isotonic. To make a solution isotonic, it is necessary to adjust the solution through addition of the adjusting substance. The adjusting substance will be required to lower the freezing point by 0.52°C of the unadjusted solution. It is possible to do so by using the following formula :

$$\frac{0.52 - a}{b}$$

where, a = the freezing point of the unadjusted solution.

b = the freezing point of 1 % w/v solution of the adjusting substance.

Where more than one solute is present

(a) is the sum of their depressions.

Effect of injecting paratonic solutions :

(a) Effect of injecting hypertonic solutions : The cell wall of a blood cell may be considered as a semipermeable membrane. The solution within the red blood cell and the plasma (second solution) is separated by the cell walls of the blood cells. Thus, the conditions for existence of osmotic pressure are fulfilled. Under normal conditions, there is an equilibrium between the two solutions and normal functions are performed. The average blood volume in human beings get five litres. On injecting large volumes of hypertonic solutions intravenously, this equilibrium gets upset and water molecules pass from the solution within the cells to the plasma and the cells collapse, assuming a undulating shape and the cells are then said to be **crenulated**. This effect is temporary and when normal conditions are restored, the cells appear normal.

(b) Effect of injecting hypotonic solutions : When large volumes of hypotonic solution are injected intravenously, the water molecules from the plasma pass into the cell in order to establish equilibrium. The cells go on swelling and a point is reached at which the cells begin to rupture. This is called **haemolysis**.

It is for these two reasons that it is necessary to adjust parenteral solutions to isotonicity.

General principles for adjustment to isotonicity :

1. In principle, all solutions intended for parenteral administration and solutions meant for eyes be adjusted to isotonicity.

2. In solutions intended for subcutaneous injection, isotonicity is desirable but is not essential, since the solution is injected into fatty tissue and not into the blood stream. It has been mentioned that the blood volume of an average individual is five litres. Injections meant for subcutaneous administration are small in volume as compared to the blood volume, and hence, there is no' appreciable change in osmotic pressure.

3. Solutions for intra-muscular administration are generally made hypertonic to promote rapid absorption and besides, these injections are administered in small volumes. Aqueous depot formulations should be isotonic.

4. Solutions intended for intrathecal administration must be isotonic for the following reason. The volume of cerebrospinal fluid in an adult is from 120 to 150 ml. Hence, even a small volume of paratonic solution will cause a variation in the osmotic pressure and consequently, bring discomfort to a patient.

5. All solutions, which are required to be administered intravenously and in large volumes, e.g. normal saline, glucose, and sodium chloride solution, glucose solution etc., must be adjusted to isotonicity.

6. All solutions applied in nostrils and also meant for application to broken skin may

7. Ophthalmic solutions should be adjusted to isotonicity with the lachrymal secretion. Generally, 0.9 % of sodium chloride is adequate.

(c) **Percentage calculations** : Before a student proceeds to undertake percentage calculations, he is advised to become familiar with weights and measures.

Per cent solutions are of the following types:

1. Per cent weight by volume (w/v) means 1 gram of solute in 100 ml of the product. In terms of grain and minims, it is grain of solute in 110 minims of product.

2. Per cent weight by weight (w/w) means 1 gram of solute in 100 grams of product.

3. Per cent volume by volume (v/v) means number of millilitres of solute (liquid) in 100 ml of product.

4. Per cent volume by weight (v/w) means the number of millilitres in 100 grams of product.

Generally, solutions are ordered in w/v or v/v, while w/w is used only when the prescriber so desires.

A revision of measures of mass and capacity, in the Imperial system, will be useful at this stage.

The standard for mass is the Imperial pound.

1 pound = 7000 grains.
 = 16 ounces avoirdupoise.

1 ounce avoirdupoise
 = 437.5 grains,

10 pounds of water
 = 1 Gallon.
 = 160 avoirdupoise ounces.

One Gallon = 8 pints.

One pint = 20 ounces avoirdupoise.

1 ounce avoirdupoise by weight
 = fluid ounce.

437.5 grains = 480 minims.

Weight by volume solutions in imperial system

Solute 1 oz Avoir, and solvent to produce 100 fluid ounces
 = 1 % w/v solutions

437.5 grains in 100 fluid ounces is 1 % solution.

Therefore, to produce 1 fluid ounce of 1 % w/v quantity of solute necessary will be,

$$= \frac{437.5}{100}$$

= 4.375 grains dissolved to produce 1 fluid ounce of 1 % w/v solution.

Or

4.375 × 4 = 17.5 grains in 4 ounces is 1 % w/v.

Or

35 grains in 8 ounces is 1 % w/v solution.

Example 7

Find the proportion of sodium chloride required to make 1 % solution of cocaine hydrochloride isotonic with plasma.

Freezing point of 1 % w/v solution of cocaine hydrochloride is - 0.09°C.

Freezing point of 1 % w/v solution of sodium chloride is 0.576°C.

Solution :

$$\frac{0.52 - a}{b}$$

$$= \frac{0.52 - 0.09}{0.576}$$

= 0.746 % w/v of sodium chloride is necessary

Example 8

Find out the required quantity of procaine hydrochloride necessary to render its solution isotonic with plasma.

Freezing point of 1 % w/v solution of procaine hydrochloride is − 0.122.

There is no unadjusted solution, i.e. (a) is zero. Using the same formula.

$$\frac{0.52 - 00}{0.122}$$

= 4.26 % of procaine hydrochloride is required to make it isotonic with plasma.

Example 9

Find the proportion of sodium chloride required to make a 2 % solution of cocaine hydrochloride isotonic with plasma.

Sodium chloride 1 % w/v
= 0.576°C freezing point.

Cocaine HCl 1 % w/v
= 0.09°C freezing point.

$$\frac{0.52 - (0.09 \times 2)}{0.576}$$

= 0.59 per cent solution of sodium chloride is necessary.

It has been mentioned before that the lachrymal secretion has the same osmotic pressure as plasma, and therefore, has the same freezing point. Sometimes, in eye lotions, it is required to issue a concentrated solution, and the patient is advised to dilute it before use. In such cases, the formula is modified by calculating the quantity, which is twice the freezing point depression.

The modified formula becomes, percentage of adjusting substance

$$= \frac{(2 \times 0.52) - a}{b}$$

Example 10

Find the quantity of sodium chloride necessary to make 100 ml of 0.3 % of zinc sulphate solution isotonic with lachrymal secretion on dilution with an equal volume of water.

Freezing point of zinc sulphate
= 0.086°C 1 % w/v solution

Freezing point of sodium chloride
= 0.576°C 1 % w/v.

Percentage of sodium chloride required

$$= \frac{(2 \times 0.52) - 0.086}{0.576}$$

= 1.65 per cent.

METHOD BASED ON MOLECULAR CONCENTRATION

The molecular concentration includes molecules, ion or both, present in a solution. The osmotic pressure is directly proportional to the number of molecules of a solute present in a solution. Hence, osmotic pressure is also proportional to the molecular concentration.

A gram molecule of any substance is the number of grams of that substance equal to the molecular weight of that substance. For example, the molecular weight of glucose is 180 and therefore, if 180 grams of glucose are dissolved in 100 gms of water, the solution is said to have a *gramme molecular* concentration of one per cent.

An aqueous solution, which has a molecular concentration of one percent, depresses the freezing point to − 18.6°C. Plasma depresses the freezing point to − 0.52.

A depression of −18.6°C is given by a molecular concentration of 1 %. Therefore, a depression of 0.52 will be given by,

$$\frac{1 \times 0.52}{18.6} = 0.03 \text{ \% of molecular concen-}$$

tration approx.

All solutions containing 0.030 gram molecular concentration of any substance will be isotonic with blood plasma.

0.03 x molecular weight
= Gram per cent.

For example, the molecular weight of urea is 60,

∴ $60 \times 0.30 = 1.8$ %

1.8 % solution of urea will be isotonic with blood plasma.

Therefore, for non-ionising substances, the following formula is used.

1 % w/v of substance required
= 0.03 x gramme molecular weight of the substance,

For ionising substances, per cent w/v of substance required

$$= \frac{0.03 \times \text{Gramme moleur weight of the substance}}{\text{Number of ions into which substance breaks}}$$

Example 11

Find the proportion of boric acid required to form a solution isotonic with lachrymal secretion.

Boric acid is practically nonionising and its molecular weight is 62.

Therefore, boric acid required
= 0.03 × 62
= 1.86 per cent solution will be isotonic with lacrymal secretion.

Example 12

Find the proportion of sodium chloride necessary to form solution isotonic with plasma.

Molecular weight of sodium chloride = 58.5
It is completely ionisable. Each molecule of sodium chloride yields 2 ions.

$$= \frac{0.03 \times 58.5}{2} = 0.884\%$$

Pharmacopoeia uses 0.9 % solution.

Example 13

1 % solution of cocaine hydrochloride is required to be made isotonic with plasma. How much of sodium chloride should be added to cocaine hydrochloride to make it isotonic with plasma ?

Molecular weight of cocaine hydrochloride is 339.5 and it is completely ionisable, each molecule giving 2 ions.

The gram molecular conc. of 1 % cocaine hydrochloride will be

$$= \frac{1 \times 2}{339.5}$$

= 0.0058 %.

The sodium chloride required will be
= 0.03 − 0.0058 = 0.0242 %

The molecular weight of sodium chloride is 58.5, and it yields 2 ions in solution.

$$= \frac{0.0242 \times 58.5}{2} = \frac{1.416}{2}$$

= 0.708 grams of sodium chloride is to be added.

Example 14

1 % solution of cocaine hydrochloride is required to be made isotonic with blood plasma. How much of dextrose may be added ?

Molecular weight of dextrose is 180,

Therefore, gramme molecular concentration of 1 % w/v solution of dextrose will be,

$$1 \times \frac{1}{180} = 0.0055$$

0.03 % gramme % will give an isotonic solution.

$$= \frac{0.0055}{0.0245} \text{ Dextrose}$$

= 0.0245 × 180 = 4.32 % dextrose will be required

PROOF SPIRIT

Proof spirit is an aqueous solution containing 50 % (v/v) of absolute alcohol. Alcohols of other percentage strength like 70 % said to be over proof (o.p.) or 30 % said to be under proof (U. p.).

Proof strength of alcohol is expressed by taking 50 % alcohol, or proof spirit as 100 proof. Then 25 % alcohol is half as strong, or 50 proof; proof strength is always twice of percentage strength (v/v). Hence, if percentage strength (v/v) is multiplied by 2, we have corresponding proof strength 35 % alcohol is 70 proof.

Alcohol and alcoholic beverages are generally measured in gallon and a unit proof gallon is frequently used to measure.

A proof gallon is 1 wine gallon of proof spirit means 1 proof gallon = 1 wine gallon of an alcohol solution containing 1/2 wine gallon of absolute alcohol and having, therefore, a strength of 100 proof or 50 % (v/v)

In India proof spirit is defined as a mixture of absolute alcohol (Pure alcohol) and water in such a way that its (mixture) specific gravity is 0.9197. From analysis it contains 57.1 % v/v of ethyl alcohol.

Proof gallons

$$= \frac{\text{Wine gallons} \times \text{Percentage strength of solution}}{50\%}$$

$$\text{Proof gallons} = \frac{\text{Wine gallons} \times \text{Proof strength of solution}}{100 \text{ (proof)}}$$

Example 1

How many proof gallons are present in 5 wine gallons of 75 % (v/v) alcohol ?

Solution :

Method - I :
$$1 \text{ proof gallon} = 1 \text{ wine gallon of 50 \% v/v strength}$$
$$\frac{5 \text{ (wine gallons)} \times 75 \text{ (\%)}}{50 \text{ (\%)}} = 7.5 \text{ proof gallons}$$

Answer : 7.5 proof gallons

Method - II :
$$75 \text{ \% v/v} = 150 \text{ proof}$$
$$\frac{5 \text{ (wine gallons)} \times 150 \text{ (proof)}}{100 \text{ (proof)}} = 7.5 \text{ proof gallon}$$

$$\text{Wine gallons} = \frac{\text{Proof gallons} \times 50 \text{ (\%)}}{\text{Percentage strength of solution}}$$

Or

$$\text{Wine gallons} = \frac{\text{Proof gallons} \times 100 \text{ (Proof)}}{\text{Proof strength of solution}}$$

Example 2

How may wine gallons of 20 % (v/v) alcohol would be the equivalent of 20 proof gallons ?

Solution :

Method - I :
$$1 \text{ Proof gallon} = 1 \text{ wine gallon of 50 \% (v/v) strength}$$
$$= \frac{20 \text{ (proof gallons)} \times 50 \text{ (\%)}}{20 \text{ (\%)}}$$

Answer : 50 wine gallons

Method - II :
$$20 \text{ \% (v/v)} = 40 \text{ proof}$$
$$= \frac{20 \text{ (proof gallons)} \times 100 \text{ (Proof)}}{40 \text{ (Proof)}}$$

Answer : 50 wine gallons

Example 3

What will be the percentage strength corresponding to 50 o.p. and 30 u. p. ?

Solution :

First convert o. p. and u. p. to proof strength.

when
$$\text{o. p. proof spirit} = \text{o. p.} + 100$$
$$= 50 + 100$$
$$= 150$$
$$\text{u. p. proof spirit} = 100 - \text{u. p.}$$
$$= 100 - 30$$
$$= 70$$
$$\text{Proof spirit} = \% \times 2$$
$$\% = \frac{\text{Proof spirit}}{2} = \frac{150}{2} = 75 \text{ \%}$$
$$\% = \frac{70}{2} = 35 \text{ \%}$$

$$\% = \frac{\text{Proof spirit}}{2} = \frac{150}{2} = 75\%$$

$$\% = \frac{70}{2} = 35\%$$

QUESTIONS

1. Name the various systems of weights and measures. Name various units of mass and mass volume in different systems.
2. Give the approx. equivalents of following in metric system.
   - 1 fluid ounce.
   - 15 grains.
   - 15 minims.
   - 1 Gallon.
   - 1 pint.
3. Name the following symbols.
   - O   m
   - C   ℈
   - ʓ   lb
   - ʓ   gl
4. What is alligation ? how it is useful in finding solutions to problems ?
5. What is Isotonicity ? Define hypertonic, hypotonic and paratonic solutions ?
6. What do you know about
   - (a) Haemolysis,
   - (b) Crenulation,
   - (c) Osmotic pressure,
   - (d) Lacrymal solution ?
7. What are the adverse effects of injecting large volume of hypertonic solutions ?
8. What precautions one must take in respect of isotonicity while injecting ?
   - (a) Intramuscularly
   - (b) Subcutaneously,
   - (c) Intrathecally,
   - (d) Intravenously.

●●●

CHAPTER 5
HEAT PROCESSES

INTRODUCTION

Heat is very important form of energy. Several processes involving the use of heat are employed conveniently for various purposes. Though most of them are used for purification, few of them are used for isolation, fractionation and preparation of pharmaceuticals. Following is the list of important heat processes practiced in pharmaceutical manufacturing.

1. Fusion
2. Calcination
3. Ignition
4. Exsiccation
5. Desiccation
6. Sublimation
7. Distillation
8. Evaporation
9. Drying.

1. Fusion : *Fusion or Liquefaction is the process of liquefying solid by the application of heat without the aid of solvent,* or it is the process of heating the solids until they melt.

Thus fusion can be used to purify certain compounds, solid at room temperature, of their impurities. The beeswax, woolfat, hard paraffin are heated to melt, filtrated while hot to remove dissolved impurities. Fusion is also used to prepare some of the inorganic medicinal substances i. e. Toughened silver nitrate, zinc chloride, sulphurated potash and even the potassium hydroxide sticks.

2. Calcination : *Calcination is the process in which inorganic substances are strongly heated to loose their volatile contents with the formation of a fixed residue.* Following are the few important examples practicing the calcination :

(i) Calcium carbonate is heated to get calcium oxide, which looses only carbon-dioxide.

(ii) Heavy magnesium oxide is prepared by heating heavy magnesium carbonate. Red mercuric oxide and light magnesium oxide are also prepared similarly.

3. Ignition : *Ignition or Incineration is the heat process and consists strongly heating an organic substance until the carbonaceous matter burns out and leaves the inorganic residue known as ash.* Ignition is a way of ensuring the inorganic matter into the substances under ignition. Thus ignition is one of the criterion to standardise the organic substances and crude drugs.

4. Exsiccation : *Exsiccation is the process of removing the water of crystallisation from the crystalline substances and making them anhydrous.* Normally, this process is carried out at 100 to 200°C. The intention of the exsiccation is to reduce the bulk and weight of the substance. Some substances loose their water of crystallisation and become variable in composition. They can be ensured of their purity by exsiccation only. Common examples of the exsiccated compounds in pharmacy are the exsiccated ferrous sulphate, exsiccated sodium carbonate, exsiccated alum and anhydrous sodium arsenate. Exsiccation is done slowly so as to prevent the fusion of the crystalline substances. Normally, the exsiccated products are in the form of fine powder.

5. Desiccation : *Desiccation is the process of removing adhered moisture from solid or liquid.* Thus, it is a dehydration process, and is accomplished by most mild heating. The objects of desiccation are, to preserve the medicinal substances properly, to reduce bulk and weight, and to facilitate powdering of chemicals and crude drugs. Desiccation is done either by mild heating as in drying over or keeping the substance in desiccator in contact with dehydrating agents. The dehydrating agents normally used for desiccation are the concentrated sulphuric acid, phosphorus pentoxide, fused calcium chloride and dried silica gel. In the laboratory a glass device is used for such a process and is known as a desiccator. In some cases desiccation at reduced process is also done.

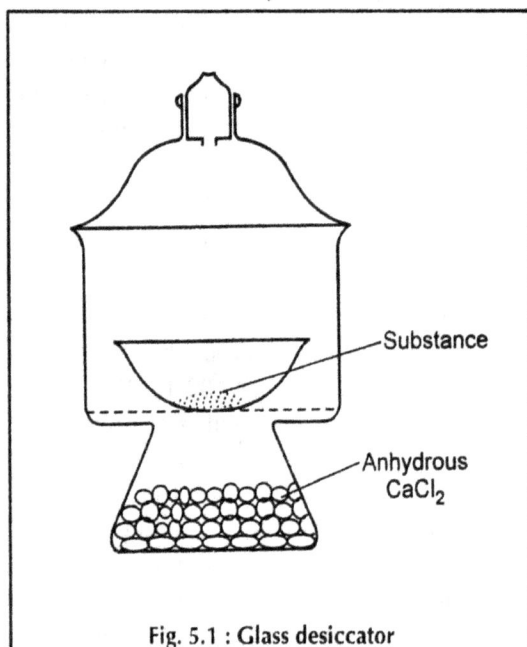

Fig. 5.1 : Glass desiccator

Substances which are very sensitive to moisture are desiccated by providing the drying agents in the container in which they are stored. The example of this type are digitalis, ergot, penicillin etc. Moisture in some of the organic solvents is removed by treating them with fused calcium chloride or anhydrous sodium sulphate.

Spray drying of the liquid is one of the method of desiccation used in pharmacy. Some of the highly hygroscopic materials and biological products are desiccated by spray drying such as papain, blood plasma and several liquid extracts.

6. Sublimation : *Sublimation is the process of heating a solid with vapour without intermediate passing through the liquid state.* In Pharmacy this process is particularly used for the purification and for the collection of volatile solids from the chemical reaction. The product is heated to vaporise and condensed to a solid and is termed as sublimate. Depending upon the physical characters three types of sublimed substances are known as (a) Cake sublimate (b) Powder sublimate (3) Crystalline sublimate.

(a) *Cake sublimate :* The substances are heated to vaporise and vapours get condensed to form a cake. The examples of cake forms are mercuric chloride and ammonium carbonate.

(b) *Powder sublimate :* Examples are calomel and sulphur.

(c) *Crystalline sublimate :* Arsenic trioxide, Iodine, benzoic acid and menthol.

No specific apparatus or device is used for sublimation, but depends upon the compound and its properties. Normally the retort known as *Paul's sublimation apparatus* and Bruhl's sublimation apparatus are used in the laboratory.

7. Distillation : *It is the process of converting liquid into its vapour and recovering the liquid by condensing the vapour by leading it in contact with the cold surface.* The vessel or container in which the substance is heated is known as *still*, which is connected to a apparatus within which lies the cold surface is known as *condenser*. The vessel which collects the product of distillation is known as *receiver*, while the condensed product is known as *distillate*. The still and condenser may be made of glass or a metal suitable for the process. The efficiency of the condenser decides the effectiveness of the process.

An ideal condenser should have the following characters :
1. It must be so constructed as to be easily cleaned.
2. The cooling surface provided by it must be larger as the rapidity of condensation is proportional to the area of condensing surface.
3. Condensing surface should be reasonable conductor of heat as the rapidity of condensation is proportional to the speed with which the surface conducts the heat.
4. The film of condensed liquid must get easily removed as quickly as possible as it acts as a conductor.
5. The water used in cooling the surface must get quickly carried from the condenser, so as to provide the cold surface.

The various types of condensers which may be used for the laboratory or commercial use are known as *Leibig condenser, Spiral condenser, bulb condenser, double surface condenser* or *multitubuler condenser*. Depending upon the techniques and the principles used following are the various types of distillation. (Fig. No. 5.2 a to e)

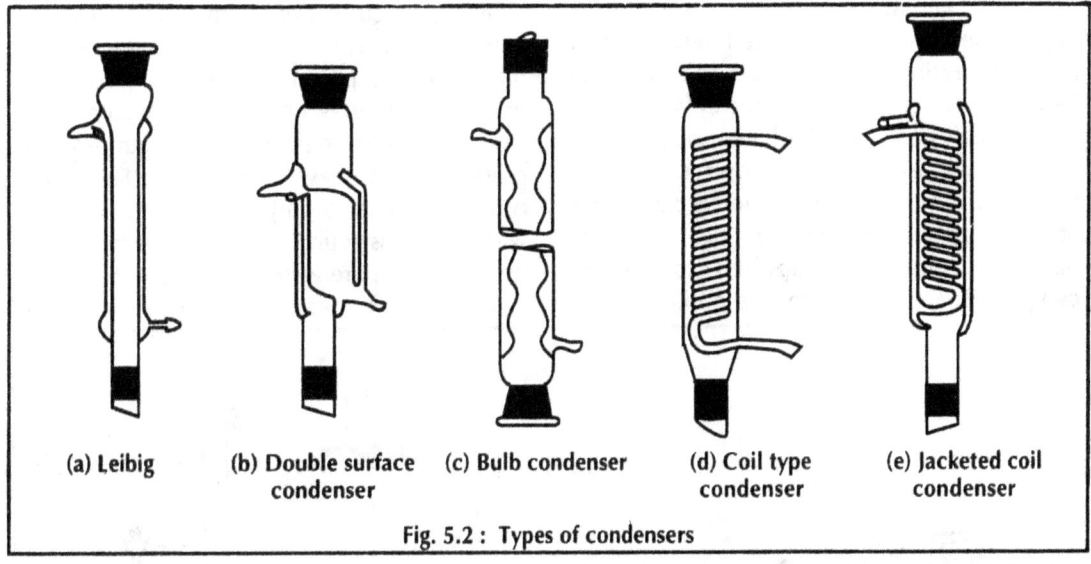

(a) Leibig   (b) Double surface condenser   (c) Bulb condenser   (d) Coil type condenser   (e) Jacketed coil condenser

Fig. 5.2 : Types of condensers

(a) **Destructive distillation :** This is also known as *dry distillation* This consists of heating the dried organic matter in suitable apparatus in absence of air. The residue left after dry distillation is said to be carbonised. The destructive distillation is only carried industrially and used to get very valuable chemicals needed for industrial and pharmaceutical use. Destructive distillation of wood and animal matter are very common. The product of destructive distillation of wood are the acetic acid, acetone creosote, methyl alcohol and wood tar. The residue left after distillation is *char-coal* The coal after destructive distillation produces coal tar, ammonia and several gases, while the residue left after the process is known as *coke*. Animal matter produces several hydrocarbons, ammonia and pyridine bases after destructive distillation. The products of destructive distillation have got a characteristic small and even they may not be present in the original matter which is being distilled in presence of air.

(b) Molecular distillation : During distillation the liquids getting evaporated are condensed on the cold surface. While doing so most of the molecules leaving the evaporating surface and reaching the condensed surface colloid with other molecules. If a high vacuum is applied the frequency of collision is decreased as the distance travelled by a molecule without collision with the another is increased which means the mean free path of the molecules is lengthened. The distance between evaporating surface and the condenser is equal to the mean free path of the vapour molecules at the very low temperature. Thus recondensation does not take place. But in case of ordinary distillation or distillation under vacuum, the conditions approaching to the equilibrium are maintained and the recondensation takes place Thus if the condenser is placed very close to the evaporating surface then the distance between them is less than the mean free path of the molecules and the distillation occurs most readily and even at the lowest possible temperature. Molecular distillation is carried out at 0.001 to 0.00001 mm of Hg. Thus this particular process is applied to certain compounds and utilized for the purification or isolation of certain pharmaceuticals. The fixed oils which were regarded as non-volatile can be distilled by the molecular distillation. Molecular distillation is conveniently used to separate vitamin 'A' from cod liver oil.

(c) Steam distillation : This is yet another method of distilling vital substances which involve use of steam. However. the distillation of immiscible liquids is more important than the miscible liquid. In case of the distillating miscible liquids the presence of each substance has the effect of lowering of vapour pressure of the other, but in case of immiscible liquids they do not have effect on the vapour pressure of the others. A immiscible liquid and water boils at high temperature but can be distilled rapidly when boiled with water by allowing the current of steam at much lowered temperature. Thus the steam distillation is based on the principle that the mixture of immiscible liquids boil when the compound vapour pressure together exceed atmospheric pressure and in case of water and liquid that ordinarily boils at higher temperature than water alone is found to boil at a temperature below that of pure water Thus steam distillation is passing the steam through liquid which

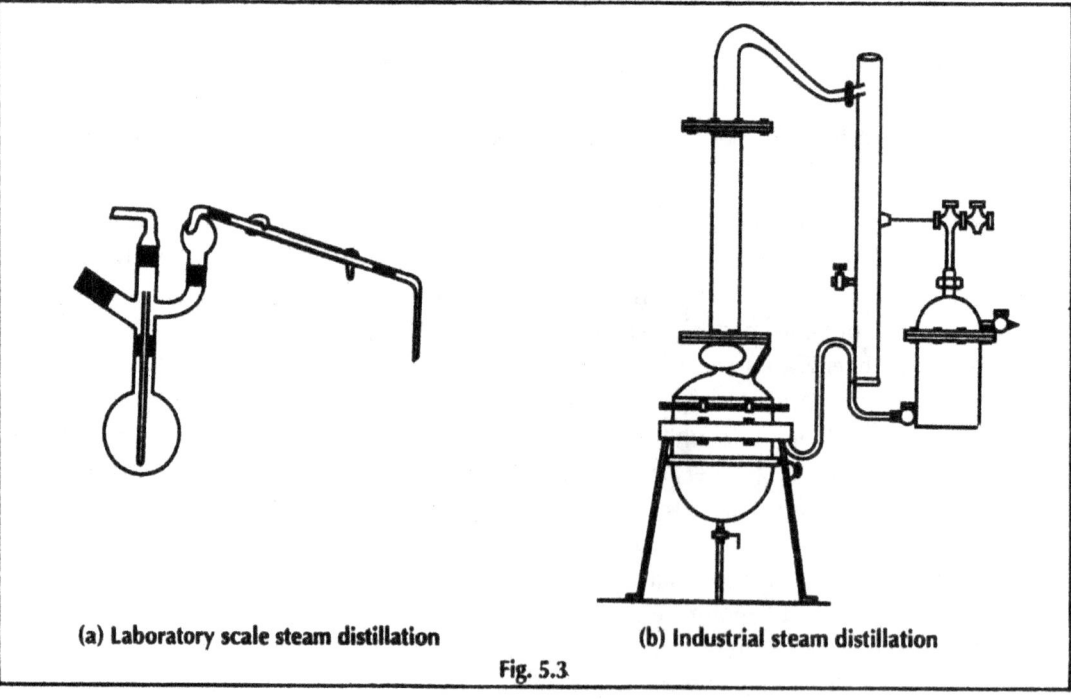

(a) Laboratory scale steam distillation (b) Industrial steam distillation

Fig. 5.3

is immiscible with water and condensing the vapour. The mixture of the immiscible liquids starts boiling when the sum of their vapour pressures equals to the atmospheric pressure. This has been stated above in case of the water and a immiscible liquid which boils at higher temperature than water. The mixture boils below the boiling point of pure water. Thus in case of a mixture of water and nitrobenzene (boiling point 206 °C) is found to boil at 99°C. Under ordinary pressure at 99°C water has vapour pressure of 733 mm of mercury and nitrobenzene 27 mm of mercury. The total being equal to the normal atmospheric pressure of 760 mm of mercury. In the above process the distillate contains about one part of nitrobenzene and four parts of water which is justified by the application of Avogadro's hypothesis stating that the weight of equal volume of different gases under the same physical condition are proportional to the weight of the mercury. The other example of steam distillation utilised for the purification are the benzene, camphor, carbon-di-sulphide.

(d) Vacuum Distillation (Distillation under reduced pressure) : A liquid boils at lower temperatures when the pressure on the surface is reduced. The rate of evaporation is more when it boils and, therefore, boiling under reduced pressure will also increase the rate of distillation. Distillation under reduced pressure becomes essential in following cases :

1. When the liquids decompose at their boiling point.
2. If the liquids are thermolabile and if the constituents extracted in the menstruum undergo chemical changes either during the recovery of the menstrum, in the preparation of tinctures or extracts or during the concentration of the galenical preparations as mentioned above.

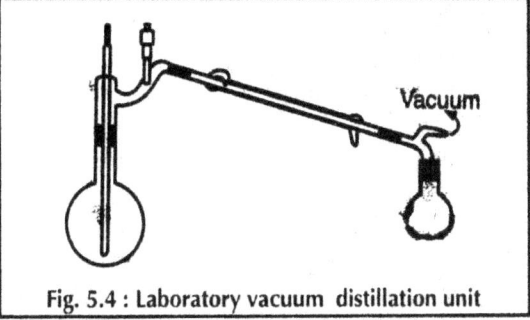

Fig. 5.4 : Laboratory vacuum distillation unit

Under these conditions there is no other suitable method except the vacuum distillation. Apparatus shown in the figure is suitable for laboratory purposes. This apparatus consists of a suitable flask known as *Clasein flask* to suit the requirement and also to check bumping which normally takes place, during the vacuum distillation and cause a considerable inconvenience. The kneck ' B ' has a arrangement of close tubing with a fine capillary and tubes into the liquid under distillation to avoid bumping. The receiver is connected to a vacuum pump to provide the suitable vacuum. The vacuum is provided above the surface of the liquid to be distilled and the flask is then heated. The reduced pressure on the surface of the heated liquid causes it to boil at lower temperature and distillation commences at a rate greater than at ordinary pressure.

(e) Fractional distillation : It is the process employed to separate two miscible liquids having different boiling points. It is very easy to separate a non-volatile solid by distillation but to separate two volatile compounds completely from each other is difficult. In case of a volatile mixture the vapour pressure of both the liquids is lowered out so that the boiling point of the mixture will be different from the alcohol and water and when the sum of the partial pressure of two vapours equals to the atmospheric pressure the mixture of the liquids starts boiling. The alcohol is more volatile and having low boiling point will be getting evaporated at a faster rate than that of water. The first part of the distillation will cover maximum amount of alcohol and less of water Towards the end it is entirely covered by water. Both the fractions can be separated and redistilled to get individual compounds. However, this process can be operated in single unit by providing the scientifically designed fractionating columns. The fractionating column is a device that considerably enhances the process of fractional distillation by condensing most of the vapour of the less volatile constituents of mixtures and return it to the distillating flask, whereas the vapours of the more volatile constituents are allowed to pass to the condenser. In the fractionating column vapour is condensed and while returning to the dissipating flask comes in contact with the rising vapour. Ultimately this results in fractionation of the liquid being distilled.

Preparation of terpeneless volatile oils like lemon and orange oils and even the isolation of several fractions like, ceneole, citral, geraneole, citranelol from volatile oil are good examples of fractional distillation.

(8) Evaporation : *Evaporation is the free-escape of vapour from the surface of a liquid.* However, evaporation differs from the vaporisation. Vaporisation is the process of converting a liquid into the vapour by application of heat under various conditions. Thus evaporation can take place even at room temperature. Evaporation and vaporisation differ from boiling in the respect that boiling takes place only at one temperature for a given pressure.

Evaporation takes place only at the surface but in case of boiling evaporation takes place from the liquid. Boiling takes place when the vapour pressure above the liquid is equal to the atmospheric pressure. Factors affecting the rate of evaporation are as under :

1. The surface exposed : The rate of evaporation is directly proportional to the surface exposed to evaporation. However, the depth of a liquid under evaporation does not affect the rate of evaporation. More the surface exposed to evaporation, higher is the rate of evaporation.

2. Saturation of the vapour : The rate of evaporation of a liquid depends upon the amount of vapour in the air above the liquid. If the air above the liquid is saturated with the vapour, the evaporation will take place effectively.

3. Pressure on the liquid under evaporation : The rate of evaporation is inversely proportional to the pressure on the surface of the liquid. If the pressure on the liquid is reduced to half, the rate of evaporation will be getting doubled and if the pressure is doubled the rate of evaporation comes to half. Thus it is justified that the rate of evaporation under vacuum is more than at normal atmospheric pressure. When the pressure is decreased above the surface of evaporation there is very less resistance to the movement of the molecules. Thus their velocity increases and the molecules of the vapour above the liquid leave to join the vapour in unit time.

4. Temperature of the vapour : A vapour of a liquid i. e. saturated at one time is unsaturated at higher temperature. It has been described earlier that in the presence of a saturated vapour no evaporation takes place. Thus-the rate of evaporation is increased by raising the temperature of the vapour. It can be explained by the following suitable examples.

At 15°C one cubic metre of air can retain about 12 gm of water vapour, whereas at 50°C about 82 gm of water vapour and at 75°C as much as 234 gm of vapour is held by one cubic metre of air.

5. Temperature of a liquid : The rise in temperature increases the rate of evaporation and thus, it is seen that the rate of evaporation is maximum at the boiling point of all liquids.

The process of evaporation is extensively used in the Pharmaceutical industry for various purposes. Since the process is time consuming and wherein large volumes of the liquids are concentrated, it is very essential to consider the characteristics or properties of which evaporaing equipment is made. Not only the chemical properties but even the heat conductivity, mechanical strength, resistances to the corrosion should also be known. Various metals or alloys are used to prepare these equipments Evaporation equipment as such can be divided into two types : (1) equipments used for small scale or for laboratory purposes, and (2) for commercial purposes.

1. **Laboratory scale :** The porcelain or even the glass equipment is used for the purpose which is very easy to handle and to clean. Moreover neither glass nor porcelain have any chemical interaction of the material to be evaporated.

2. **Large scale :** The evaporating equipments may be made of the following metals or the combinations thereof.

(i) **Aluminium :** It is very light and resistant to fatty acids, phenol, dilute nitric acid and is good conductor of heat. It is also suitable for alkaline liquids.

(ii) **Copper :** It is resistant to alcohol, volatile oils and most of the organic liquids. However, it is very sensitive to acids and ammonia. It is good conductor of heat hence preferred.

(iii) **Stainless steel :** Resistant to atmospheric corrosion, high pressure steam, weak acids and alkaline.

(iv) **Nickel :** It is resistant to the corrosion by alkalies or weak acids and oxidation by heating.

(v) **Lead :** It is resistant to corrosion by acids like hydrochloric, sulphuric, nitric acid and even the concentrated sulphuric acid. It is highly malleable but a poor conductor.

To achieve the evaporation perfectly, following few points should also be considered :

1. **Temperature :** As far as possible Evaporation should be carried at low tmperature since most of the active principles of the plants are either rendered insoluble and get precipitated by heat at high temperature, while some others get decomposed. In most of the cases the evaporation of the extracts for concentration, is done at very low temperature. For example Liquid extract of malt not above 55°C Liquid extract of hyosyamus not exceeding 60°C, Dried extract of belladonna in exceeding 80°C and so on. Wheresoever possible evaporation should be carried in vacuum so as to avoid the high temperature. The product obtained by evaporation under reduced pressure is friable and very light. The example being dried extract of cascara sagrada.

2 **Time :** As far as possible evaporation should be carried out for short time. If the heating is continued for long duration the dissolved contents get decomposed.

3. **Agitation :** During evaporation the upper layer of liquid under evaporation has tendency to form the scum or film which results in lowering down the rate of evaporation, and it is necessary to agitate or to stir the product under evaporation. This will also prevent the degradation of the product at the bottom, due to excessive heat and will also prevent depositing of the solids.

4. **The material of the evaporator :** As far as possible the material of the evaporator selected should be inert chemically and good conductor of heat.

Types of evaporators : Taking into consideration the factors which affect the rate of evaporation as discussed above, various types of evaporators are practised in the pharmaceutical industry.

The steam jacketed evaporating pan is used on large scale. Since it is much wider effective evaporation takes place. Tilting arrangement may also be used if desired.

Multiple effect evaporator : Where large volumes of aqueous liquids are to be evaporated this type of evaporator is preferred. Normally it is steam operated. The steam is introduced in the first chamber while the vapours resulting from different evaporators are used to evaporate the second quantity, while the vapours from the second are used for the contents of the 3rd chamber. This is economical and a tripple effect is observed.

Film evaporators : In case of film evaporators numerous advantages are claimed since the vertical tubes are provided in the equipment. The large evaporating surface is provided. This is also steam operated and the steam is introduced into the jacket which results in the boiling. The volume of vapour formed ascends and forms into the core in the centre of a tube, carrying with heat the liquid is filled around the inner surface of the steam. The vapour passes through at a high velocity and the liquid gets concentrated The concentrate is collected from the separator. In the horizontal film evaporator, the same principle is used for evaporation.

Calandria evaporator : To get the better heating surface the tubes used in the evaporators are heated on the distance and the liquid concentrates. Heating medium is normally steam and it occupies the space between tube and plates, outside of the tubes. The liquid under evaporation boils inside of the vertical tubes raising through the tubes and falls back to the central column. During the boiling process the liquid and the vapour raises rapidly up the pipe and thus it is effective utilisation of the heat.

(9) Drying :

Drying is an important operation in pharmaceutical practice, since it is usually the last stage of manufacturing before packaging and it is important that, the moisture remaining should be low enough to prevent product deterioration. In the preparation of medicinal chemicals, drying is usually the final stage of processing and is designed to yield a stable homogeneous product, which is easy to manipulate in subsequent operations of packaging or formulating. A rigid definition of drying that shall sharply differentiate it from evaporation is difficult to formulate. The term **drying** usually infers the removal of relatively small amounts of water from solid or nearly solid material, and the term evaporation is usually limited to the removal of relatively large amounts of water from solutions. In drying processes, the major emphasis is usually on the solid product. In most cases drying involves the removal of water at temperatures below its boiling point, whereas evaporation means the removal of water by boiling a solution. Another distinction is that, in evaporation, the water is removed from the material as practically pure water vapour, mixed with other gases only because of unavoidable leaks. In drying, on the other hand, water is usually removed by circulating air or some other gas over the material in order to carry away the water vapour, but in some drying processes no carrier gas is used. The above definitions hold in many cases, but there is also notable exceptions to every one of them. In the final analysis, the question of whether a given operation is called evaporation or drying is largely a question of common usage.

In some cases, drying involves, converting a wet filter cake into a free flowing solid, in others such as spray-drying or drum-drying, a solution is both evaporated and dried in a single operation. Vegetable drugs are fired prior to extraction, partly in order to avoid deterioration on storage and transport and partly to facilitate grinding. Drying is also an important stage in some formulating operations, notably during tableting by "wet granulation". Various methods and equipments are available and choice of these methods and equipments depends on :

(a) the heat sensitivity of the product.
(b) its physical characteristics, prior to drying.
(c) the nature of the solvent to be removed.
(d) the need for asepsis.
(e) the scale of operation.
(f) available sources of heat.

Theory : When a material is exposed to air at definite temperature and humidity, it will either gain or lose moisture until an equilibrium is established. The moisture content at equilibrium varies with the nature of the material and with the temperature and humidity of the air. Thus, starch exposed to air at a relative humidity of say 60 per cent at room temperature may contain at equilibrium upto 15 per cent of water. Conversely, a non porous insoluble solid such as talc has a very low equilibrium moisture content at all temperatures and humidities. At this stage, understanding of the progressive stages in the drying is important. Consider, for example a slab of material of sufficiently high moisture content so that its surface is wet. In contact with a current of warm air superficial water diffuses through the surrounding stationary air film and is carried away rapidly by the moving air stream.

The rate of evaporation is determined by the temperature and the humidity of the air, when the air is moving at constant velocity. Provided that, water can move freely from the interior of the slab to the surface to replace the water lost by evaporation, the rate of evaporation proceeds at a constant rate, as shown by the line AB in the figure, 5.5.

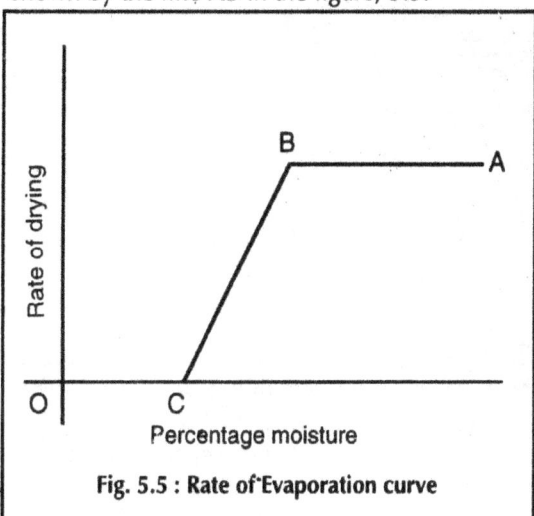

Fig. 5.5 : Rate of Evaporation curve

At this stage, the rate of drying is controlled by the rate at which the vapour can diffuse through the surface air film. As drying continues, the surface is no longer completely wetted and the drying rate falls; line BC represents this "falling rate" period, which will vary according to the thickness of the slab. The limiting factor is now the rate of movement of water from the interior to the surface; water molecules may diffuse through the solid or capillary forces may be responsible for this movement. The point "B" at which the falling-rate occurs is known as the "critical moisture content." As drying proceeds further, the curve eventually approaches zero rate at point "C", which corresponds to the water content in equilibrium with the air. Thus, in order to dry a material, two processes are necessary, firstly, heat must be supplied to provide the latent heat of vaporization, and secondly, the liberated vapour must be removed, generally by a moving air stream.

The rate of mass-transfer of water from the solid to the moving air during the constant rate period is directly proportional to the difference between the humidity of the air at the liquid surface of the solid and bulk of the air, and the area of surface exposed to the air.

Thus, the rate of mass transfer

$$= A (H - h) K \text{ where}$$

A = area of the interface.
H = humidity of the saturated air
h = humidity of the air stream.
K = mass transfer coefficient.

The rate of heat transfer from the air to the wet solid can be expressed as follows :

Rate of heat transfer = $U.A. \Delta t$

where,

U = overall coefficient of heat transfer.
Δt = temperature difference between the air and surface of the solid.

Combining these equations for rates of mass transfer and heat transfer, the following expression is obtained.

$$U.A.\Delta t = A(H-h)K.L.$$

where L = Latent heat of vaporization

Then $H - h = \dfrac{\Delta t.U}{K.L.}$

DRYING EQUIPMENTS

(a) Tray dryer : This is essentially, a hot air oven in which the material is placed in thin layers in trays. There are many variations of design according to the source of heat used and also as a result of added modifications such as vacuum, forced air circulation and thermostatic control. In small, laboratory dryers the material is placed on trays, which slide into the drying cabinet, while in large installations the interior may be designed for the wheeling in of trolleys containing the trays. The simplest form of heating places the source of heat (e.g. a steam coil) at floor level and relies

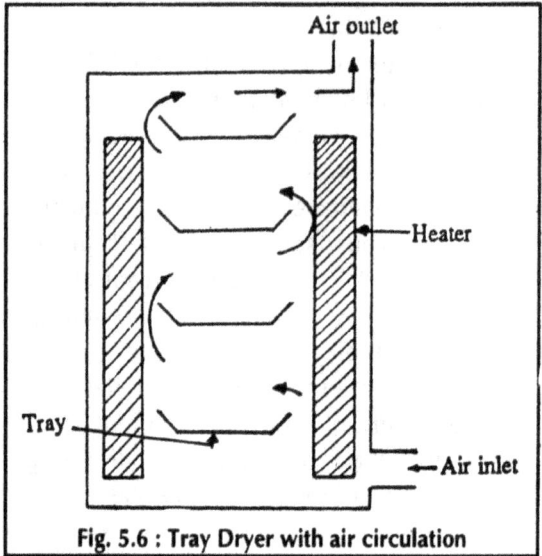

Fig. 5.6 : Tray Dryer with air circulation

on natural convection. Most modern equipment, however, uses fans to provide a forced circulation of air across the trays. In small ovens, there may only be provision for a single passage of heated air while in larger units thermal efficiency is improved by recirculation of air which is reheated after its passage over each shelf as shown in the Fig. 5.7.

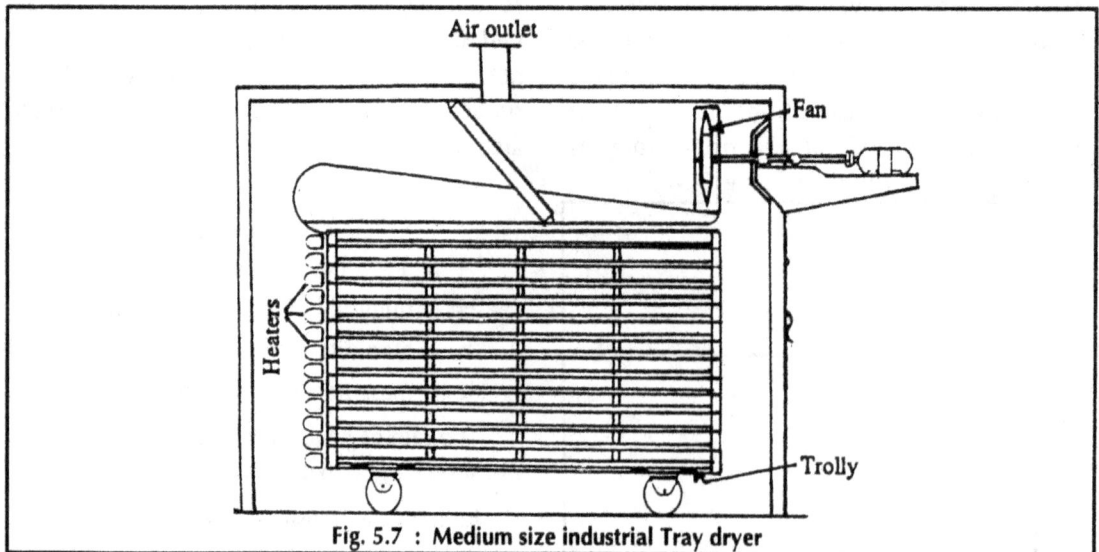

Fig. 5.7 : Medium size industrial Tray dryer

Air flows in the direction of the arrows over each shelf in turn. The wet material may be spread directly on the shelves or on shallow trays resting on the shelves. Electrical elements (healers) or steam heated pipes are positioned so that air is periodically reheated after it has cooled by passage over the wet material on one shelf before it passes over the material on the next shelf. Tray dryer is a type of Fixed bed dryers i.e., the bed of the material to be dried is stationary. Tray dryers are comparatively less efficient because of the stationary nature of the bed. The same surface of the material is exposed every time, the drying of the material may not be very uniform, since same area and surface of the material exposed every time to the heated air, and the lower layers of the material remain comparatively unexposed. When the material is on trays it is easy to handle it in both loading and unloading without losses and therefore, valuable products or small batches are handled by this method.

(b) Fluidized Bed Dryer : This is a type of "Dynamic convective dryers". In this type of dryer the bed of the material to be dried is not stationary and is always in a state of continuous movement i.e. the bed of material is dynamic.

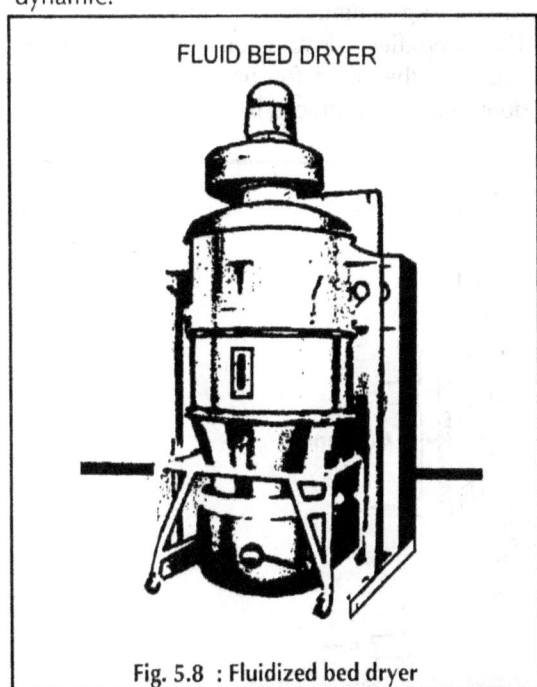

Fig. 5.8 : Fluidized bed dryer

Fluidized bed dryers operate by the passage of heated air through a fine mesh which supports the bed of powder. The dryer consists of a conical vessel of either plastic or stainless steel with a perforated bottom, into which the material to be dried is placed. Filtered air, drawn in by the induction fan is heated and filtered and then passes through the powder bed. An air filter above the bed retains any airborne particles. The temperature of drying, can be controlled by regulating both the inlet air temperature and the flow rate of air. As the velocity of the air is increased, the pressure drop of the air through the bed becomes at a certain point equal to the net effective weight of the solid per unit area and the bed begins to expand. Further increase beyond this point is known as "Onset of fluidization", where the

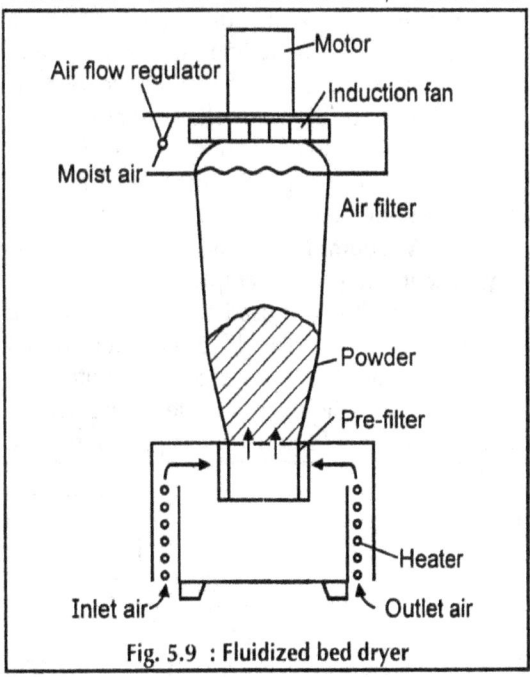

Fig. 5.9 : Fluidized bed dryer

particles are supported by the air, causes rapid expansion of the bed and particles begin to show turbulent motion. The particles are not in direct contact with each other and efficient heat exchange occurs between the particles and the flowing air, the moist air being carried away rapidly. The drying cycle of tablet granules can be as little as 30 minutes compared with 24 hour cycle of conventional tray dryers. The intense agitation of granules may cause attrition but the use of suitable binders for making the granules can overcome this. Many organic powders develop electrostatic charges during fluidization particularly near the end of the drying process, so that efficient electrical earthing of the drying chamber and cloth filter is necessary.

The floor space required for fluidized bed dryer is small compared to tray dryer. In case of fluidized Bed dryer, the turbulent air leads to high head and mass transfer rates. Therefore, it is the rapid process. Efficient heat and mass transfer give high drying rates, so that drying times are shorter than static bed convection dryers. The fluidized state of bed gives drying from individual particles and not from the entire bed hence most of the drying will lie at a constant rate, and the falling rate period is very short. The temperature of a fluidized bed is uniform and can lie controlled precisely. The fluidized state also produces a free flowing produce. Short drying time means that the unit has a high output from a small floor space.

(c) Vacuum dryer (Vacuum oven) : This equipment is a good example of a conduction dryer though it is not used so extensively. The vacuum oven consists of a jacketed vessel sufficiently stout in construction to withstand vacuum within the oven and steam pressure in the jacket. In addition, the supports for the shelves form part of the jacket, giving a larger area of conduction heat transfer.

The oven can be closed by the door that can be locked tightly to give an airtight seal. The oven is connected through condenser and receiver to a vacuum pump, although if the liquid to be removed is water and the pump is of the ejector type that can handle water vapour, the pump can be connected directly to the oven. Operating pressure is usually about 0.03 to 0.06 bar, at which pressure water boils at 25 to 35°C.

Some ovens may be large and continuous forms have been devised, but for pharmaceutical purposes an oven of about 1.5 m. cube and with 20 shelves is commonly used. This gives an area of about 40 to 50 m^2 for heating. In an alternative design there are number of small compartments rather than one large one. This simplifies construction and operation by avoiding the need for one large and heavy door, which is replaced by small doors to each compartment.

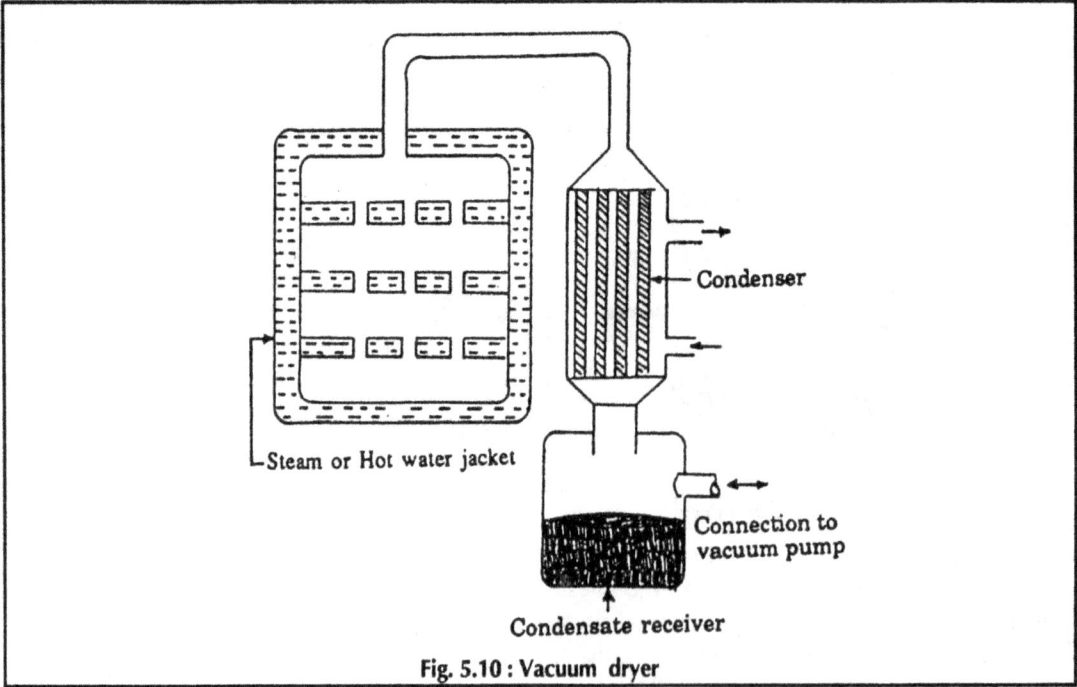

Fig. 5.10 : Vacuum dryer

The main advantage of vacuum oven is that drying takes place at a low temperature and there is no risk of oxidation. The temperature of the dry solid will rise to the steam or water temperature at the end of the drying but this is not usually harmful. A serious drawback is the limited capacity and high labour cost of operation. There is a danger of finely powdered material being drawn off by the vacuum pump and filters that require frequent cleaning have to be provided.

(d) Freeze dryer : The removal of water vapour from a frozen solution by sublimation forms the basis of freeze drying. The process of drying from the frozen state is carried out by subjecting the material to be dried to low pressures, after it has been frozen at temperatures below – 40°C. Under these conditions the frozen water will sublime i.e. pass from the solid to the gaseous state without becoming liquid. The water vapour is removed from the system by condensation in a cold trap maintained at a lower temperature than the frozen material.

Number of substances of pharmaceutical importance are very sensitive to heat and are decomposed readily especially in the presence of water. Recovery or drying of such heat sensitive substances is carried out at very low temperature. The principle of the process of freeze drying is to freeze such substances when placed in a vacuum chamber at the reduced pressure. *Thus, freeze drying or lyophilisation is the process of sublimation of ice at reduced pressure.* Ice has a vapour pressure of 4.6 mm of mercury at 0°C. Hence it is possible to evaporate the ice completely without forming water. The vapour of the ice formed is continuously removed by the application of vacuum. Thus, in freeze-drying frozen water will sublime without becoming liquid.

The presence of solute depresses the freezing point of the solvent, and therefore, it is necessary to cool the solution below the triple point of the solution, to ensure the absence of liquid phase. The vaporisation of ice occurs only at the surface, and hence, it is necessary to expose a large surface area of the frozen material for immediate sublimation. When large volume of liquids are to be freeze-dried commercially, the vessels containing the liquid are continuously rotated during freezing to obtain a thin layer of frozen material around the inner periphery of the vessel. For the most effective, sublimation, the highest possible temperature below the triple point should be used. The first consideration, in the freeze drying of any solution is the temperature at which it must be held, for sublimation to occur from the solid state. To facilitate the sublimation of ice, from the material, the latent heat of sublimation of ice is supplied by means of radiant heat. In the pharmaceutical industry, freeze drying has very important role, as several biological products, blood plasma, antibiotics, hormones, enzymes are dried by this process. These substances are either hydrolysed, oxidised, or otherwise unstable for long period when kept in the form of a solution. These substances should be free from moisture and should be stored at refrigeration temperatures to prevent their spoilage. Freeze drying has a special advantage over vacuum drying and spray drying since vaporisation in case of freeze drying takes place from the frozen solution and liquid water does not come in contact with the active ingredient. Hence, there are hardly any chances of degradation of the active ingredient or denaturation of plasma proteins, when the product is dried by freeze drying process. A freeze-dried material differs considerably in physical properties from a solid prepared by evaporation of a liquid under reduced pressure or by spray-drying or roller drying. This can by readily seen by comparing samples of human serum or human plasma dried by different methods. If water is removed by distillation under reduced pressure, there is a general concentration of the solution of the serum solids into a glue-like substance which ultimately contains from 5 to 10 per cent moisture. This glue like substance is not completely soluble in water, which indicates some denaturation of the proteins. Spray-dried plasma also shows some evidence of slight denaturation. In freeze-drying, evaporation takes place from the solidified solution, no concentration occurs and the evaporated solid occupies practically the same volume as that of the original frozen solution: In these circumstances, no denaturation of the plasma proteins occurs. Freeze drying therefore embodies three stages :

(a) **Preliminary** freezing,
(b) Vacuum evaporation, and
(c) Heat requirement for evaporation.

In preliminary freezing the containers containing the material to be dried are first cooled to 2°C and then transferred to the deep-freeze cabinet where they are rapidly cooled to – 50°C. The more rapid the rate of freezing the smaller the crystals and more amorphous and more readily soluble is the final product. The frozen containers are then loaded into the vacuum desiccators. In high-speed vertical spin-freezing, the bottles containing the product to be dried, are spun on their axes at 750 to 1000 revolutions per minute. The liquid is thereby distributed uniformly inside the bottle round the periphery. The liquid, after super cooling, freezes suddenly in this position, giving small crystals and a very soluble product. If this is done in the vacuum chamber, frothing and foaming is avoided and both evaporation and freezing occurs. Thus, pre-freezing is abolished and the freezing becomes the first stage of the drying process.

In vacuum evaporation, the maintenance of the contents in the solid frozen condition during the application of the vacuum is of vital importance. Air is exhausted by double-stage, high vacuum pumps, until a suitable vacuum is obtained. (a vacuum of 0.01 mm of mercury is possible). During evaporation, some water vapour must be carried over into the pump, from which it must be removed either by heating or centrifuging. A condensing coil at the bottom of the **chamber is maintained** at – 50° by **means** of special refrigerating plant. When **the pressure** is sufficiently low, ice evaporates **and** condenses on the coils. As ice forms on the condenser, it acts as an insulator (does not conduct heat) and the heat interchange becomes less efficient.

Heat requirement for evaporation is necessary and a small source of radiant heat is therefore placed in the chamber head and evaporation takes place rapidly with the frozen material remaining at – 20°C., until all the ice has sublimed. The freeze dried material always has more solubility.

HEATING BATHS

Water bath : In the case of solutions of flammable liquids having a boiling point below 100°C, the stainless-steel electrically heated water bath or steam bath provided with a constant level device must be used. The individual circular type, provided with a lid of series of concentric rings in order to accommodate flasks and beakers of various sizes are available. A rectangular type, suitable for use in classes, has several holes each fitted with a series of concentric rings. In both the cases the water bath is fitted with an immersion heating element controlled by a suitable regulator.

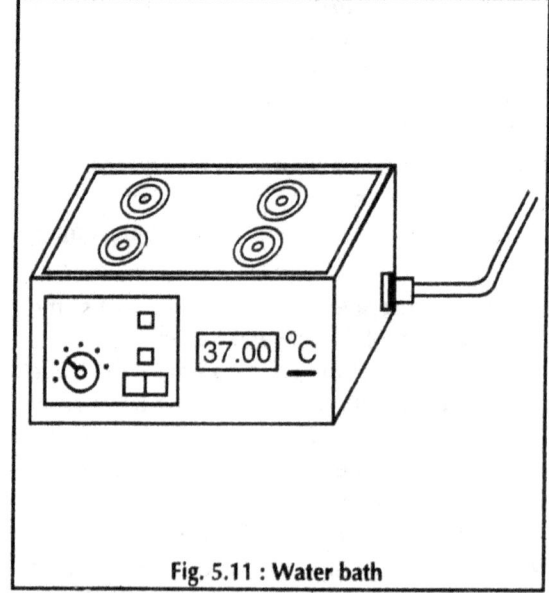

Fig. 5.11 : Water bath

Oil bath : For temperature above 100°C, oil baths are generally used. Liquid paraffin may be employed for temperature upto about 220°C. Glycerol and dibutyl phthalate are satisfactory upto 140 – 150°C; above these temperature fuming is usually excessive and the odour of the vapours is unpleasant. For temperature upto 250°C, 'hard hydrogenated' cotton seed oil, (m. p. 40 – 60°C), is recommended. The silicone fluids are probably the best liquids for oil baths but are somewhat expensive for general use. A satisfactory bath suitable for temperatures upto about 250°C may be prepared by mixing four parts by weight of 85 per cent ortho-phosphoric acid and one part by weight of meta-phosphoric acid; the mixed components should first be heated slowly to 260°C and held at this temperature until evolution of steam and vapour has ceased. This bath is liquid at room temperature. For temperature upto 340°C, a mixture of two parts of 85 per cent ortho-phosphoric acid and one part of meta-phosphoric acid may be used. This is solid at about 20°C.

High temperatures may be obtained with the aid of baths of fusible metal alloys, e.g. wood metal – 4 parts of bismuth, 2 parts of lead, 1 part of tin and 1 part of copper – melts at 71°C; Rose's metal – 2 of bismuth, 1 of lead and 1 of tin – has a melting point of 94°C; a eutectic mixture of lead and tin, composed of 37 parts of lead and 63 parts of tin, melts at 183°C. Metal baths should not be used at temperatures much in excess of 300°C owing to the rapid oxidation of alloy.

An air bath is a very cheap and convenient method of effecting even heating of small distillation flasks (say, 25 ml or 50 ml).

QUESTIONS

1. Name and define various heat-processes. Distinguish clearly between exsiccation and desiccation.
2. Define the following terms with suitable examples (a) Molecular distillation, (b) Vacuum distillation, (c) Destructive distillation, (d) Steam distillation.
3. Distinguish between evaporation and drying. Name and describe the factors affecting the rate of evaporation.
4. Define "Drying" Enlist the factors on which the choice of method for drying a pharmaceutical products depend.
5. With the help of "Drying curve" discuss the theory of drying of pharmaceutical product. Give the equation for rate of mass transfer of water or moisture from the material to be dried.
6. With a neat and labelled diagram describe the working of a tray dryer.
7. What do you understand by "Fluidised Bed" ? With a neat and labelled diagram describe the mechanism, construction and working of fluidised bed dryer.
8. For which type of materials you will use "Vacuum Oven" for drying ? Give construction and working of vacuum oven
9. What do you understand by "Freeze Drying" ? Give different stages involved in freeze drying and mechanism of freeze drying. What are the applications of freeze drying in pharmaceuticals ?

●●●

CHAPTER 6
GALENICALS

INTRODUCTION

Crude drugs play very vital role in medication. They are obtained from various sources like minerals, animals and vegetables. At times they are used in their natural form, normally, they are extracted by various means and methods for their constituents which they contain. The utility of crude drugs as medicament is due to their active chemical constituents. The crude drugs contain several substances categorised as active chemical constituents and inactive chemical constituents, only the proven active constituents of the crude drugs need to be extracted for medicinal purposes. Taking into consideration the vividness of occurrence and chemical nature, crude drugs are to be extracted scientifically. The proper knowledge of the solubility and behaviour with the solvents various extraction processes at variable conditions (such as temperature, pH, oxidation etc.) should be given due importance while extracting the crude drugs. It was GALEN a Greek pharmacist of Rome (131 - 200 AD), who described various methods of extracting the crude-drugs for the first time and hence, the branch dealing with the extraction of plant and animals drugs is known as **Galenical Pharmacy** and the products as *Galenicals*.

Extraction of the crude drugs can be done by various processes depending upon the chemical properties of the active constituents of the drugs. Various methods used for the extraction are shown as under :

Infusion, dicoction, digestion, maceration and percolation.

The choice of selection of a proper solvent capable of extracting the active constituents depends upon the chemical properties of the active constituents as stated above. Thus, the solvent capable of penetrating, the plant or animal tissues and dissolving the active medicaments present in them is known as *menstruum*, while the inert insoluble material after exhausting the drug is known as *marc*.

Processes like infusion, decoction, digestion are rarely used now-a-days with few exceptions for extraction of crude drugs and hence, will be described in short.

1. Infusion : Infusion is the process of extracting the vegetable drugs, wherein water is used as menstruum. The process consists of treating vegetable crude drugs with boiling water but the drugs are not boiled with the menstruum. The entire mixture is allowed to cool, filtered and supplied. Infusion for use should be freshly prepared all the while. Process of infusion is used to prepare the following preparations.

(a) Infusion of senna, and
(b) Infusion of quassia.

Since the active constituent of quassia i.e. quassin is more soluble in cold water, cold menstruum is used in the preparation of infusion of quassia.

Concentrated infusions : These differ from the infusions in the respect that they either use alcohol as a menstruum or alcohol is used as a preservative. They are prepared by method of maceration similar to the tinctures. Concentrated compound chirata infusion is official in IP.

Fig. 6.1 shows the device used to prepare the infusion. This contains perforated earthenware tray at specific height over which drug is placed and menstruum poured.

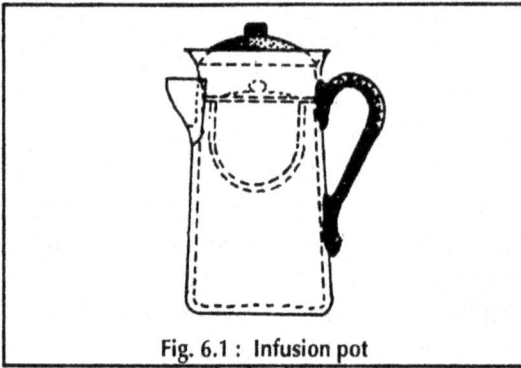

Fig. 6.1 : Infusion pot

2. Decoction : Decoction is the process of extracting the hard and woody crude drugs wherein the water is used as menstruum and the crude drugs are boiled along with menstruum. Decoction differs from the infusion in the respect that the crude drugs in infusion are not boiled with the menstruum but only boiling menstruum is poured over the crude drugs. Freshly prepared decoction should only be dispensed, as it also extracts mucilagenous and albuminous matter as in infusions. No decoction is official at present in IP or BP.

3. Digestion : This process of extracting the drugs consists of the application of gentle heat to the substance which is being extracted. This is only applicable where moderately elevated temperature is not objectionable and will help the menstruum to dissolve more contents from the drugs.

4. Maceration : Several official preparations in various pharmacopoeias are recommended to be prepared by this process of extraction and hence, it is comparatively more important than the processes described earlier. This has got several advantages over the other processes and differs in many respects from the infusion and decoction described above. As indicated in the pharmacopoeia the process consists of the following :

" Place the solid materials with whole menstruum in the closed vessel and allow to stand for seven days shaking occasionally. Strain press the marc and mix the liquid obtained. Clarify by subsidence or filtration. "

This process is normally used for the preparation of tinctures or extracts and menstruum is usually alcoholic, hydroalcoholic (in case of tinctures) or may be aqueous. Drug is kept with the menstruum for a long period. The process is carried out at ambient temperature. At the end of the process the marc is either pressed or the menstruum is decanted depending upon nature of the drugs to be extracted in the process. There are two types of maceration i.e. simple maceration and double or triple maceration.

Depending upon the type of the drugs to be extracted by maceration two different methods are adopted. The type of the drugs to be extracted by maceration are either organised drugs or unorganised drugs. Organised drugs are either the parts of the plants like roots, seeds, barks etc., which have got the cellular structure. They contain alkaloids glycosides, tannins etc.,as their active constituents. While the unorganized drugs are derived from the parts of the plants and are acellular (Non-cellular) in nature. They either contain volatile oil, resins, or oleo-gum-resins as their active constituents. The following is the detailed account of the methods of extraction normally followed for the organised or unorganized drugs with the reasons thereto.

Double and Triple Maceration

Repeated maceration is more effective than a single maceration depending upon the nature of drug, (i.e. organised or unorganised) to be macerated. The process of double or triple maceration in respect of suitability should be considered thoroughly. Since the appreciable amount of active principles retain in the first pressing of the marc, the necessity of double or triple maceration gets justified. Double maceration is applied in the preparation of *concentrated compound gentian infusion*. The triple maceration is applicable in case

Table 6.1 : Maceration of organised and unorganised drugs

Tinctures made from organised drugs	Tinctures made from unorganised drugs
1. Drugs and whole of the menstruum shaken occasionally for seven days in closed containers.	1. Drug and 80/% of the menstruum shaken occasionally for 2 to 7 days in closed vessels.
2. Strain, press the marc, clarify by subsidence or filtration.	2. Supernatant liquid is dacanted and the marc is not pressed. If necessary decanted, liquid is then filtered.
3. Filtrate is not adjusted to volume. Herein liquid is uniform at all the points either in contact with the drug or above the drug.	3. Rest of the (i.e. 20 %) menstruum is passed through the filter.
4. The marc is usually bulky and contains good proportion of liquids.	4. The supernatant liquid decanted contain all dissolved chemical constituents separated from the lower acellular part which occupies a small part of the solution and is normally gummy in nature.
5. The drug in process is organised (i.e. cellular) and hence can be pressed. The volume is not adjusted because the pressing if carried by various means and methods may not be uniform, and if the product is adjusted to volume, may result in ununiform strength of the solution. Examples are : Tincture of orange, Tincture of lemon, etc.	5. The pressing of the gummy marc is neither practicable nor necessary. The supernatant liquid contains maximum soluble constituents and a small amount adheres to the gummy matter. The 20 % of the menstruum washes the gummy matter and after filtration can maintain the strength of the entire solution. Examples are : Tincture Benzoin, Tincture of Tolu.

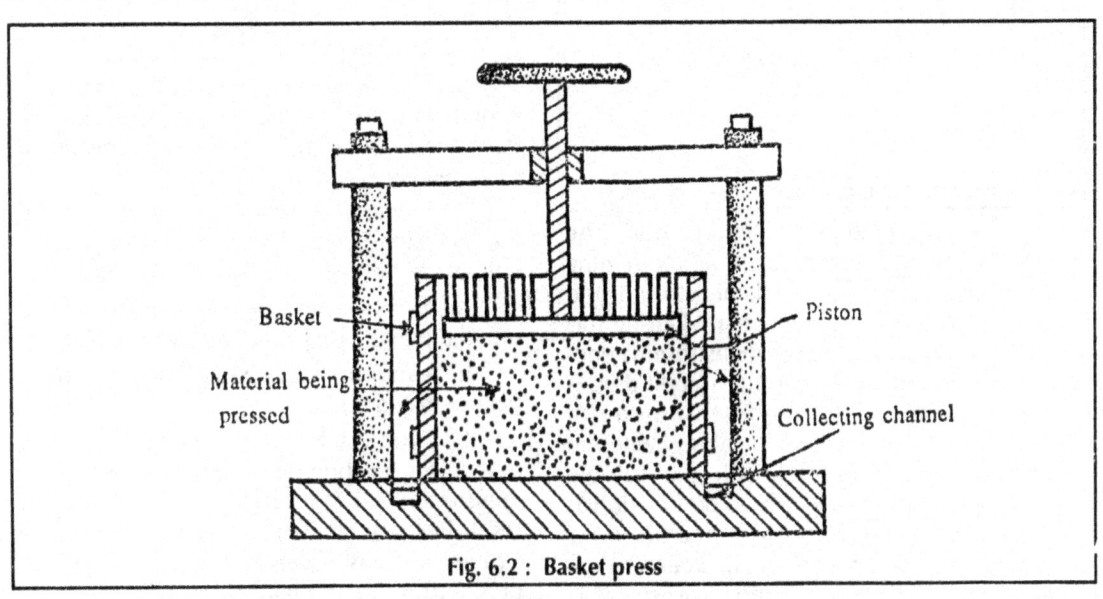

Fig. 6.2 : Basket press

where the marc cannot be pressed. Physico-chemical nature of the menstruum sometimes call for few changes during the maceration process i.e. to enhance the solubility of the chemical constituents or even to prevent the solution of gummy material in the tinctures. *Liquid extract of glycyrrhiza* is prepared by triple maceration process.

5. Percolation : This is another official method of extracting the drugs used in the preparation of tinctures or extracts. The process in short consists of three stages viz.

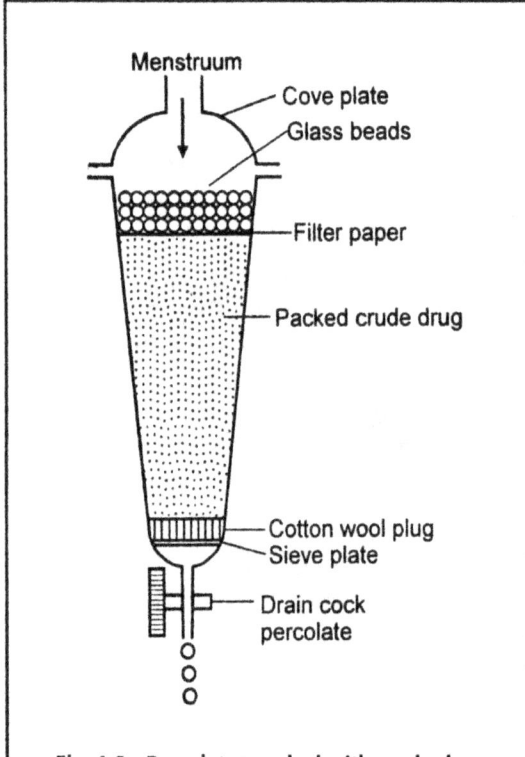

Fig. 6.3 : Percolator packed with crude-drug

Imbibation, maceration and percolation. The process of imbibition is nothing but moistening drug under percolation with menstruum and allowing it to stand for four hours. During this period the drug swells and menstruum penetrates, the cell walls. During maceration drug is kept in contact with the menstruum for 24 hours with occassional shaking wherein menstruum gets saturated with the soluble constituents of the drugs. Thus, percolation is the process *wherein the maceration is followed by downward displacement of saturated menstruum* and the drug is exhausted by the slow passage of the menstruum through the column of the drug. To perform percolation special devices are used separately for laboratory or for industrial purposes.

Normally, a percolator in conical form is made either to be open or closed. In case of water as a menstruum, open type of percolator can be preferred as it is cheap and very convenient for the arrangement of automatic supply of menstruum. In case of alcohol, ether or in other volatile menstruum only the closed percolator is to be used. Resting upon the size and material to be percolated several other types of percolators can be used. They may be made out of glass, copper, stainless steel etc. If the percolation is to be carried at elevated temperature it is either provided with a steam jacket or arrangements to circulate the hot water. Percolator is conical vessel having a lid at the top and is provided with perforated false bottom on which filter paper is placed to support the column of the drug and allow all the menstruum, to escape.

In the process of percolation after the selection of the proper percolator, the material to be percolated needs to be packed into percolator properly. The material to be percolated is moistened (imbibation) with the menstruum for the following reasons :

1. The dried tissues are allowed to swell, so as to reduce the porosity of the material in the percolator, which may also result (if not done) in choking the percolation column.

2. The swelling helps further for menstruum to penetrate the cells of the vegetable drug to dissolve their chemical constituents more readily.

3. The moistening of the material helps the fine particles less liable to be washed out of column as they get increased in the size.

The imbibed material is then packed neatly into the percolator for the following reasons :

1. Uniform distribution of the material to be exhausted.

2. Even packing of the material in the percolator ensures the uniform run of the menstruum downwards. Uneven packing may result in the inefficient extraction as the menstruum will pass freely without extracting the drug through large channels.

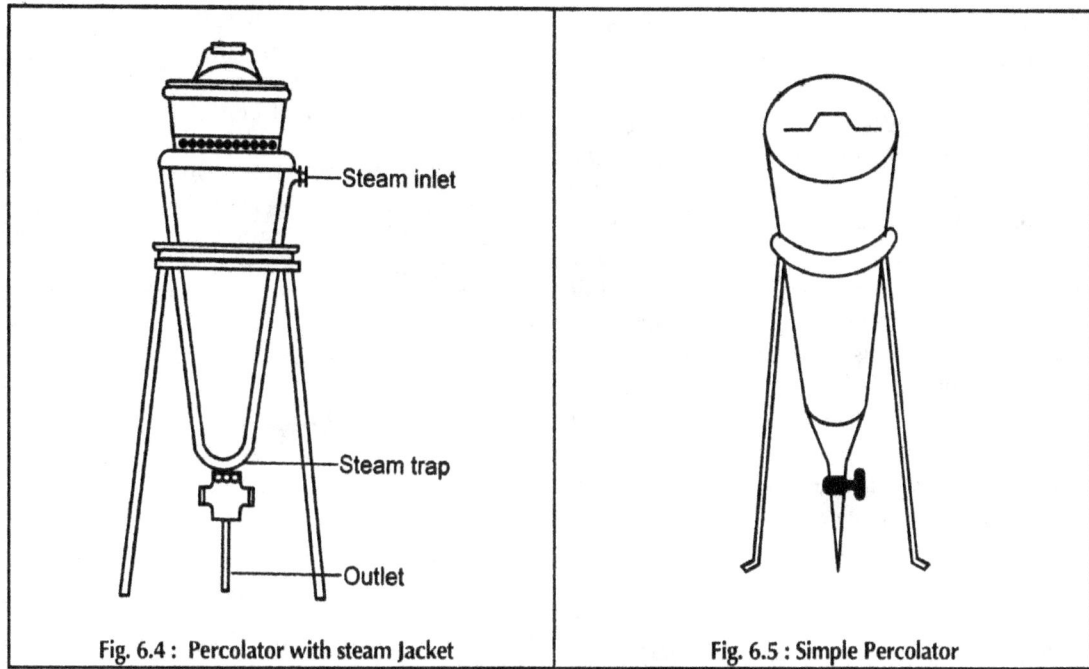

Fig. 6.4 : Percolator with steam Jacket   Fig. 6.5 : Simple Percolator

The drug under percolation is tapped with a rod or a suitable device to give the proper compression. The drug is placed in the percolator, layer by layer, which will not disturb, even if sufficient menstruum is added to the percolator. To avoid the disturbances the packing material is covered with a filter paper at the top and is covered with sand. Normally, the conical percolators should be used for the extraction, so that the sloping side of the percolator will allow the further expansion of the bed due to swelling, if any. Moreover, in case of cylindrical percolator menstruum fails, to penetrate through the material near the sides at the bottom and may result in uneven extraction. The material in the percolator all the while be kept in contact with the sufficient quantity of the menstruum so as to avoid the cracking of the bed. Sufficient quantity of the menstruum should be added to the percolator and can be tested by opening the tap at the bottom wherein the percolate begins to drip. Then the drug is kept in contact with the menstruum for twenty four hours to allow the penetration and the solvent action of the menstruum.

Reserved percolation : The process of percolation is more rapid and results in complete extraction of the chemical constituents of the drug as compared to the maceration. However, it has certain limitations and also needs certain modifications wherever desired. One should remember that percolation cannot be accepted uniformly, because it is not suitable process for extracting the drugs, all the while.

It is accepted that the liquid extracts are more concentrated preparations as compared to the tinctures and other related products. If the crude drugs are to be exhausted thoroughly quantity of menstruum required will be too much. And as a whole, process will be difficult to manage. Under these circumstances, it is essential to reduce the volume of menstruum. This can be done by simple, process of evaporation. Taking into consideration,

1. the time required for the evaporation,
2. volume of the percolate to be evaporated,
3. the chemical changes that may take place during the evaporation (which are not desired), and
4. the economy of the process.

It is not possible to subject the entire percolate to evaporation. *And as such certain volume of the percolate is reserved.* This reserve percolate is the first operation of the process and *contains the major bulk of the active constituents* owing to the preliminary maceration. The rest of the percolate is collected separately and also processed separately. The drugs are percolated until exhaustion, confirmed by the specific test, and the entire volume is subjected to the evaporation. The product of evaporation is a concentrated form of the percolate and it is mixed with the earlier reserved percolate. The combined product is then standardised and met with specifications as mentioned in pharmacopoeia.

Percolation of volatile liquids : As mentioned above at times volatile menstrua are used to extract certain drugs. The menstrua being ether, acetone, ethyl ether and other hydrocarbons. These being comparatively volatile are responsible for the huge loss under commercial scale. However, it can be avoided by using suitable device. The equipment shown in the Fig. 6.6 is suitable for the purpose.

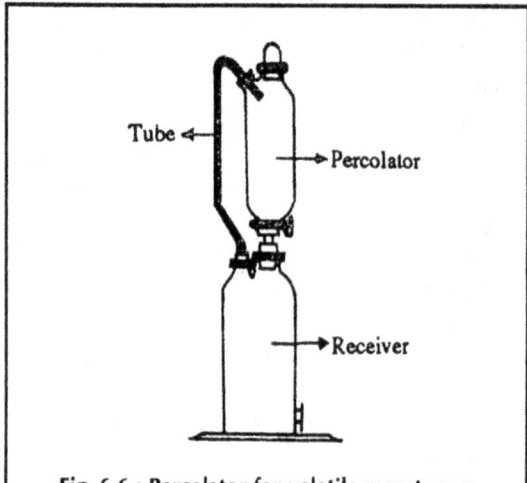

Fig. 6.6 : Percolator for volatile menstruum

The percolator and the receiver receiving the percolate are inter-connected by a tube. This tube helps in taking the displaced air by the liquid from the percolator into the receiver and thus, may pass into the space above the menstruum in the percolator. The partial vacuum created into the percolator may result in stopping the descent of the liquid through the drug to be percolated, but this displacement is maintained by the tube provided. Percolation by using very volatile menstruum is performed in case of *Liquid extract of malefern, Liquid extract of lobellia,* and also for isolation of *oleo-resin from capsicum.*

Percolation may be expedited applying the pressure or by reducing the pressure. Suitable apparatus for the same is shown in Fig. 6.7.

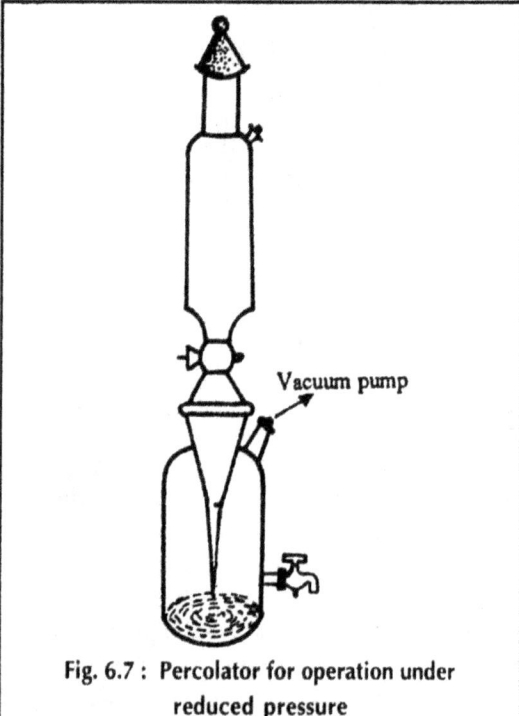

Fig. 6.7 : Percolator for operation under reduced pressure

SOXHELATION OR CONTINUOUS HOT EXTRACTION

It becomes very essential sometimes to extract the crude drug by the action of hot menstruum for a long period of time. For specific reasons which may be due the constituents, as they are rarely soluble in the menstruum or the penetration of the cellular tissue by the menstruum is very slow, and under these circumstances the drugs are extracted by continuous heat extraction process; i.e. canthardin from cantharides with benzene, alkaloids from the nux-vomica seeds and even extraction of fixed oils from the seeds are the ideal examples.

Continuous hot extraction is also known as **soxhelation** since it is performed by using

Continuous hot extraction is also known as **soxhelation** since it is performed by using the equipment known as soxhelet apparatus. Fig. 6.8.

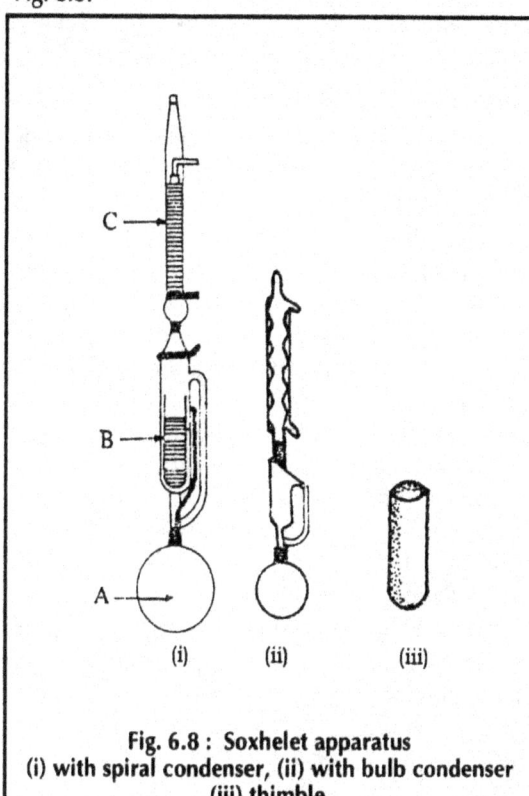

Fig. 6.8 : Soxhelet apparatus
(i) with spiral condenser, (ii) with bulb condenser
(iii) thimble

Part ' A ' is nothing but a container in which the menstruum to be used is placed. Part ' C ' is a specific type of condenser while ' B ' is extracting chamber. ' B ' consists of a thimble holding the drug to be extracted.

The container contains the suitable menstruum and when the heat is supplied to it the vapour of the same passes through large side tube of ' B ' into the condenser ' C ' wherein it condenses and drops into the thimble of the extracting chamber. It extracts the soluble constituents of the material in the thimble till the upper level of the condensed liquid reaches the tip of the siphoning tube. The whole of the percolate siphons over into the container 'A'. Thus, a limited amount of hot menstruum is made to percolate the drug repeatedly and thus, it extracts the active constituents and then are passed to the container A. The process is continuous one and can be continued as desired.

Following is the list of various official preparations made by using either percolation or reserve percolation methods for their preparation.

Table 6.2 : Percolation methods for tinctures

Tinctures prepared by Percolation method	Preparations made by Reserve percolation
1. Tincture belladonna I. P.	1. Liquid extract of vasaka I.P.
2. Compound cardamom tincture I. P.	2. Liquid extract of datura I.P.
3. Strong ginger tincture I. P.	3. Liquid extract of hyoscyamus I.P.
4. Tincture digitalis I. P.	4. Liquid extract of ipecacuanha I.P.
	5. Liquid extract of nux-vomica I.P.

SPIRITS :

These are the liquid preparations containing pleasant volatile liquids and ethyl alcohol. i.e.

(i) Spirit of chloroform
(ii) Aromatic spirit of ammonia
(iii) Spirits etherons nitrosi

METHOD OF PREPARATION OF SPIRIT

There are four classic methods of preparation of spirits :

1. Simple solution : This is the method by which the majority of spirits are prepared. The formula and procedure given for Aromatic spirit of ammonia USP illustrate the method of preparation.

Aromatic Spirit of Ammonia USP	
Ammonium carbonate, in transluscent pieces	– 34 G
Strong ammonia solution	– 36 ml
Lemon oil	– 10 ml
Lavender oil	– 01 ml
Nutmeg oil	– 01 ml
Alcohol	– 700 ml
Purified water, to make	– 1000 ml

Dissolve the ammonium carbonate in the strong ammonia solution and 195 ml of purified water by gentle agitation and allow the solution to stand for 12 hours. Dissolve the oils in the alcohol contained in a graduated bottle or cylinder, and gradually add the ammonium carbonate solution and enough purified water to make the product to measure 1000 ml.

Set the mixture aside in a cool place for 24 hours, occasionally agitating it, then filter, using a covered funnel.

2. Solution with Maceration : In this procedure, the leaves of a drug are macerated in purified water to extract water-soluble matter. They are expressed and the moist, macerated leaves are added to prescribed quantity of alcohol. The volatile oil is added to the filtered liquid. Pippermint spirit USP is made by this process.

3. Chemical Reaction : No official spirits are prepared by this process. Ethyl nitrite is made by the action of sodium nitrate on a mixture of alcohol and sulfuric acid in the cold. This substance then is used to prepare ethyl nitrite spirit, a product no longer official.

Evaluation of Galenicals :

As a rule, every product alter formulation needs to be evaluated by confirmation of identify and quality.

Identity can be done by physical or chemical tests as applicable in monograph. Most of the pharmacopoeias are also giving guide-lines now-a-days for specific type of products, the minimum parameters to be followed, in respect of quality such as disintegration time, dissolution time, weight variation, contents of active ingradients in case of tablets and capsules, sterilization and test for pyrogens in case of parenterals and many others depending upon the product (formulation) under study.

The same principle can be applied to gelanicals and following parameters play important role in their evaluation.

1. Density or weight per ml
2. pH
3. Alcohol content (if applicable)
4. Total solids
5. Optical rotation
6. Refractive index

QUESTIONS

1. Define the following :
   (i) Infusion, (ii) Decoction, (iii) Maceration, (iv) Percolation, (v) Spirit.
2. Describe the method of preparation of maceration and percolation, alongwith a note on modified maceration and reserve percolation.
3. Draw a well-labelled diagramme of soxhelet percolator ? Differentiate between soxhaletion and percolation.
4. Draw a well labelled diagramme of percolator and state the importance of percolation. Name five extracts prepared by reserve percolation method.
5. How galenicals are evaluated, explain with suitable examples.

CHAPTER 7

SURGICAL AIDS

DEFINITION

Surgical aids are the materials used to protect the wound, to correct deformities, tying blood vessels and sewing tissues after minor operation e.g. Bandages, ligature and sutures.

SURGICAL DRESSINGS

The word surgical dressings are used to include all the materials either used alone or in combination to cover the wound. The purpose of application of dressing is to protect the wound and favour its proper healing. A material which holds the dressing in desired position is known as bandage. Fibres are used for the preparation of surgical dressings.

Dressings are meant for the following functions.

(1) To reduce or prevent infections
(2) To offer protection to healing wounds
(3) To offer mechanical support to the tissues

Surgical dressings should comply the following requirements as mentioned in Pharmacopoeia.

(1) They should be sterilized before use.
(2) They should be stored in dry and well-ventilated place at a temperature not exceeding 25°C.
(3) They should be used with permitted antiseptics in prescribed concentrations only.
(4) They should not be dyed unless mentioned in the monograph.
(5) Adhesive products should not be allowed to freeze.
(6) There should not be any loose threads, fibre-ends in dressings.

Surgical dressings are classified as :

(A) Fibres

(a) Non-medicated fibres

Absorbent cotton, wool, rayon, silk etc.

(b) Medicated fibres

Boric acid wool, Capsicum wool.

(B) Fabric

These are woven materials and may be

(a) Medicated, and
(b) Non-mediated.

Gauses, bandages and plasters are various forms of fabrics.

Absorbent lint, Absorbent ribbon gauze, Boric acid lint, Absorbent gauze, X-ray detectable, are the examples of bandages.

(C) Bandages

These are the products used to retain dressings in place and provide support for application of medicaments to the skin. They are water proof. And offer mechanical support and may be fastenable. They may be elastic, or non-elastic, adhesive or non-adhesive.

(a) Non-medicated bandages

Crepe bandage, Domette bandage, Calico bandage, Cotton and rubber elastic bandage

(b) Medicated bandages

Plaster of Paris bandage, zinc paste bandage, zinc paste Ichthamol bandage.

(D) Rubber and Oil Impregnated Materials

Belladonna self-adhesive plaster, zinc oxide self-adhesive plaster, etc.

British Pharmacopoeia recognizes the following types of surgical dressings.

(1) Fibres and related materials

i.e. viscose, wood cellulose wadding.

(2) Carded products

i.e. Absorbent cotton, viscose wadding, etc.

(3) Non - extensible, non-adhesive woven products

i.e. Absorbent muslin; domette bandage, etc.

(4) Non-extensible adhesive woven products

i.e. Belladonna adhesive plaster, zinc oxide surgical adhesive tape,

(5) Extensible non-adhesive woven products

i.e. Cotton bandage, elastic web bandage, etc.

(6) Extensible adhesive woven products

i.e. Elastic adhesive bandage, extension plaster

(7) Non-woven products,

i.e. Impermeable plastic surgical adhesive tape, permeable plastic surgical adhesive tape, etc.

Following are the few commercially available woven dressings in the market.

Cotton, silk and wool are used to prepare a number of woven dressings. They should also comply the pharmacopoeial requirements. Few of them are described below.

1. Absorbent Lint : It is cotton cloth of plain weave from the warp yarn of which a nap has been raised.

2. Flannel Bandage : It consists of a raised fabric of plain weave and is made up of entirely wool.

3. Domette Bandage : It consists of a combination of fabric of plain weave, where the warp yarn are of cotton and weft yarns are entirely of wool.

4. Crepe - Bandage : It consists of fabric of plain weave, wherein warp threads are of cotton and wool, whereas the weft threads are entirely of cotton only.

5. Gauge and cellulose wadding tissue : Cellulose tissue consists of layer of cellulose wadding enclosed in tubular absorbent gauze.

SUTURES

These are the sterile threads, strings or strands specially prepared for use in surgery meant for sewing tissues together. Sutures must possess the following properties.

(a) They must be sterile and should cause no irritation.

(b) They should have finest possible guage and adequate strength.

(c) If absorbable, their time of absorption must be known.

(d) They are intended to be used for one occasion only.

Sutures may be prepared from intestinal tissues and tendons of animals and birds; vegetable fibres; camel hair; human hair; synthetic threads or metallic wires. Depending upon their characteristic of absorption, i.e. digestion in the tissues of the body, sutures are known as absorbable or non-absorbable sutures.

Various methods are used to sterilize sutures. (To make them free of pathogenic micro-organisms). A few of the important methods are :

1. Chemical sterilization

2. Sterilization by irradiation, and

3. Sterilization by heat.

Heat sterilization involves two processes and sutures are classified into two categories depending upon heat resistance,

(a) boilable (in anhydrous liquid) and
(b) non-boilable.

The sterilization should not affect the properties of sutures or their utility. In irradiation method, sterilization is carried out by electron particles or by gamma rays from cobalt 60. The recognized dose of gamma rays treatment is 2.5 megarad.

Sutures may be of the following types :

1. **Absorbable sutures**
   (a) Sterile catgut (small intestine of sheep, ox and appendix of deer)
   (b) Sterile reconstituted collagen suture

2. **Non-absorbable sutures**
   (a) Sterile non-absorbable sutures (silk and cotton)
   (b) Sterile linen suture
   (c) Sterile polyamide sutures (nylon)
   (d) Sterile polyester sutures (terylene)
   (e) Sterile braided sutures
   (f) Sterile stainless and silver sutures

3. **Haemostatics**
   (i) Oxidised cellulose
   (ii) Absorbable gelatin sponge

Uses

Depending upon the physical and chemical properties and also the desired effect, various sutures are effectively used under different conditions.

Silk sutures are strong, smooth inactive and also available in various diameters. The braided form is compact one and has a special advantage of not getting twisted when drawn through the body tissues. Nylon sutures are strong enough and enjoy the merit of their utility in skin and plastic surgery. Cotton sutures due to their low order of tissue reactivity are preferred, but suffer from poor tensile strength. Linen, though very much economical and quite effective, lacks in uniform diameter for practical purposes. Kangaroo tendons are specially used in hernia, while metallic sutures are used in surgery in general.

ABSORBABLE GELATIN SPONGE

Absorbable gelatin sponge is a sterile, white, tough and finely porous spongy material, which is absorbable and water insoluble.

For the preparation of this material, the warm solution of gelatin is whisked to a foam of uniform porosity and then it is dried, cut into pieces of specific size and finally, sterilized at 150°C for one hour.

Though, it is insoluble in water, it is absorbed in body fluids. It takes up not less than 30 times its weight of water. About 9 gm of absorbable gelatin sponge takes upto 45 times its weight of well agitated oxalated whole blood.

It is used as a haemostatic. It is moistened with sterile sodium chloride solution and put within a surgical incision where it gets absorbed in 4-6 weeks. It is also used as a local coagulant and haemostatic.

LIGATURES

A ligature is a thread, used to constrict and seal off a blood vessel, vein or artery hence to ligate.

Ligatures are classified as absorbable or non absorbable, depending on the materials from which they are made. Absorbable ligatures are absorbed by the tissue in which they are implanted. Absorbable materials are catgut (non-boilable and boilable), reconstituted collagen, synthetic absorbable polymers, kangaroo tendon and ribbon gut.

Non absorbable ligatures are not absorbed by tissue, they are on the surface, and remain in the body after the wound has heated. The most commonly used materials are silk, Linen, nylon (Polyamides), polyester, polyolefines and stainless steel wire, and to a small extent: Cotton, horse-hair, human-hair, silkworm gut and wires of other metals, e.g. tantalum, silver, phosphor bronze, etc.

Method of Preparation of Sutures and Ligatures

Sutures and ligatures are prepared by using the following steps.

1. Splitting
2. Cleaning of submucosa
3. Spinning
4. Polishing
5. Gauging

Standards for sutures and ligatures :

1. Length
2. Tensile strength
3. Sterility.

Labelling : The label on the container must state the length of strand, the gauge number, whether the strands are plain, hardened or chronicized.

The label on the box must state the name and percentage of any bactericide in the fluid in which the sutures are immersed.

Storage : Sterilized surgical catgut should be protected from light and stored in a cool place.

Packaging : Surgical catgut is packed either in glass tube sealed by fusion of the glass, flexible packages based on aluminium foil or plastic films, and the bottle packs.

Sterilization of Catgut

Following methods are used to sterilize catgut :

1. **Chemical method :** The main substances like formaldehyde, hydrogen peroxide, hypochlorite, glutaraldehyde, ethyl iodide, methyl bromide, iodine, ethylene oxide and β-propiolactone.

2. **Heat sterilization :** All heat sterilizing processes, are based on the fundamental necessity of removing this combined moisture before the string can be raised to sterilizing temperature of 150° to 165°. Heating above 80° in presence of moisture leads to hydrolysis of absorbable materials.

3. **Radiation sterilization :** Irradiation by electron particle or gamma rays.

QUESTIONS

1. Define the following with suitable examples :
   (i) Surgical aids, (ii) Surgical dressings, (iii) Sutures, (iv) Ligatures.

2. Differentiate between :
   (a) Sutures and ligatures
   (b) Bandages and surgical dressings
   (c) Biological and non-biological sutures
   (d) Woven and non-woven dressings.

3. What are the ideal requirements of surgical dressings ?

4. Write short notes on :
   (i) Sterilization of ligatures, (ii) Absorbable and non-absorbable sutures, (iii) Domette bandage, (iv) Crepe bandage.

●●●

CHAPTER 8

POWDERS AND GRANULES

INTRODUCTION

Powders are a useful dosage form and usually consists of mixtures of two or more powdered medicaments meant for internal use. The size of the particles ranges from 10,000 microns (μ) to 0.1 micron (0.1 μ) depending upon the method employed for grinding. The size of the particle determines the effectiveness of physiological properties. Powders are economical and easy to manufacture as compared to tablet triturates, granules and cachets.

Tablet triturates or Moulded tablets : These are small tablets prepared extemporaneously. The potent medicament is diluted with lactose, moistened with 50-60 % alcohol, and then the paste is filled in mould and dispensed.

Granules : These are the formulation's of medicinal substances with small irregular particles of 2 to 4 millimetres. Granules contain pharmaceutical adjuvants. These are provided in sachets each containing 5 gms of granules, i.e. Bephenium, Methylcellulose granules are official.

Cachets : These are the dosage forms like capsules made of rice flour and water moulding into suitable shape to enclose the medicaments with unpleasant taste. There are two types of cachets, dry closing and flanged type, to hold the drug material from 0.2 to 2.0 gms. Cachets are official products. They are required to be immersed in water for a few seconds placed on tongue and swallowed with water.

Advantages of Powders :

1. The dose variation depending on the condition of the patient, is possible.
2. Powders are more stable than liquid dosage forms.
3. Many a times, the desired effect depends on the particle size and where a diffusion is desired, powder meets the required need i.e. it diffuses more rapidly than the tablets and pills.
4. Relatively easy to swallow.

Disadvantages of Powders :

1. Bitter powders cause discomfort.
2. Powders affected by atmospheric conditions, cannot be safely handled.
3. Time consuming.
4. Quantity less than 60 mg or so cannot be weighed conveniently on dispensing balance.

Mixing of Powders : In small scale work, it is better to use hand mixing methods.

1. Spatulation : Small amounts of powders with the same range of particle size and densities, may be mixed with the help of spatula, the powders being placed on a tile.

2. Trituration : This is carried out in mortar. In case of combination of small amount of one drug, with a large quantity of a diluent it is better to triturate first with one volume of drug, with equal volume of the diluent, and then adding twice as much diluent and continue the trituration. This procedure i. e. adding twice as much diluent as there is material in the mortar is continued until the total bulk of powder is in the mortar.

By the term trituration, it is meant the pestle be moved (with pressure) in circle, starting from the centre, reaching the periphery and returning to the centre of the mortar. This cycle is repeated several times or until the mixing is satisfactorily completed.

Sifting : Brushing of powders through sieves is known as sifting. Sifting is useful where free flowing light powders are desired, as in case of snuffs.

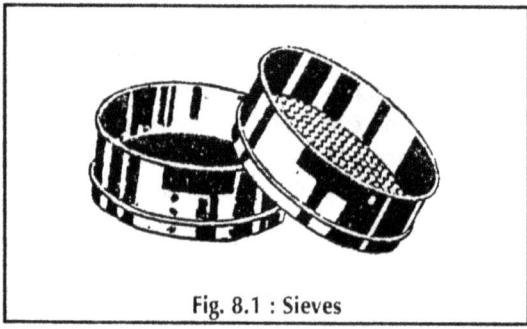

Fig. 8.1 : Sieves

Tumbling : Tumbling is carried out in a wide mouth closed container. It is obvious that this procedure avoids pressure gradient.

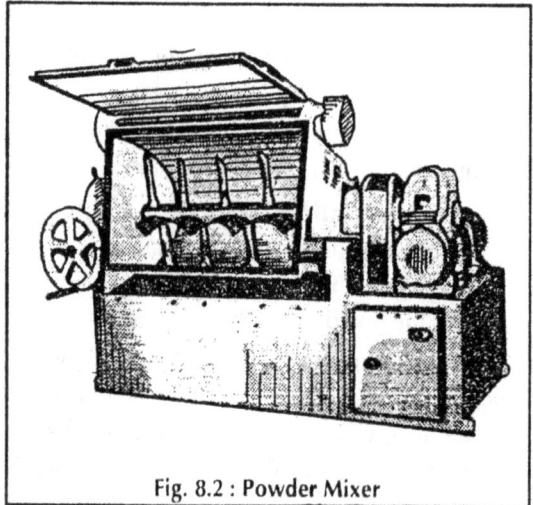

Fig. 8.2 : Powder Mixer

The powders are **required** not to occupy more than half or less **than half the** capacity of the container. The container is rotated in such a manner that during the motion the powder particles float in the air. Tumbling is used for mixing powders with density differences.

On large scale, powders are mixed in mixers, a typical of which is shown in Fig. 4.2.

Special types of powders :

(a) Hygroscopic Powders : Powders which absorb moisture from the atmosphere are called hygroscopic powders. Some powders absorb moisture to such a great extent that they go into solution. Such powders are called **deliquescent powders**. Remedy lies in dispensing these powders in granular form in order to reduce surface area of powders and to expose less area to the air. If powdering is necessary, it may be carried out in dry mortar. Double wrapping of powders as described is to be carried out.

(b) Efflorescent Powders : Some substances loose their water of crystallization on exposure, particularly to dry atmospheric conditions. Such substances are said to **efflorescent**. Such powders may loose water of crystallisation during trituration causing the powder to become pasty. This difficulty can be overcome by using corresponding anhydrous salt or by drying the crystalline form to constant weight. When such steps are being taken, the dose is required to be adjusted.

(c) Eutectic Mixtures : Many substances, when combined with other, powders turn into liquid or give rise to a pasty mass. This is undesirable when powders are being dispensed. Such combinations which liquify are known as **Eutectic Mixtures.**

Examples : Acetanilide, antipyrine, menthol, camphor, chloral hydrate, phenol, salol, thymol and acetyl salicylic acid.

When two ore more of these are combined, liquefaction occurs. Liquefaction is avoided in the following way :

1. If each substance is in sufficient quantity, dispense each separately advising the patient to use one powder each as a dose.

2. Alternatively, use starch, talc or calcium phosphate as an adsorbent powder equal in proportion of liquefiable substances. Each liquefiable substance is triturated with equal quantity of adsorbent powder. The second liquefiable substance is separately triturated with the adsorbent powder and then both the mixtures are lightly mixed.

(d) Explosive Mixtures : These are generally a mixture of oxidising and reducing substances. For example a combination of potassium chlorate and tannic acid is an explosive mixture particularly so when pressure is applied. In trituration there is a pressure gradient. In order to avoid explosion, the substances should be powdered separately and then combined by mixing lightly.

Oxidising agents are chemically incompatible with reducing agent, so serious explosion may occur. To overcome this problem,. triturate lightly and pack separately.

Oxidising agents	Reducing agents
Potassium chlorate	Charcoal
Potassium dichromate	Hypophosphites
Potassium nitrate	Sulfur
Potassium permangnate	Sulfides
Sodium peroxide	Tannic acid
Silver nitrate	Volatile oils
	Oxalic acid

Example of Explosive Powder :

Potassium chlorate	10 grains
Tannic acid	5 grains
Sucrose	5 grains

In above powder mixture, potassium chlorate is an oxidising agent, while tannic acid is a reducing agent.

When oxidising agent and reducing agent is triturated in mortar, a violent and dangerous explosion is possible, so triturate separately and mix lightly .

List of Volatile and hygroscopic substances :

Camphor, Chlorbutol, Menthol, Thymol and Volatile Oils.

Hygroscopic substances include citric acid, Iron and ammonium citrate, potassium citrate, pepsin and sodium chloride.

Containers and closures for powders :

Powders may be wrapped or sent out in bulk. In wrapped powders, each dose is enclosed in a paper. For powders less than six powder packs, a suitable size of box is chosen. The wrapped powders may be placed flatty if the number of powders is less and when the number is large, they may be stacked on edges.

Powders are supplied in plain white glass bottles or jars with close fitting lids. Deliquescent or powders containing volatile ingredients are wrapped in waxed paper which further can be enclosed in metal foils. Individually wrapped powders are enclosed in cartons or rigid slide boxes of paper of plastic material . Now a days they are supplied in aluminium sachets.

Wrapping of powders : Take a clean paper of a suitable length, generally 1/8 inch less than twice the inside length of box. The width of paper may be three times the inside width of the box.

Turn up one edge of paper to 1/7 th of its width. Weigh out material for each powder and put it in the centre of the paper. The free end of the paper is then folded and placed under the previously folded edge. Fold this through the centre. Turn the ends symmetrically so that the size is now less than inside length of the box. Pair off the powders and place a rubber band so that the paper does not unfold itself.

Double Wrapping : Double wrapping is carried out with the help of two sheets of papers. The inner sheet of paper is a waxed paper. Double wrapping is carried out exactly as the single paper wrapping. It is necessary for powders containing volatile or hygroscopic substances.

Bulk Powders :

Generally, the quantity prescribed is more and is required to be taken in teaspoonfuls or tablespoonfuls and consequently they are sent out in wide mouth screw capped bottles.

A powder is considered to be simple if it has one ingredient. While a compound powder is a mixture of two or three or more ingredients.

Labelling of powders : Label on the container must provide the direction for taking the powder, along with all other details, like name, quantity, batch no. date of manufacture, date of expiry and dose.

Number of powders to be dispensed should be stated by the prescribers.

Storage of powders : Powders be stored in air tight well closed containers in cool place away from moisture.

Example 1

Acetyl salicylic acid	5 grains

Send 4 powders.

Label : Take one every 4 hours

Type : Simple powder.

Each powder contains 5 grains. Weigh out excess of total quantity of Acetylsalicylic acid and powder it. Weight out 5 grains of the powder four times, wrap, label and dispense. Reject the excess.

Before a student begins to study and carry out exercises on compound powders, he should bear the following points in mind :

1. Weigh out material for one powder more, than required.

2. If the total quantity arrived at, is a fraction and not directly weighable, take sufficiently (nearest) extra number of powders which will give directly weighable quantities.

3. If the total quantity of each powder includes a fraction, calculate the quantity of lactose (diluent) necessary to make it directly weighable.

4. If the prescription contains a liquid, adjusting the mixed material by adding lactose so that each power is directly weighable.

5. While mixing, mix the powdered ingredients in ascending order of their weight.

Supposing 1 mg of a substance is to be mixed with second substance (say about 12 mg) do it as follows :

1 mg + 1 mg of second substance.

2 mg of mixture + 4 mg of second substance

6 mg of mixture + 6 mg of second substance or the remaining

Example 2

Aspirin	0.25 g
Paracetamol	0.25 g

Let a powder be made.

Type : Compound powder

Send such nine powders.

Label : One to be taken when the pain is severe

Nine powders are to be sent. Calculate for ten powders

Aspirin	2.5 g
Paracetamol	2.5 g

Each powder must contain 0.5 g of the mixture.

Method :

Mix by trituration and dispense in a powder box or in an envelope.

Example 3

Tragacanth powdered	15 g
Acacia powdered	20 g
Starch powdered	20 g
Sucrose powdered	45 g

Type : A compound powder

Use : Suspending agent, for use in pharmacy

Method

Finely powder the substances; and mix them in a laboratory mixer.

Example 4

Mercurous chloride	gr 1/5
Sodium bicarbonate	gr (iii)
Powdered rhubarb	gr ss

Let powder be made. Send twelve powders

Label : Take one, three times a day between meals.

Type : Compound powder

Taking one extra powder will give 13/5 grains of mercurous chloride. This is not a directly weighable quantity, hence calculate for 15 powders.

Mercurous chloride	3 gr
Sodium bicarbonate	45 gr
Powdered rhubarb	7.5 gr
	55.5 gr of mixture

55.5 gr is again a quantity not weighable. Therefore, use lactose as diluent 4.5 grains of lactose may be added. The total would then be 60 grains of mixture and each powder will amount to 60/15 = 4 grains.

Method :

Mix mercurous chloride with lactose, and rhubarb powder and then sodium bicarbonate. Wrap 15 powders.

Powder containing small doses

At times potent medicaments are prescribed in fractions or in too small a bulk. In such cases the following rules are applicable.

For imperial quantities : Make the weight of the ingredient upto 2 grains for each powder by addition of lactose (diluent).

For metric quantities make the weight for each powder upto 100 mg with lactose. Exercises 5 and 6 illustrate the point.

Example 5

Codeine phosphate	gr 1/6

Send five powders

Label : Take one before going to bed

Calculate for six powders

Take Codeine phosphate $1/6 \times 6 = 1$ grain.

Each powder must weigh two grains. Hence quantity of lactose would be $6 \times 2 = 12$ grains. We already have 1 grain of Codeine phosphate. Weigh 11 grains of lactose.

Method :

Triturate Codeine phosphate with 11 grains of lactose mixing being carried out in ascending orders of weight. Dispense five powders.

Exercise 6

Diazepam	5 mg

Send nine powders

Label : Take one at bed time.

Type : Powder containing small dose.

Calculate for ten powders.

Diazepam $5 \times 10 = 50$ mg

But each powder must weigh 100 mg

Therefore, quantity of lactose to be taken is $(100 \times 10) - 50 = 950$ mg.

Method

Weigh out 50 mg of diazepam and triturate with 950 mg. of lactose. Weigh out powder (100 mg) and dispense nine.

Example 7

Hyoscine hydrobromide 1/150 grain

Send 12 powders.

Label : Take twice a day

Type : Powder containing small dose.

Calculate for 15 powders

Hyoscine hydrobromide

$$15 \times 1/150 = 1/10 \text{ gr.}$$

Take one grain of Hyoscine hydrobromide and triturate with nine grains of lactose. 1 grain of the mixture will contain 1/10 grains of Hyoscine hydrobromide.

Method

1 grain of mixture + 29 grains of lactose (repeated) be triturated and twelve powders dispensed.

Example 8

Diazepam	1/9 grain
Aspirin	3 gr
Paracetamol	3 gr

Send ten

Label : use one at bed time

Type : Compound Powder containing small dose.

Calculate for 11 powders :

Diazepam	$11 \times 1/9$	= 11/9 gr
Aspirin		33 gr
Paracetamol		33 gr

Diazepam is not directly weighable

Take 2 grains and triturate with 16 grains of lactose.

Total 18 grains of mixture. One grain of this mixture will contain 1/9th grain of diazepam and

11 grains will contain $1/9 \times 11 = 11/9$ grains.

Method

Take 11 grains of the mixture and triturate with 33 grains each of Aspirin and Paracetamol respectively.

Total bulk would be 33 + 33 + 11

= 77 grains

Each powder will therefore weigh 77/11 = 7 grains

Wrap and dispense the powders.

Example 9

Sodium bi - carbonate	gr X
Powdered rhubarb	gr iii
Oil of Peppermint	mss

Let a powder be made. Send nine

Label : Take one after meals

Type : Powder containing a liquid volume

Calculate for ten powders

Sodium bicarbonate		100 gr
Powdered rhubarb		30 gr
Oil of peppermint		5 minim
Lactose	q. s.	140 gr

Method

Mix the dry ingredients. Then add oil of peppermint. Each powder will weigh between 13 and 14 grains. Weigh the mixture. Then add lactose to weigh 140 grains. Each powder will now be 14 grains. Double wrap the powders as the oil of peppermint is volatile. The inner wrapper must be waxed paper. Wrap and dispense nine powders.

EFFERVESCENT POWDERS

As the name indicates, a powder of this type effervescences on coming in contact with moisture.

Obviously, it will be a mixture of acid and substance like sodium bi carbonate. Generally, medicaments may also be incorporated. Effervescent granules effectively mask the taste of a nauseous drug.

The commonly used acids for preparation of effervescent granules are, citric and tartaric acids together with **sodium** bicarbonate. The acids are slightly more in quantity than is necessary to neutralise the bicarbonate. This imparts pleasant sour taste.

If a medicament is being incorporated it is best to heat it at 100° C in order to let it loose water of crystallisation because the effervescent granules are required to be treated at 100° C.

Laboratory method of Preparation of Effervescent powders :

Preheat a porcelain dish over a boiling water bath. Finely powder the acids and bicarbonate of soda is ascending order of weight.

Place the mixture in the preheated porcelain dish. The citric acid loses the molecules of water of crystallization and this is sufficient to make mixture of powders, moist and coherent. This operation takes about five minutes. As soon as the powder mixture balls into the hand pass it through a No. 8 sieve superimposed by No. 20 sieve. The finer granules will fall through number 20 sieve. Collect these granules and place them in a warm place for drying.

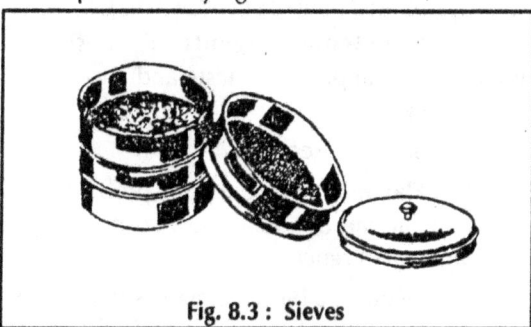

Fig. 8.3 : Sieves

Pack the granules in a wide mouth bottle for easy removal and dispense.

Note : If there is no effervescence when in contact with water, the preparation is considered to be useless

Example 10

Sodium bicarbonate	20.4 g
Sugar	60.0 g
Tartaric acid	10.80 g
Citric acid	07.2 g
Iron and ammonium citrate	2.15 g

Follow the above procedure.

Example 11

Menthol	12 grains
Camphor	12 grains
Ammonium chloride	72 grains
Light magnesium carbonate	144 grains

Let a insufflation be made.

Label : For the nose

Type : Powders containing liquefiable substances

Method

Separately powder each ingredient and weigh out the required quantities of each. Lightly mix menthol with ammonium chloride and camphor with magnesium carbonate and then mix both. Pass the mixture so obtained through No. 80 sieve and then dispense the sieved mixture of powders as usual.

POWDERS FOR EXTERNAL USE

There are three types :

1. Dusting Powders : The characteristics of these powders is that the powders are in the state of very fine particles capable of passing through and required to pass through a No. 80 sieve. They are mixture of such substances as zinc oxide, starch, boric acid kaolin and talc. The last two are obtained from mineral sources and generally expected to contain the pathogenetic organism viz. *Clostridium tetani*. Hence when kaolin or talc, are natural mineral ingredients included in a formula, they must be sterilised by dry heat (160°C) for one hour (from the time that the powder attains 150° C temperature) before use. The dusting powders are not meant to be applied to open wounds.

Unless otherwise directed, 50 g of powder be dispensed for external use.

2. Insufflations : These powders are intended for body cavities or areas where direct access to affected part is not possible. They are sent out in wide mouth bottles from which the required quantity is removed and transferred to an insufflator (a device to blow the powder) for use.

3. Snuffs : These are sent out in hinged boxes similar to a pill box and meant to be inhaled through nose for local action.

Example 12

Zinc oxide	20 g
Salicylic acid	0.2 g
Starch	78 g

Let a powder be made

Label : The dusting powder

Method : Each of the ingredients is finely powdered in a little excess and mixed in ascending order of weight. The mixture is passed through a No. 80 sieve and then dispensed in bottles with a perforated cap.

Example 13

Magnesium oxide	2.5 g
Starch	5.0 g
Purified talc sterilized	50.0 g

Label : The dusting powder.

TOOTH POWDERS

A powder, or preparation for the rubbing or cleansing of the teeth.

Requirements for tooth powder :

1. When used properly with an efficient toothbrush, it should clean the teeth adequately, i.e., remove food debris, plaque and stain.

2. It should leave the mouth with a fresh, clean sensation.

3. Its cost should be economical so as to encourage regular and frequent use by all.

4. It should be harmless, pleasant and convenient to use.

5. It should be capable of being packed economically and should be stable in storage during its commercial shelf-life.

6. It should conform to accepted standards in terms of its abrasivity to enamel and dentine.

Ingredients :

Basically, tooth powder contains following ingredients,

I. An abrasive.
II. A surfactant or detergent.
III. A sweetening agent.
IV. Flavour.
V. Colour (if required)

I. Abrasive : Clearly the main purpose of abrasive (Cleaning and polishing agent) is to remove any adherent layer on the teeth. They may be

e.g. Dental grade sillica,
Dicalcium phosphate dihydrate
Hydrated Alumina
Calcium Carbonate

II. Surfactants : Surfactants are use in the tooth powder to aid in the removal of the surface film on the tooth by lowering the surface tension. They also provide secondary benefits of providing foam to suspend and remove the debris.

e.g. Sodium lauryl sulfate.

III. Sweetening agents : These are important to improve the taste and for product acceptance.

e.g. Sodium saccharin.

IV. Flavours : Flavours are probably the most crucial part of a tooth powder because of consumer preference.

The flavour is a blend of many suitable oils, with peppermint and spearmint being the major base components. These are always fortified with other components such as thymol, menthol (to give a pleasant cooling effect), clove oil, cinnamon, eucalyptol, aniseed, etc.

V. Colours : Important in influencing consumer preference and purchase intent.

General Method of Preparation of Tooth Powder

This is done by simple mixing. Mixing is done in ascending order of weight thus ingredients of small quantity are premixed and then mixed with other ingredients in ribbon-type or agitator type of mixer. Flavour can be sprayed on to the bulk or can be premixed with part of some abrasive or polishing agent and then mixed with bulk.

Calcium carbonate	75 g
Kaolin	13.0 g
Sodium lauryl sulphate	02 g
Powdered pumice	10 g
Saccharine sodium	q. s.
Flavour	q. s.
Colour	q. s.

Herbal (Ayurvedic) tooth powder

Basically herbal tooth powders are classified into two types :

1. Red tooth powders
2. Black tooth powders.

Black tooth powders generally contain charcoal as base, and pudina, Ajowan, Kapoor, Nilgiree, and at times sweetening agent

Red tooth powder contains mixture of polyherbs like Babhul, Jambhul, Bor, Acrod, Khair, Bakul, Manjishtha, Trifala, and anti-dusting agents, etc.

Main ingredients required for the formulation of herbal or Ayurvedic tooth powders are :

1. Abrasives
2. Base
3. Astringents
4. Flavouring agents
5. Sweetening agents.

Typical polyherbal recipe may be as under :

Each gm of powder contains :

Acrod	02 mg
Akkal kadha	10 mg
Anant mool	10 mg
Arjuna	10 mg
Babhul	50 mg
Bakul	225 mg
Bor	20 mg
Dalchini	03 mg
Jambhul	50 mg
Jeshthamadh	35 mg
Kabab-chini	50 mg
Katha	30 mg
Lavang	05 mg
Maifal	20 mg
Manjishtha	60 mg
Ova	10 mg
Vajradanti	40 mg
Trifala powder	q. s.

Black tooth powder

A typical formula for preparation of black tooth powder may be as under.

Ajowan satva	0.75 %
Asmantara	0.25 %
Camphor	10 %
Charcoal to make	100 %
Kapoor tel	10 %
Mentha oil	2.0 %
Nilgiri tel	01 %
Sankhjira	25 %

Evaluation of tooth powder

Following are the important parameters on which tooth powders are to be evaluated irrespective of their types.

1. Abrasive action
2. Lustre
3. Consistency
4. Specific gravity
5. pH
6. Odour, colour and taste
7. Moisture
8. Humectants
9. Sweetening agents

Abrasive action :

(a) **Method of evaluation of abrasive action :** The teeth are fixed in brass holders which are then placed in a apparatus where they are brushed mechanically by reciprocating arms to which tooth brushes are attached. The brushes are trimmed and adjusted, so that a uniform pressure is exerted in all instances. The abrasiveness of powder on both tooth enamel and bone is determined by using micrometer gauge sensitive to 0.001 inch. On the basis of bone abrasion results, powders are classified as abrasive, moderately abrasive, or non-abrasive.

(b) Average abrasiveness : Average abrasiveness is determined by using formula.

Average abrasiveness

$$= \frac{1}{3} \frac{E \times 100}{24} + \frac{D \times 100}{335} \times \frac{C.E.J \times 100}{190}$$

where E = measure of wear on enamel in 0.001 mm

D = measure of wear on dentine in 0.001 mm

C.E.J = measure of wear on cemento-enamel junction in 0.001 mm

The abrasiveness of calcium carbonate set arbitrarily at 100.

(c) The tooth powder is placed on chemically clean glass and rubbed with a metal instrument having a hardness and surface similar to the curved surface of a small coin. Freshly distilled water is added to confer a paste like consistency before rubbing with the metal instrument. One hundred double strokes are made, applying a thrust of one pound. A control test is performed near to the spot where the tooth powder tested, using a lubricant such as glycerol, petroleum jelly. After both tests are completed, the glass is placed in hot nitric acid to remove particles of alloy adhering to glass. The glass is observed in transmitted and reflected light for scratches. The test is repeated for three times.

(d) The tooth powder shall not deteriorate when cooled to a temperature of 15°C for one hour or when heated to a temperature of 50°C for 72 hours.

(e) Tooth powder samples are placed in an atmosphere of 75 % relative humidity at room temperature for several days, and determine the amount of moisture absorbed under the standard conditions.

(f) Apply the tooth powder to mucous membrane of the cheecks and gums for 2 minute. It must not produce irritation or unpleasant symptoms.

QUESTIONS

1. What are powders ? How powders are prepared ?
2. What are advantages of powders over other dosage forms of medicaments ? Describe the containers for cosmetic powders ?
3. Describe various types of powders for internal and external use.
4. What are effervescent powders and how are they prepared ?
5. What are tooth powders ? How are they classified ?
6. What you know about evaluation of tooth powder ?
7. What is tooth-powder, explain the role played by abrasive, surfactant and flavour in tooth powders ?

CHAPTER 9
MONOPHASIC DOSAGE FORMS

VEHICLES FOR MIXTURES

As the name indicates these products consist of only one phase, and various vehicles used to formulate these products are as under.

Water :

Tap water should never be used as vehicle for mixtures. Trace metallic salts and dissolved gases in tap water give rise to incompatibilities, particularly with sensitive drugs. Distilled water is to be used. Sterility of purified water is to be maintained. Any evidence of contamination calls for rejection of the lot and fresh supply be used. For this purpose, it is better to go for a distill-water still. It is better to have as much purified water as is necessary for day's work. Purified water is by far the most cheap and inert vehicle for mixtures. Purified water can be obtained by ion-exchange or reverse osmosis method.

Concentrated Aromatic Waters

The strength of conc. aromatic water is 40 times the strength of ordinary aromatic water. One volume diluted with 39 volumes of purified water will produce the ordinary strength. Most of the aromatic waters are carminative in nature and generally, improve palatability and impart flavour to the mixtures containing nauseating drugs. Examples of aromatic waters are peppermint water, cinnamon water etc.

Concentrated Infusions

One volume added to seven volumes of purified water produces the ordinary strength of infusion. The carminative properties as well as the property of being bitter is associated with infusion. They are not frequently used.

Syrup Vehicles

Solution of sugar in water is known as *syrup*. Naturally, these are sweetening agents. The syrups are good vehicles for salines. A simple syrup is one which is the solution of sugar in purified water. Raspberry and cherry syrups impart their characteristic flavour since they are prepared from the juice of fresh ripe fruits.

Diabetic Syrup

A diabetic patient requires non-glycogenetic vehicle. Only one formula for this type of syrup is being given below :

Orange oil	0.05
Tween 20	3.00
Citric acid	0.35
Carboxy methyl cellulose solution..... ad	50.00

(The C. M. C. solution contains 1 % sodium carboxy methyl cellulose and 0.1 % sodium cyclamate, non-carbohydrate sweetening agent.)

Elixirs

Elixirs are sweetened and flavoured solutions in alcohols. At times a, hydro-alcoholic vehicle is needed to dissolve drugs.

Tinctures and Spirits

They are not frequently used, as they are rather potent preparations and have a high alcoholic content.

Linctuses :

These are viscid solutions of medicines meant to be licked. They have local action on the throat. A viscid vehicle is used to ensure prolonged action. They are generally simple solutions.

Stabilizers :

These are the substances, which make the solution, suspension, or mixture stable and hence are known as *stabilizers*.

Even the substances which retard the rate of reaction or preserve a chemical equilibrium or act as antioxidants keep pigments and other components in emulsion and prevent the particles in a colloidal suspension from precipitating, are also stabilizers.

Thus sodium citrate an anti peptizing agent, sodium meta bisulphite as antioxidant and gums as emulsifying or suspending agents are the good examples of stabilizers in pharmacy.

Colorants :

Substances which impart colours to the solutions or mixtures are colorants for colouring agents. They are added for any of the following purpose -

1. for identifying similar looking products,
2. To mask the undesired colour.
3. To improve the aesthetic value or marketing value.

Since availability of natural and safe colours is limited many synthetic colours are used in pharmaceutical industry. But these colours must be safe and approved by food and drug administration. They are water soluble or slightly soluble in water or alcohol. Most of them are anthraquinone, azodyes or coal-tar compounds. They are used in very small concentration. Some of the natural safe colours are curcuma (turmeric) carmine, litmus, saffron, indigo, chlorophyll and walnut oil. Animal dye like cochineal may also be used safely.

Flavours :

Flavours are added to mixture to mask undesired smell of the substances normally, the flavours are volatile oils or synthetic compounds like vanilline.

These are used in very small concentration upto 1.0 % either alone or by dissolving in alcohol as found suitable. Examples - Lemon oil, orange oil, cardamom oil, peppermint oil, etc.

STUDY OF MONOPHASIC LIQUIDS

Following is the account of few monophasic liquid dosage forms with suitable examples alongwith method of preparation, containers used and type of labeling for them.

MOUTH WASHES

Mouth washes are simple aqueous solutions intended to wash oral cavity and impart a deodorising analgesic, astringent or antiseptic action. The vehicle may be water or a combination of water and alcohol.

Containers : These are dispensed in white fluted bottles.

Labelling : Proper directions for diluting the mouth wash, before use should be clearly indicated on the label.

Example 1

Liquified phenol	1.5 ml
Peppermint oil	0.5 ml
Purified water	ad 100 ml

The mouth wash

Method

Dissolve phenol in water add the peppermint oil and make up the volume.

Label : Dilute it with twice the warm water before use.

> For external use only.

Example 2

Potassium permangnate	50 mg
Water	ad 100 ml.

The mouth wash.

Label : Warm and use the solution.

Use freshly prepared.

Method

Powder potassium permangnate in a glass mortar. Add a little of water. Transfer the solution to a measure. Repeatedly wash the mortar with water and add the washings to the measure. Finally make up the volume by addition of more of vehicle.

Use as directed by physician. For external use only.

GARGLES

The aqueous solutions usually highly medicated and intended for administration only after dilution, in the treatment of an infection of throat.

Containers : White fluted bottles, to distinguish them from preparations for internal use. Coloured bottles are to be used if the gargle needs protection from light.

Labelling : Directions for proper dilution should be stated on the label. It should also include the words " **For external use only** ."

Example 1

Alum	2.0 g
Purified water	ad 100 ml.

"The Alum gargle."

Label : Use as directed.

Method

Dissolve alum in purified water and dispense.

Example 2

Acetyl salicylic acid	2.5 g
Amaranth solution	1.0 g
Sodium citrate	0.5 g
Water	ad 100 ml.

The gargle.

Label : Use as directed by physician.

It should be freshly prepared.

Method

Dissolve the sodium citrate in about 50 ml of water and then add acetyl salicylic acid. Add the amaranth solution and then make up the volume.

Example 3

Phenol	4.0 g
Glycerin of Tannic acid	20 ml.
Peppermint water	ad 100 ml.

Label : The gargle.

Dilute one Tablespoonful with a pint of warm water and gargle, morning and night.

THROAT PAINTS

Throat paints are the liquid preparations for application to the mucous membrane of the buccal cavity.

Glycerin, liquid paraffin, propylene glycol or resinous substances like balsams are employed as bases.

Throat-paints may be antiseptic, astringent or analgesic in action.

Containers

Wide mouthed bottles are used where the paint is to be used with a brush or swab. If the paints contain a poison, vertically fluted bottle may be used in order to distinguish from ordinary medicines for internal use. A few of the glycerines are also used as throat paints.

Labelling : Containers should be labelled "For external use only."

Storage : Throat-paints should be stored in air tight containers and in cool place.

Example 1

Phenol	1.5 g
Glycerin	ad 25 ml.

The throat paint.

Label : Use as directed, "**For external use only.**"

Method

Dissolve phenol by adding it to glycerine and gently warm until solution is obtained.

It should be diluted with water.

Example 2

Iodine	10.4 g
Potassium iodide	05.0 g
Peppermint oil	01.0 ml.
Glycerine	100 ml.

The throat paint.

Label : Apply with a swab.

Shake well before use. "**For external use only.**"

Method

Powder iodine and potassium iodide crystals. Dissolve the powders in about 25 ml. of glycerine. Transfer to a measuring cylinder . cy Add the peppermint oil. Rinse the mortar with a little of glycerine. Add this to the measuring cylinder Make up the volume. Filter if necessary and then dispense.

EAR DROPS

Ear drops are meant to be instilled into the ear. They are usually solutions or suspensions of drugs in water, diluted alcohol, glycerine, propylene glycol or ethylene glycol. The non-aqueous vehicles are more favourable than aqueous vehicles, since aqueous vehicles promote and enhance ear infections. If water is used as vehicle purified water boiled and cooled must be used.

Containers : Ear drops must be dispensed in coloured fluted glass bottles fitted with plastic screw-cap along with glass dropper tube fitted with rubber teat or a suitable plastic cap and a droping device.

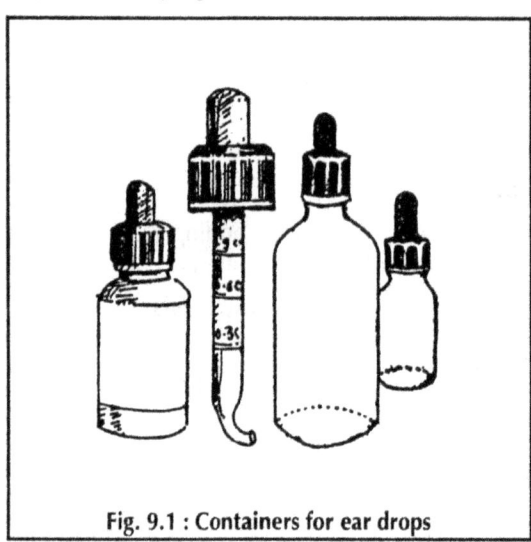

Fig. 9.1 : Containers for ear drops

Unless otherwise directed 15 ml of ear-drops be dispensed.

Labelling : Label should indicate the words **"For external use only"**

In absence of any instructions 3 to 4 drops to be put into affected ear, should be stated on the label.

Example 1

Phenol	05 g
Glycerine	ad 100 ml.

Label : Place 5 drops in affected ear.

Note : An additional warning may be put on the label.

" Dilute with glycerine only " or "Not to be diluted with water."

Method

Dissolve phenol in glycerine, if necessary warm, to dissolve.

Label : For external use only.

Example 2

Sodium bicarbonate	7.0 g
Phenol	0.5 g
Glycerine	50 ml.
Purified water	ad 100 ml.
The ear-drops	

Label : Use as directed.

For external use only.

Method

Take about 60 ml of purified water, boil it for half an hour and cool it. Dissolve sodium bicarbonate in about 40 ml of water. Separately dissolve phenol in glycerine. Mix the two solutions, transfer to a measure and make up the required volume.

Example 3

Amethocaine	1.5 g
Phenol	2.0 g
Glycerine	ad 100 ml.
The Ear drops.	

Label : Use as directed by the physician.

For external use only.

Mix.

Example 4

Picric acid	01 g
Boric acid	02 g
Alcohol 95 %	30 ml.
Purified water	ad 100 ml.

The Ear-drops.

Label : Use as directed.

For external use only.

Caution : Handle picric acid carefully. It explodes if triturated or heated.

Method

Boil and cool excess of purified water. Dissolve boric acid and picric acid in 30 ml. of boiled purified water. Add 30 ml. of 95 % alcohol. Transfer to a measure and adjust to volume with purified water.

Example 5

Salicylic acid	01 g
Alcohol 90 %	ad 100 ml.

Salicylic acid ear drops.

Label : Use as directed by physician.

"For external use only."

Mix.

Example 6

Chloramphenicol	250 mg.
Propylene glycol	ad 25 ml.

The Ear drops.

Label : Use as directed.

"For external use only."

Mix.

NASAL DROPS

These are the aqueous or oily preparations to be instilled into the nostrils by means of dropper.

Since the oil retards the ciliary action of the nasal mucous, a oily nasal-drops are not to be utilised for long periods.

Containers : Similar to the ear-drops, nasal-drops be dispensed in coloured fluted glass bottles, fitted with plastic screw cap along with glass dropper tube, fitted with rubber teat or a suitable plastic cap and a dropper device.

Unless otherwise directed 15 ml of ear drops be dispensed.

Labelling : Label should indicates the words

"For external use only".

Prescribers instructions be included on the label.

In absence of any instructions, 3 to 4 drops to be put into affected ear, should be stated on the label.

Example 1

Penicillin (Sodium salt)	2,500 units
Normal saline	ad 100 ml.

The Nasal-drops.

Label : Use as directed.

Mix.

Example 2

Ephedrine hydrochloride	100 mg.
Normal saline	ad 10 ml.

The Nasal-drops.

Label : Use as directed.

Mix.

Example 3

Atropine sulphate	50 mg.
Normal saline	ad 10 ml.

The Nasal-drops.

Label : Use as directed.

Note : These drops are meant to lessen mucous production,

Method : Mix.

LINIMENTS

Liniments are solutions or suspensions or emulsions intended for external application. They are generally applied with massage.

Therapeutic properties depend on the penetration of medicaments through skin and layers below, and will depend on the nature of medication as well as on the degree of massage employed. They possess analgesic, rubefacient, soothing, or stimulating properties.

Containers of Liniments :

The containers must be easily distinguishable by touch from those used for internal medicine. Coloured fluted bottles may be used. If poisonous substances are present, then the solution may be coloured by adding colouring agents such as amaranth, sulphan blue etc.

Unless otherwise mentioned 50 ml of liniments be prepared.

Be supplied in coloured bottles.

Fig. 9.2 : Containers for liniments

Labelling : Labelling is similar to mixtures. It should include the words,

'For external use only.'

Should not be applied to broken skin.

Storage : Depending upon the nature of medicaments. These are to be stored in well-filled, well closed, air tight containers and in cool place.

Example 1

Soft soap	09 g
Camphor	05 g
Turpentine oil	69 ml
Purified water	to 100 ml

Prepare Liniment

Label : Use as directed.

For external use only.

Method

Take the required quantity of soft soap in the mortar and add water in thrice the quantity as soft soap. Triturate to make a soapy solution. Take the required quantity of oil of turpentine in a dry measure glass and dissolve camphor in it. Add this solution drop by drop in the mortar, triturating continuously and rapidly, till the primary emulsion is formed.

Add a small quantity of water and transfer it to the previously calibrated, round, vertically ribbed and blue or amber coloured bottle. Adjust to the required volume by adding water. Cork and label it.

LINIMENT OF TURPENTINE

30 ml.

FOR EXTERNAL USE ONLY

FOR   MR. X. Y. Z.

Direction : To be applied externally on the affected part with friction

SHAKE WELL BEFORE USE

Date : 17/10/2001   Prepared by : Arm

CIVIL HOSPITAL - BELGAUM

Use

Liniment of turpentine is used externally in a patient suffering from arthralgia (joint pain), myalgia (muscular pain), fibrositis, and sprain.

MECHANISM OF ACTION

It acts as an irritant and counter-irritant.

Irritants and counter irritants : The practice of applying irritants to the skin in internal diseases was known long before, as it was originally believed that disease was a malignant entity which might be drawn from the deeper organs of the surface by irritating the skin.

Irritants are agents which produce more or less local inflammatory reactions when used locally.

The initial symptoms of irritation are congestion and redness of the part; such drugs producing only this degree of irritation are known as rubefacients. Stronger irritants cause blistering and are known as vesicants like cantherdin: while some drugs which cause irritation and small discrete suppurations are called pustulants.

Counter-irritants are the drugs or agents which are applied locally to irritate the intact skin for the purpose of relieving deep-seated-pain.

Visceral disease is often accompanied by tenderness of the skin and underlying muscles, and pain arising in such cases may be referred to this area of the skin and not to the organ involved. For example, in heart disease, pain is often felt in the left chest wall and shoulder extending down the left arm.

The physiological basis of counter-irritation is not precisely known but it is presumed to act by the following mechanisms :

1. **Local :** Counter-irritants cause vaso-dilation and redness of the part (rubefacient action) accompanied by sensory stimulation. This is associated with a feeling of warmth and comfort. The vasodilation is due to the axon reflex i. e. the vasodilator effect with all its accompaniments occurring without the impulse passing through a nerve cell.

2. **Focal :** Vasodilation may affect the more deep-seated tissues and permit the dispersal of pain producing substances. The vasodilation is produced by stimulation of sensory nerve endings in the skin and relay of afferent impulses in the cerobrospinal axis to efferent vasomotor fibres supplying the internal tissue.

Strong sensory irritation of segment of the skin either alters or completely depresses the pain arising from an internal organ which is innervated by the same segment and following the common sensory pathway to the brain. This effect is due to cortical pre-occupation. There is a crowding of sensations which result in inability of brain to receive all impulses which are directed to it. This helps in relieving internal pain.

Counter irritants can be either physical or chemical agents.

Physical counter-irritants are :
(a) hot water bottles,
(b) short wave diathermy,
(c) radiant heat,
(d) galvanic electric current.

Chemical counter-irritants are :
(a) Volatile oils e. g. oil of turpentine, camphor, menthol, thymol, methyl salicylate etc.
(b) Black mustard powder or oil

Example 1

Menthol	4 g
Camphor	4 g
Thymol	4 g

Let a liniment be made

Label : Apply with camel hair brush to the affected part.
For external use only.

Method

The above three substances when combined together form an oily liquid. Hence triturate together in a dry mortar until a liquid is formed. Then transfer to a dry bottle.

Example 2

Salicylic acid	1.2 g
Resorcinol	3.6 g
Alcohol 70 %	120 ml

Let the Liniment be made.

Label : Use as directed.
For external use only.

Method

Dissolve salicylic acid and resorcinol in about 100 ml. of alcohol. Transfer to a measure and make up the volume by addition of 70 % alcohol.

Example 3

Calamine	1.0 g
Zinc oxide	2.0 g
Olive oil	15 ml
Solution of Cal. hydroxide	15 ml

Make a Liniment

Label : To be used daily.
For external use only.

Note : The free fatty acids in olive oil react with solution of calcium hydroxide forming a divalent soap giving a water in oil emulsion. The solution of calcium hydroxide must be freshly prepared.

Method

Triturate calamine and zinc oxide in mortar and continue trituration after adding the olive oil. Add calcium hydroxide solution and triturate briskly until a cream is formed.

Example 5

Triethanolamine	1.0 ml
Oleic acid	4.0 ml
Benzyl benzoate	24 ml
Water	120 ml

Benzyl benzoate liniment

Label : Apply as directed.

For external use only.

This is a soap emulsion. The soap is formed due to interaction between triethanolamine and oleic acid (the fatty acid).

Method

Mix triethanolamine with required quantity of water, 120 ml. Mix oleic acid and benzyl benzoate. Add both mixtures and stir gently.

Example 6

Camphor	4.0 g
Oleic acid	4.0 g
Alcohol 90 %	70 ml
Potassium hydroxide	q. s.
Flavour	1.5 ml
Purified water	ad 100 ml

Prepare Liniment

Label : Use as directed by physician

For external use only.

Method

Dissolve the oleic acid in about 50 ml of alcohol and add potassium hydroxide solution until one drop of solution diluted with ten drops of carbon-dioxide free water gives full blue colour with one drop of bromothymol blue and a full yellow colour with thymol blue. which indicates a pH between 7.6 and 8.0. Dissolve camphor and the flavour in remainder of alcohol and mix the two solutions. Make up the volume to 100 ml. Allow the liniment to stand for seven days then filter and dispense.

Example 7

Methyl salicylate	13 ml
Arachis oil	ad 50 ml

Mix. Prepare liniment

Use as directed by physician.

For external use only.

LOTIONS

Lotions are aqueous suspensions intended for external application to the skin without massage on lint, or other soft absorbent fabric. (distinction from liniments).

A few are emulsions. Use of homogenisers serves to give better dispersion of insoluble substances.

Lotions are used for their cooling, soothing anti-allergic, antiseptic, astringent or drying properties depending on the ingredients used.

Table 9.1 : Difference between liniments and lotions

Liniments	Lotions
1. Most of them are to be applied with a slight friction.	1. These are to be applied without friction.
2. These are used for application to the unbroken skin only.	2. Lotions are used for application to skin (even broken or inflamed).
3. Act as irritants and counter irritants.	3. Have antiseptic, anti-inflammatory and cooling properties.
4. May contain camphor	4. Do not contain camphor.

Containers for lotions : Lotions must be dispensed in coloured (blue or amber coloured) fluted bottles or in suitable plastic containers.

Unless otherwise directed 100 ml of lotion be prepared.

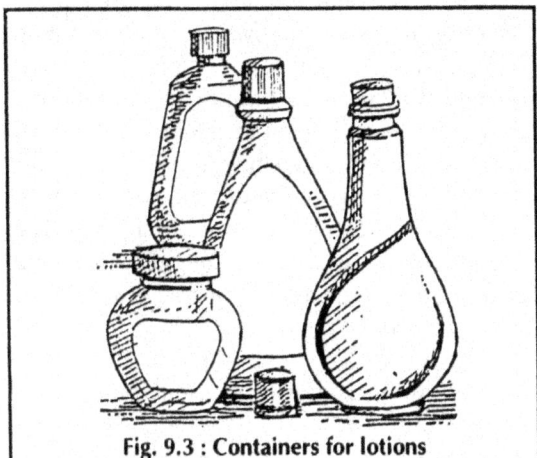

Fig. 9.3 : Containers for lotions

Labelling : It should cover the words **'For external use only'**. Proper instructions for lotions, if diluted to use within one month of dilution.

Storage : In well-filled well closed containers in cool place.

Classification :

1. Simple lotions containing soluble ingredients i. e. potassium permanganate lotion (0.1 %), Cetrimide lotion (1 %), etc.
2. Lotions containing insoluble ingredients, e. g. Calamine lotion.
3. Lotions exhibiting intentional incompatibility, e. g. Lotion nigra (Black wash)

Example 1

Prepared calamine	3.50 g
Zinc oxide	1.50 g
Bentonite	0.90 g
Sodium citrate	0.15 g
Liquified phenol	0.15 g
Glycerin	0.15 g
Rose water upto	30 ml

Mix and prepare a lotion.

Direction : To be applied externally on the affected part without friction.

Method

Take the required quantities of calamine, zinc oxide and bentonite in the mortar, finely powder them and mix. Measure about three quarters (20 ml) of the vehicle and dissolve in it, the quantity of sodium citrate; pour a portion of it in the mortar and triturate to form a smooth cream; add the remaining amount of sodium citrate solution and mix well. Add the required quantity of glycerin and liquefied phenol into it: add more of the vehicle to produce the prescribed volume (30 ml). Transfer it into the bottle; cork and label it. The bottle should be round, vertically ribbed and blue or amber coloured.

Label

```
              CALAMINE LOTION
                   30 ml
            FOR EXTERNAL USE ONLY
FOR        MR. X. Y. Z.
Direction : To be applied on the affected
           part without friction
            SHAKE WELL BEFORE USE
Date : 19/10/2001    Prepared by : SBG
          AJAY-PHARMACY, GULBARGA
```

Note : In addition, to the direction ' For external use only'. ' **Shake well before use:**' should be written on the label

Use :

1. To allay pain and swelling of sunburn.
2. In pruritus.
3. In any irritating skin disease e. g. dermatitis eczema, ringworm psoriasis, etc.

Mechanism of action

1. Astringent, 2. Antipruritic,
3. Antiseptic.

Example 2

Calamine	8.0 g
Zinc oxide	8.0 g
Sodium carboxymethyl cellulose	2.2 g
Dioctyl sodium sulphosuccinate	0.08 g
Glycerin	0.4 ml
Purified water	ad 120 ml

The calamine lotion, send 60 ml

Label : Apply as directed

Method

Mix calamine and zinc oxide in a mortar. Add glycerine to levigate the mixed powders. The sodium carboxymethyl cellulose and dicotyl sodium sulphosuccinate are dissolved in sufficient water. This solution is added to the levigated paste. The volume is then made upto 120 ml Pass through a homogeniser.

Label : 'For external use only'
        Shake well before use'

Example 3

Precipitated sulphur	05.0 g
Glycerin	05.0 ml
Sodium lauryl sulphate	0.25 gm
Alcohol	15 ml
Rose water	ad 100 ml

Let a lotion be made, send 50 ml

Label : Apply every night.

Method

Triturate the sulphur with glycerin (glycerin is used to wet the sulphur) add 0.25 gms of sodium lauryl sulphate, and the alcohol. Finally add the rose water to make up the required volume.

Example 4

Zinc sulphate	4.0 g
Sulphurated potash	4.0 g
Water	100 ml

Let a lotion be made.

Mop on face each night.

It should be freshly prepared.

Note : Sulphurated potash is a mixture of potassium sulphides and other potassium compounds. Zinc sulphate reacts with sulphurated potash forming zinc sulphide which is diffusible.

Method

Mix zinc sulphate with water to produce 50 ml and similarly, mix Sulphurated potash to produce 50 ml of mixture. Add the two mixtures together and dispense.

Eye Lotions

Eye lotions are required to be used while warm. It, therefore, follows that the eye lotion be diluted with warm water before use. Consequently they are issued in double strength and the patient is instructed to dilute it with equal volume of warm water before use. Eye lotions are not used for open wounds or damaged eye. There is always a danger of infection. The eye lotions are used for washing or bathing the eyes. Patient is required to be told to clean and wash the eye before use.

Eye lotions are sterilized products.

Following exercise represents preparation of eye lotion.

Example 5

Potassium permangnate solution 8 ounces (1 in 5000)

Label : The eye lotion.

Use freshly prepared.

For external use only.

To be used thrice a day with equal volume of warm water.

Calculations : 35 grains in 8 ounces is 1 in 100 solution.

Therefore, No. of grains required in 8 ounces to make 1 in 5000 solution will be

$$\frac{35 \times 100 \times 8}{5000 \times 8} = 0.7 \text{ grains}$$

will make 8.0 ℥ of 1 in 5000 solution.

This quantity (0.7 gr) is not directly weighable. Therefore, dissolve 1 grain in ten drachms of boiled distilled water. Seven drachms of this solution will contain 0.7 grains of potassium permangnate. Make up the volume of 8 ounces and dispense.

Example 6

Chlorinated lime	01.25 g
Boric acid	01.25 g
Water upto	100 ml

Prepare a Lotion

Label : Use as directed by physician

It should be recently prepared.

ENEMAS

Enemas are aqueous or oily solutions or suspensions that are introduced into the rectum for cleansing, therapeutic or diagnostic purposes.

Cleansing preparations are used to evacuate faeces in constipation or before an operation. They act in one of two ways -

1. By stimulating peristalsis because either -

   (a) Their volume is large (0.5 to 1litre) : e.g. plain water, soap (soft soap 1 in 20) and turpentine enemas; the last-named also relieves flatulence; or

   (b) They cause osmotic retention of water in the bowel. This type of enema is of smaller volume, e.g. Sodium-phosphate enema (100 ml) and magnesium sulphate enema.

2. By lubricating impacted faeces e.g. olive and arachis oil enemas (100 to 500 ml).

Therapeutic enemas may be used as -

Sedatives - Chloral hydrate, paraldehyde.

Anthelmintics - Quassia (for thread worms)

Anti-inflammatory agents - Corticosteroids (for ulcerative colitis)

Nutrients - When absorption by mouth is impaired.

Barium sulphate enema, which is a suspension, is used for X-ray examination of the lower bowel.

Large volume enemas are administered from a douche can and should be warmed to body temperature before use. Some commercially available, small volume enemas (e.g. sodium phosphates and prednisolone) are in disposable polythene or polyvinyl chloride bags sealed with a rectal nozzle.

Container : Enemas should be supplied in coloured fluted glass bottles or in single use plastic packs fitted with rectal nozzle.

Storage : These are stored in cool place.

Labelling : It should be labelled "for external use only".

COLLODIONS

Collodions are liquid preparations consisting of a solution of pyroxylin in a mixture of organic solvents, usually ether and alcohol. They are intended for local external application and are applied by painting on the skin and allowing to dry. A flexible cellulose film is formed, covering the site of application.

Collodions may be used to seal off minor cuts and wounds or as a means of holding a dissolving medicament in contact with the skin for long periods.

Salicylic acid collodion BP

Salycylic acid	120 g
Flexible collodion	to 1000 ml

Label : As directed by physician.

> For external use only

Flexible collodion is a solution of colophony in a mixture of castor oil and collodion.

Colophony	25 g
Castor oil	25 g
Collodion sufficient to produce	1000 ml

Mix the ingredients and stir until the colophony has dissolved; allow any deposit to settle and decant the clear liquid.

Collodion for the preparation of flexible collodion :

Collodion is a solution of pyroxylin in a mixture of solvent ether and ethanol (90 per cent).

Method : It may be prepared by adding 100 g of pyroxylin to 900 ml of a mixture of 3 volumes of solvent ether and one volume of 90 % of alcohol.

QUESTIONS

1. Define Gargles, throat paints and mouth washes. Describe the way of labelling them along with the note on suitable containers for them.

2. Differentiate the following :
   (a) Mouth wash and throat paint
   (b) Gargles and mouth wash.

3. Differentiate lotions and liniments. Write a note on containers for liniments and lotions.

4. Write the various purposes for which liniments and lotions are used. How liniments are prepared and dispersed ?

5. What are eye-lotions ? How are they labelled ?

6. What is role of oil in lotions ? What for camphor is used in lotions ?

7. Define the following with suitable examples : (a) Stabilisers, 'b) Adjuvants, (c) Flavours.

8. Name any three vehicles, alongwith their merits and demerits, in formulations.

9. Define the following terms and state their uses :
   (a) Enema, (2) Collodion, (3) Nasal-drops, (4) Ear-drops, (5) Colourants.

10. Comment on the "containers" for (a) Liniments, (b) Nasal-drops, (c) Lotions, (d) Mouth washes.

CHAPTER 10

BIPHASIC DOSAGE FORMS

SUSPENSIONS

INTRODUCTION

Suspension is the dispersion of particles of insoluble liquid or of partially soluble or insoluble solids in liquid.

Depending upon the particle size of dispersed solid, it may be further classified as coarse suspension, fine suspension and colloidal suspension. Suspension's may be for parenteral, external or oral administration.

Containers : Depending upon the viscosity suspensions can be dispensed either in narrow mouth fluted or wide mouth bottles.

Labelling : In case of liquid preparations *"shake well before use"* label be used. In case of dry-suspension powders the specified amounts of vehicle to be used for dilution be indicated clearly.

Many pharmaceutical preparations are prepared in the suspension form for one reason or the other.

A good suspension

1. After shaking, should remain in suspension for long time, particle size of solid in suspensions vary from 0.5 to 5.0 μ.
2. Should have easy redispersion of solids.
3. Be pourable from the container.
4. Be elegant in appearance.
5. Have uniform small particles which on standing should not form aggregates.
6. Should have solid particles with adequate stability in the vehicle used.

Solids in suspension are classified according to their wettability as under :

(a) Diffusible solids and
(b) Indiffusible solids

Diffusible solids remain in dispersed form for a sufficiently long time till they are consumed.

Indiffusible solids settle down on standing. Indiffusibility depends on various factors such as

1. Wettability
2. Viscosity
3. Particle size.

Hence surface active agents, thickening agents and use of fine powder helps to obtain good suspension.

General method for preparation of suspensions containing diffusible solids :

Grind all the ingredients of suspension to obtain fine powder. Then mix the powders as per ascending order of their weights as under :

Example : If the suspension contains following powders :

Powder A	1 g
Powder B	3 g
Powder C	4 g
Powder D	8 g

Mix 1g of powder A with 1g of powder B. Then mix the 2g of mixture with the remaining 2g of powder B. Total mixture quantity becomes 4 g. Now mix this 4g mixture with 4g of powder C and finally prepare homogeneous mixture of this 8g powder with 8g of powder D.

After mixing the powder, add little amount of vehicle to form a paste. Then add required amount of vehicle to obtain the volume. Observe the suspension for any suspended impurity and then transfer it in a bottle and rinse the mortar. Collect the rinse and transfer it in a bottle. Shake the bottle to obtain a uniform suspension. If any volatile ingredient is present in the formula, add in the bottle and shake it to disperse uniformly.

Thin suspensions (low viscosity) can be filled in a narrow mouth bottle. High viscosity suspensions require wide mouth bottle for storage. Temperature variations adversely affect the preparation, hence it is stored in a cool place.

Indiffusible solids, settle down quickly it becomes difficult to maintain the uniformity of dose. However, preparation can easily be stabilised by incorporating thickening agent in the preparation. It increases the viscosity of the preparation and rate of sedimentation is decreased.

Different types of thickening agents are given below:

1. **Acacia** : Dried exudate of *Acacia senegal*. It forms colloidal solution in water and increases the viscosity.

2. **Tragacanth** : Dried extract from *Astragalus gummifer* and certain other species of *Astragalus*. It forms gel with water. The mucilage or gel is viscous and less sticky than acacia.

3. **Compound powder of Tragacanth** : It is a good thickening agent and used in the concentration of 2 g per 100 ml of final mixture. It is prepared by mixing acacia 20 per cent, tragacanth 15 percent, starch 20 per cent and remaining sucrose. When tragacanth alone is used, then 0.2 gm per 100 ml suspension may be used.

4. **Starch** : Sometimes starch mucilage is used as a suspending or thickening agent. Maize, wheat or rice starch may be used.

5. **Sodium alginate** : It is a sodium salt of alginic acid. Alcohol 2 to 4 per cent is used while preparing the mucilage. Being an anionic compound, it is incompatible with many cationic substances. Hence while using, its incompatibility with other ingredients should be ascertained.

6. **Methyl cellulose** : In the cellulose there are three hydroxy groups in the monomers, one or more is replaced by methoxy group to give methylcellulose. It can be used for internal as well as external preparations. High viscosity grade methyl cellulose is used as thickening agent. Normally 0.5 to 2 per cent is sufficient to give adequate viscosity.

7. **Hydroxy ethyl cellulose** : When hydroxy ethyl group is substituted for hyroxy group in the cellulose monomer, the compound formed is called *hydroxy ethyl cellulose*. It is soluble in hot and cold water.

8. **Sodium carboxymethyl cellulose (SCMC)** : It differs from methyl cellulose in having one of the hydrogen atom of methyl group is replaced by carboxy group. ($-CH_2COOH$) Because of carboxyl group, salts can be produced various grade of S.C.M.C. are available with viscosity 6 to 4000 centipoises for 1 per cent solution. It is used in the concentration 0.25 to 1 per cent in the suspension.

9. **Microcrystalline cellulose** : Solution of high molecular weight polymer crystallises, to form microcrystals. These are separated microcrystals of cellulose has a molecular weight around 36000. They are dispersible but not soluble. These produce colloidal dispersion. It is sometimes used in combination with S. C. M. C.

10. **Bentonite** : Formula of bentonite is $Al_2O_3, 4\ SiO_2 \cdot H_2O$ with little magnesium, iron and calcium carbonate. It is hygroscopic powder. About 2 per cent is used as suspending agent in external preparations when used on the broken skin it should be sterilised. *Clostridium tetani* spores are many a times seen associated with bentonite.

11. **Aluminium-magnesium silicate** : It is also called as Veegum 0.5 to 2 per cent is used in the suspension. Heat and presence of electrolytes, reduce the viscosity of solution.

12. Hectorite : It is used in the suspension for external use.

Bentonite, veegum and hectorite are of mineral origin and are used in the preparations to be used externally only.

13. Aluminium hydroxide : Colloidal hydrated aluminium hydroxide is sometimes used as a suspending agent. It assists wetting of unwettable substances.

14. Carbomer (Carboxy vinyl polymer) : It is a high molecular weight polymer of acrylic acid. In low concentration (0.1 to 0.5 per cent) it is effective as a suspending agent.

15. Colloidal silicon dioxide : Silicon compounds such as Silicon tetrachloride when hydrolised in vapour phase give Silicon dioxide. In water it forms a network and thus remains in a suspended form. It is used in the suspension in the concentration of 1.5 to 4 per cent.

Commonly used diffusible and non diffusible substances are :

Diffusible solids :
    Powders for Internal use
        Light kaolin
        Light magnesium carbonate
        Calcium carbonate
        Magnesium trisillicate
        Rhubarb powder

Indiffusible solids :
    Succinyl sulphathiazole
    Phenobarbitone
    Chalk
    Sulphadimidine
    Aspirin
    Aromatic chalk powder

Following are used for External preparations only.
    Calamine
    Zinc oxide
    Precipitated sulphur
    Hydrocortisone

Wetting agents : These are the substances which help the wetting process, which is nothing but is a spreading of liquid over a solid surface.

The surfactants having HLB value from 8-10 are satisfactory wetting agents and they are used to cause homogenisation where it is badly desired.

Example 1 :
R_x

Acacia	40 g
Chloroform water	60 ml

Label : A suspending agent

Method

Remove adhered impurities from acacia by washing with chloroform water. Put 40 g of acacia and add 60 ml of chloroform water stirr slowly to obtain solution.

Example 2 :
R_x

Tragacanth	0.2 g
Ethyl alcohol	02 ml
Chloroform water to 100 ml.	

Label : A suspending agent

Method

Put tragacanth in a beaker. Moisten it with alcohol and mix with chloroform water to form mucilage.

Example 3 :
R_x

Starch		25 g
Water	to	1000 ml

Label : A suspending agent

Method

Keep 25 g starch in a beaker and add 3/4th of water. Mix it thoroughly and heat on a low flame to gelatinise the starch. Cool it under current of water and then adjust the volume with water. It should be prepared freshly.

Example 4 :

℞

Eucalyptus oil		10 ml
Menthol		03 g
Water	ad	200 ml

Note : When volatile oil or solid is to be incorporated in water diffusible solid is used as a distributing agent.

In this prescription light magnesium carbonate is used as a distributing agent. For 2 ml of volatile oil or 2 g of volatile solid 1 gm of light magnesium carbonate give a good result. The preparation is used for adding the preparation in water at 65°C for inhaling purpose.

Final formula

Eucalyptus oil		10 ml
Menthol		03 g
Light magnesium carbonate		6.5 g
Water	ad	100 ml

Method

Dissolve finely powdered menthol in oil and add light magnesium carbonate powder. Mix it thoroughly. Slowly pour water with constant trituration to form pourable paste. Transfer the paste in the bottle.

Label : As a inhaler or as directed by physician.

Example 5

℞

Sulphadimidine		12 g
Syrup of orange		15 ml
Water	ad	160 ml
Send 50 ml.		

Label : Take twenty ml every four hours,

Type : Mixture containing indiffusible solid.

Note : Sulphadimidine is indiffusible and hence, compound powder of tragacanth is used in the proportion of 2 g 200 ml of final suspension

Method

Sulphadimidine is powdered in the mortar. Then 3.2 g of compound powder of tragacanth is added. Both the powders thoroughly mixed. Add water in small succession with constant trituration till the pourable paste is formed. Transfer it in bottle. Rinse the mortar with water. Add the rinse in the bottle and finally add syrup of orange. Make up the required volume by water.

Example 6 :

℞

| Strychnine hydrochloride | 0.4 mg |
| Chloroform water | 15 ml |

Prepare a mixture
Send 180 ml

Label : Take three times a day

Note : This is a mixture containing potent medicament in a fraction, non-weighable.

Calculations : Each dose contains 0.4 mg of strychnine hydrochloride. Total doses are twelve. Hence quantity of strychnine hydrochloride is $0.4 \times 12 = 4.8$ mg which is not weighable.

Hence, accurately weigh 100 mg of strychnine hydrochloride.

Prepare 100 ml solution in chloroform water. Pipette out 4.8 ml of solution which contains 4.8 mg of drug.

Method

Take 4.8 ml of above solution and dilute it with chloroform water to make the volume 180 ml.

Example 7 :

℞

Magnesium sulphate		31 g
Magnesium carbonate		04 g
Peppermint water	ad	180 ml
Send 60 ml		

Label : Take two tablespoonful half an hour before breakfast

Type : Mixture containing diffusible solid
Shake well before use, label is necessary.

Method

Magnesium sulphate and magnesium carbonate are powdered. Three fourth of vehicle is then added slowly with trituration to form a cream. Cream is then transferred to measure. The volume is then adjusted with vehicle label it.

Example 8 :

R$_x$

Bismuth carbonate	1.0 g
Sodium bicarbonate	0.7 g
Tincture of belladonna	0.4 ml
Water ad	30 ml

Label : Take 30 ml before each meal;

Shake well before use. Send 60 ml.

Type : Mixture containing diffusible solids

Method

Powder bismuth carbonate and sodium bicarbonate and mix. Add a small amount of water to it, form pourable paste. Transfer it in bottle. Then add tincture of Belladonna and adjust the volume with water.

Example 9 :

R$_x$

Quinine sulphate	1.6 g
Potassium iodide	0.8 g
Water add	180 ml

Label : Take 15 ml every four hours.

(Quinine sulphate is diffusible) '*shake well before use*' label is necessary.

Follow method for mixtures containing diffusible solids.

Magnesium hydroxide mixture B. P. and Aluminium hydroxide gel B. P are some of the official suspension preparations.

SUSPENSIONS PRODUCED BY CHEMICAL REACTION

In this method, the reacting constituents in dilute solutions are made to react to produce a suspension of active constituent. In this method, the reactants are dissolved separately in half volumes of the vehicle and then the two solutions are mixed. The advantage of this method is that, we get diffusible precipitate.

Example 10 :

R$_x$

Sulphurated potash
Zinc sulphate
Concentrated camphor water

Use : Scabicide

Direction : To be applied as directed.

Sulphurated potash is a mixture of potassium polysulphides and other sulphur compounds.

It reacts with zinc sulphate to form diffusible precipitate of zinc sulphide.

Method

Dissolve sulphurated potash and zinc sulphate separately in 40 ml water. The sulphurated potash solution is slowly added to zinc sulphate solution with constant stirring. Camphor water is added slowly with vigorous shaking. Volume of solution was made up.

Other suspensions prepared by chemical reaction include Magnesium hydroxide gel, Aluminium hydroxide gel, etc.

FLOCCULATED AND NON-FLOCCULATED SUSPENSION

At some concentration of the added ion, the electrical forces of repulsion are lowered sufficiently and the forces of attraction predominate. Under these conditions, the particles may approach each other more closely and form loose aggregates which are called flocs. Such a system is said to be flocculated system.

Electrolytes, polymers and surfactants are commonly used as flocculating agents. In a deflocculated system containing a distribution of particle sizes, the larger particles naturally settle faster than the smaller particles. The very

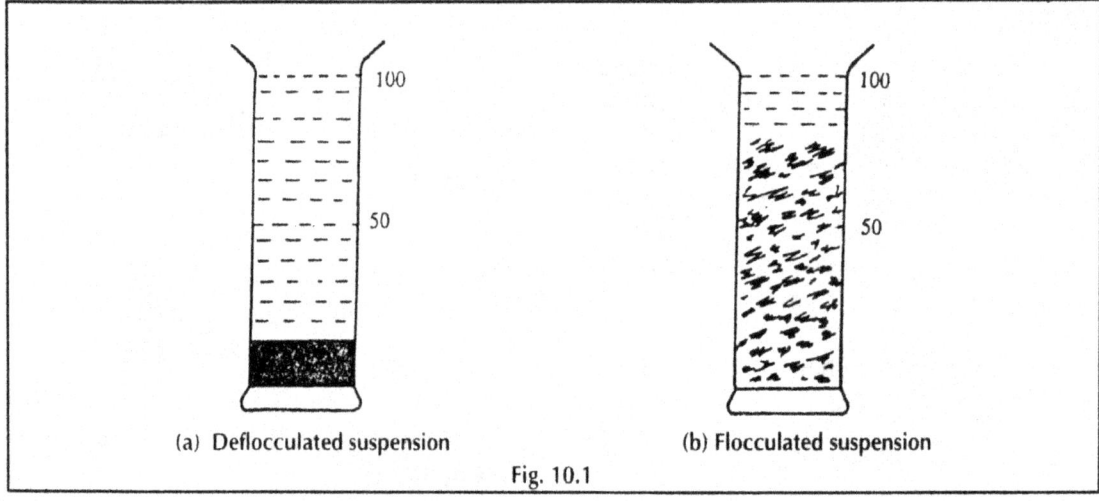

(a) Deflocculated suspension   (b) Flocculated suspension
Fig. 10.1

small particles remain suspended for a considerable length of time with the result that no distinct boundary is formed between the supernatant and the sediment. When the same system is flocculated, two effects are immediately apparent. First, the flocs tend to fall together so that a distinct boundary between the sediment and the supernatant is readily observed and second the supernatant is clear, showing that the very fine particles have been incorporated into the flocs. The initial rate of settling in flocculated system is determined by the size of the flocks and porosity of the aggregated mass.

Frequently, the pharmacist needs to assess a formulation in terms of the amount of flocculation in the suspension and to compare this with, that found in other formulations. The two parameters commonly used for this are :

(i) Sedimentation volume

(ii) Degree of flocculation

I. Sedimentation Volume : The sedimentation volume F is the ratio of the equilibrium volume of the sediment V_u to the total volume of the suspension, V_0

Thus, $F = \dfrac{V_u}{V_0}$

As the value of F, which normally ranges from nearly 0 to 1, increases the volume of suspension that appears occupied by the sediment increases. In the system where F = 0.75 for example, 75 % of the total volume in the container is apparently occupied by the loose, porous flocs forming the sediment. In a particular suspension therefore, if F can be made to approach the value of unity, the product becomes more acceptable. When F = 1 no sediment is apparent even though the system is flocculated. This is the ideal suspension, under these conditions, no sedimentation wig occur and caking will be absent.

II. Degree of Flocculation : A better parameter for comparing flocculated system is the degree of flocculation, β.

Degree of flocculation relates the sedimentation volume of the flocculated suspension, F to the sedimentation volume of the suspension when deflocculated, F_α. It is expressed as -

$$\beta = \dfrac{F}{F_\alpha}$$

The degree of flocculation is, therefore, an expression of the increased sediment volume resulting from flocculation. If for example, ,B has a value of 5.0, this means that the volume of the sediment in the flocculated is five times that in the deflocculated state. The flocs are quite porous and the desirable scaffold-like structure is present.

Table 10.1 : Relative Properties of Flocculated and Deflocculated particles in Suspension

Deflocculated	Flocculated
1. Particles exist as separate entities.	1. Particles form loose aggregates.
2. Rate of sedimentation is slow because each particle settles separately and particle size is minimum.	2. Rate of sedimentation is high because particles settle as floc, which is a collection of particles.
3. A sediment is formed slowly but the sediment eventually becomes very closely packed and hard cake is formed which is very difficult to redisperse.	3. The sediment is formed rapidly but the sediment is loosely packed. Particles are not bonded tightly to each other and a hard dense cake does not form. The sediment is easily redispersible.
4. The suspension has a pleasing appearance since the suspended material remains suspended for a relatively long time.	4. The suspension is somewhat unsightly due to rapid sedimentation and the presence of an obvious clear, supernatant region.

EMULSIONS

INTRODUCTION

Oil and water if taken together, the two phases remain separated. This is because oil is immiscible with water. Now shake the mixture rigorously, small globules of one phase gets formed. These globules disperse in the other phase. The globules are called dispersed phase and the medium is called continuous phase. The mixture formed is called as an **emulsion**. Still this mixture is unstable and the globules come together to form big globule formed. Thus the immiscible phase separates. In order to obtain a stable emulsion, third substance which keeps the globules separated is used. This substance is called as an **emulsifying agent** or **emulgent**.

Hence, emulsion can be defined as a mixture containing two immiscible liquids, in which one liquid is dispersed in the form of small globules in the other liquid (continuous phase) and stabilized by the third substance called as an *emulsifying agent*.

In general, two immiscible liquids form an emulsion. However, in pharmaceutical emulsions one of the liquids is water and the other is oil. Therefore, we get two types of emulsions.

1. Oil globules in water (o/w type emulsion)
2. Water globules in oil (w/o type emulsion)

In o/w type, oil is in the dispersed phase and water in continuous phase. While conditions are reversed in w/o type of emulsion.

However, in Pharmaceutical practical, the term "emulsion" is used to indicate oil in water (o/w) type of emulsion only for internal use. An emulsion for external use may be water in oil (w/o) type. Normal globule size of Macro-emulsion is 100 to 1,00,000 n.m and of micro-emulsion it is 10 to 100 nm.

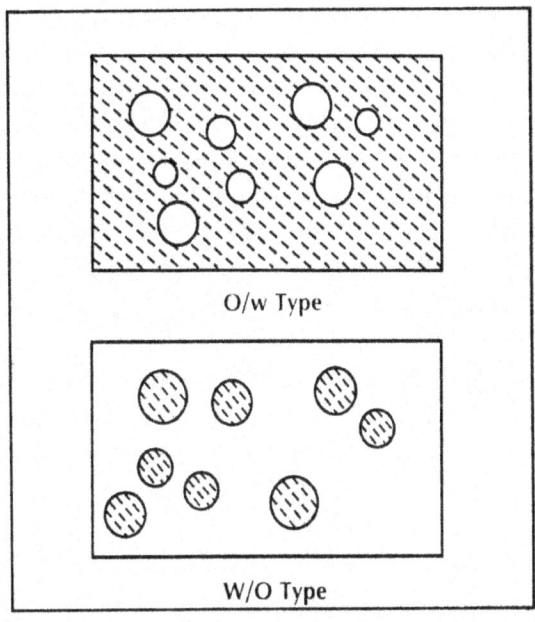

Fig. 10.2 : Type of emulsion

Examples : Natural emulsions are such as milk and latex of plant. Artificial emulsions are liquid paraffin emulsion, castor oil emulsion, cod liver oil emulsion etc.

Containers : Emulsions are dispensed in wide-mouthed glass bottles, since normally they are viscous preparations.

Unless otherwise mentioned 100 ml emulsion be dispensed.

Labelling : Bottles containing emulsions must be labelled as **"Shake Well before Use."** Emulsion intended for external use must be labelled as **"For External Use Only."**

Identification of type of emulsion can be done by the following methods.

1. **Dilution test :** If continuous phase is added in the emulsion it will not crack or separate into phases. For example if water is added in o/w type of emulsion it will remain stable.

2. **Staining :** Add oil soluble dye such as scarlet red in oil and prepare an emulsion with water and emulsifying agent. Observe a drop of emulsion under microscope. You will see red globules dispersed in water. Background will be colourless and globules will appear red. The test can be carried out using water soluble dye such as methylene blue.

3. **Electrical conductivity :** Dip the electrodes in an emulsion. Put an electric bulb in the circuit. Switch on, if the bulb glows the emulsion is o/w type because continuous phase water conduct the charge and circuit is completed. If water is in dispersed form, the bulb will not glow or it may flicker.

Concentration of Disperse Phase

Theoretically all the globules are spherical and of a uniform size. They do not occupy more than 75 per cent of total volume of an emulsion. In reality, the globules are not of a uniform size and shape hence it is possible to have emulsion containing more than 75 per cent disperse phase. Such emulsions are prepared by machine.

Emulsion containing less than 10 per cent of disperse phase is also not stable. If it is required to prepare an emulsion of medicinal oil of less than 10 per cent then the volume of the oil can be increased by using inert fixed oil to obtain stability to the preparation.

Concentration less than 10 per cent of disperse phase lead to creaming which is not desirable.

The type of product that is formed is dependent to some extent on characteristics of oil, but it is much more dependent on the emulsifying agent used. However, when the oil phase is less than 2 per cent without emulsifying agent, it is o/w type.

Phase Inversion - Dual emulsions

In the phase inversion process the internal (disperse) phase and external (dispersion medium) phase interchange. The inversion in the emulsion may take place by mechanical or chemical action. If the emulsion contains 10 to 45 per cent of water and it is agitated or pumped, then phase invention may occur. The chemical reaction between one of the phases and emulsifying agent may change the emulgent to give phase inversion. Change in pH or change in solubility of phases on aging also causes a phase inversion. An emulgent (emulsifying agent) with adequate solubility in both the phases cause such a change.

When the emulsion is partially converted into other type, it is called as **dual emulsion.** Small amount of continuous phase is present in the droplet of the globules in the dual emulsion.

Lecithin forms dual emulsion with cresol, linseed oil, light petroleum, chloroform and hexalin. Albumin, casein and gelatin also form dual emulsions.

Monovalent soaps such as sodium and potassium forms o/w type and divalent soaps such as calcium gives w/o emulsion. If both are present in the emulsion, then phase inversion occurs on standing.

Emulsion stability :

An emulsion may be considered as stable when it retains its colour, appearance, consistency, odour, chemical nature etc., at the time of manufacture till consume on aging. Instability of an emulsion may be of the following types :

(i) Creaming,

(ii) Cracking.

Creaming

Creaming may be defined as formation of a layer of dispersed phase in relatively concentrated form at the surface. Such an emulsion on vigorous shaking results in homogeneous emulsion. On standing again, the cream forms on the surface. It is undesirable because this leads to cracking of emulsion resulting in inaccurate dose.

Intensive study has been carried out to find the factors responsible for creaming on emulsion. Stokes law explains the rate of creaming

Stoke's Law :

$$V = \frac{2r^2 (\Delta P) g}{g n}$$

Where,

V = rate of creaming.

r = radius of globules

n = Viscosity of continuous phase.

ΔP = density difference between two phases.

g = gravitational constant.

Rate of creaming can be decreased by reducing the globule size and increasing the viscosity. Use of unstable thickening agent may form lumps on standing and increase the globule diameter with increasing the rate of creaming.

Cracking

Separation of dispersed phase from the emulsion is referred as cracking. Once the emulsion is cracked it is difficult to correct it.

Following are the reasons for cracking of an emulsion :

1. Decomposition of an emulsifying agent;
2. Precipitation of thickening agent;
3. Addition of opposite type of an emulgent;
4. Increase in temperature;
5. Microbial attack;
6. Excessive creaming; and
7. Addition of solvent which dissolve both phases.

Miscellaneous Instabilities

Deterioration of emulsion in the presence of light and extreme low or high temperature is a common feature. Hence, it is to be stored in coloured bottle and air tight bottles at moderate temperatures. Phase inversion is another physical instability of the emulsion.

Evaluation of Emulsions : This can be done by using the following parameters :

1. **Globule size :** Increase in globule size by coalescence rate on aging is the indication of physical instability of the emulsion. Microscopic and coulter counter measurement at a frequent interval of time gives indication of the rate of coalescence of globules. If these studies continue to give increase in globule size, it indicates poor emulsion.

2. **Temperature :** Exposure to high (60°C) and low (0 to 4°C) temperature alternatively gives indication of emulsion stability. However, effect of thermal stresses on different emulsions vary from formulation to formulation.

3. **Flow Properties :** Flow property is the manifestation of globule size, concentration of emulgent and phase volume ratio. So the study of flow property over an extended period of time gives a clue for emulsion stability. Any suitable instrument for the measurement of viscosity can be used for such studies.

4. Phase separation : The rate at which coalescence of globule occurs definitely indicates the stability pattern of emulsion. The test can be carried out by keeping emulsion in the measuring cylinder and observing the rate of separation of the phase. This is a lengthy process and can be accelerated using a high speed centrifuge. If emulsion stands such stress, it can be considered as a stable emulsion.

Good emulsion should possess the following characteristics :
- (i) Dispersed globules should not separate or coalescence;
- (ii) Should maintain flow property throughout its shelf life;
- (iii) No phase inversion; and
- (iv) Should stand to mechanical and physical stresses.

Additives in the Emulsion

1. Preservatives : Preservatives act as an antimicrobial agent. The growth of microorganism is in aqueous phase. Hence preservative should have adequate solubility in water. If it has more solubility in lipid phase, the activity reduces. Concentration of preservative should be adequate to retard the growth of microbes some of the preservatives used in emulsion are benzoic acid, formic acid salicylic acid P-Chlorobenzoic acid, benzalkonium chloride, hexachlorophene, phenyl mercury nitrate, hexamine etc.

2. Thickening agents : Viscosity plays a major role in stability of emulsion. Thickening agents are sometimes included in the formulation to get adequate consistency. Hydrocolloids in aqueous phase or long chain waxes serve the purpose. Selection depends on the type of emulsion formulation and actual amount of substance needed for the required consistency.

3. Elegance : In order to improve the taste, flavour and colour of the emulsion, different additives are included in the preparation. These are normally vanillin, raspberry, rose etc. for flavour, sweetner for taste and permitted colours.

4. Antioxidants : Butylated hydroxytoluene, or tocopherol are the common antioxidants used in emulsion. Oily constituent of emulsion may get rancid on standing, inclusion of antioxidant preserve the preparation from such deterioration.

THEORIES OF EMULSIONS

Extensive research has been carried out to study the mechanism of emulsification and role of emulgent. Outcome of the work is the postulation of theories of emulsion formation. However, no single theory is sufficient to explain the nature of emulsification because of the various factors such as pH, proportion of water and oil, effect of electrolyte on the stability of an emulsion.

All the liquids possess force at its surface and assume a shape having minimum surface that is a sphere. When two drops come in contact, they combine to form bigger drop occupying less surface area than did the two smaller individual drops. The force (energy) at the surface is known as surface tension of the liquid when it is in contact with its own vapour or air. However, it is called as interfacial tension when one liquid is in contact with another liquid. Surface active agents or wetting agents reduce the interfacial tension at the boundary of the liquids. The interfacial tension can be overcome to form the globules of the liquid. Hence some mechanism should be present to keep these globules separate; other wise they coalescence and the emulsion brakes. In order to stabilize emulsion, any of the following mechanisms is useful :

1. Formation of a thin film of a substance around the globule to separate it from other globules.
2. Substance should orient in such a way that its ends separate the globules from dispersion medium.
3. Substance that lowers down the interfacial tension between the liquids.

Basically, all these mechanisms are physical phenomenon, and hence, the action of emulsification in the presence of emulgent is also physical .

Some theories of emulsification are discussed here.

1. Surface Tension theory

The substance which lowers down the interfacial tension between two immiscible liquids and thereby reduces the tendency of the globules to coalescene, gives stable emulsion. Surface active agent lowers down the surface tension and thus acts as an emulsion stabilizer.

2. Oriented - Wedge Theory

In this theory, it is presupposed that the emulsifying agent has two groups with affinity for two immiscible liquids and it forms a monomolecular layer at the surface of one liquid (globule). It orients in such a way that the other group project towards the continuous phase forming a wedge. Oil in water or water in oil emulsion formation depends on the quantity of oil soluble portion or water soluble portion in the molecule. the main drawback of this theory is

(i) Improbablity of the formation of monolayer;

(ii) Absence of definite polar groups in many of the common emulsifying agents; and

(iii) It does not explain why some substances, not themselves emulsifying agents, favour the formation of emulsion and others do not.

3. Plastic Film Theory

According to this theory, the emulgent forms a plastic thin film around the globules, and thus hinder the coalescence. This effect is purely mechanical and is not dependent on the surface tension. The formation of oil in water and water in oil emulsion can be explained on the basis of selective solubility of the emulsifying agent. Water soluble emulgent will give o/w type and oil soluble emulgent will form w/o type emulsions. The plastic film formed around the globule will keep the globules away from each other. If the viscosity of the continuous phase is increased by the addition of emulgent or any other substance, it will restrict the movement of the globule and thus stabilize the emulsion. On the. other hand, the substance which reduces the viscosity, if added to the emulsion, reduces the stability of the emulsion.

This theory is in agreement with most of the observed facts concerning emulsion formation, but does not explain the effects of pH, particle size and electrical charge developed on the globules.

EMULSIFYING AGENTS

In order to obtain stable emulsion, it is necessary to choose a suitable emulsifying agent or a suitable combination of emulsifying agents. This is a difficult task considering a wide variety of emulsifying agents. This is simplified by Griffin who introduced Hydrophil-Lipophile Balance system (H.L.B. system). **The HLB is weight per cent of the portion of the hydrophlic surfactant divided by five.** The HLB of an oil soluble substance will be low i.e. between 2 to 10, and for water soluble substance it will be high i.e. 10-20.

Oils can also be classified on this scale by the HLB required by a surface active agent to emulsify them. The HLB can be calculated for most polyol fatty acid esters as -

$$HLB = 20\left[1 - \left(\frac{S}{A}\right)\right]$$

S = saponification number of ester.

A = the acid no. of the recovered acid.

Once the required HLB of oils- is determined; the HLB of emulsifying agent (s) should equal this figure for best stability. For a blend of emulsifying agent the HLB is assumed to be an additive quantity.

Substances with 3-6 HLB value produce w/o emulsion and 8 to 18 LHB value produces o/w emulsion.

Following are the HLB values of few important emulsifying agents.

Table No. 10.2 : HLB values

Emulsifying agent	HLB value
Sorbitan trioleate	01.8
Glyceryl monostearate	03.8
Sorbitan mono-oleate (span 80)	04.3
Sorbitan mono-palmitate (span 40)	06.7
Acacia	08.0
Gelatin	09.8
Tri-ethanolamine oleate	12.0
Tragacanth	13.2
Tween - 20	16.7
Potassium oleate	20.0
Sodium lauryl sulphate	40.0

Classification of Emulsifying agents

Emulsifying agents are classified in two ways the first method is base on the ionizing characteristic of the substance

(A) Non ionizing substances : These are esters of higher fatty acids. If the polar group dominates, it is useful as o/w emulsifying agent and in pressure of dominance of-non-polar group, w/o type of emulsion is formed. Polyethylene glycol esters of higher fatty acids and polyethylene glycol ethers of higher fatty acids under the trade name span 20, Tween 40, span 40, span 60 span 80 and Tween 20, Tween 80 are the examples of this type.

(B) Ionizing substances

(i) Anionic Emulsifiers : Substances which ionizes and the emulsifying property lies in the anion are called anionic emulsifiers sodium and potassium soaps belong to this group. Mono-valent soap from o/w type of emulsion, divalent soap (calcium, aluminum soap) from w/o type of emulsion. Organic sulphates and sulphonates also belong to this group. Examples are sodium lauryl sulphate, Lanette wax S^x (mixture of acetyl and stearyl alcohol and sulphate) and sodium cetyl sulphonate.

(ii) Cationic - Emulsifier : Quaternary ammonium compounds such as cetyl trimethyl ammonium bromide and benzalkonium chloride are the representatives of this group.

Second method of classification of Emulsifying agents

In this method the agents are divided into the following groups.

1. Carbohydrates

Acacia : gum acacia is used as emulsifying agent; for o/w type. This gives good extempore preparation of emulsion. The proportion of acacia used as emulsifying agent is 1/4 for fixed oil, 1/2 for volatile oil and equal for oleo resin. Incompatibilities are found with alcohol, solution of ferric chloride and lead acetate. Being carbohydrate it undergoes bacterial decomposition.

Tragacanth : This is another gum with comparatively weak emulsifying action. One part with forty parts of fixed oil is used in combination with acacia. Tragacanth being viscosity builder stabilizes the emulsion.

Other emulsifying agent of this group are Agar, chondrus, gum, resins, methyl cellulose etc.

2. Proteins

Gelatin : Gelatin is prepared from bones, skin of an animal. Homogeniser is normally used when gelatin is used as emulgent. Two forms of gelatin are available pharma gel A is used as pH 3 to 3.5 and Gel B is used in alkaline medium. It undergoes slow hydrolysis loosing the viscosity. Hence the emulsion requires preservative.

Egg yolk : This gives excellent emulgent properly to form o/w type of an emulsion with nutrient value. An average egg yolk emulsify 120 ml of fixed oil and 60 ml of volatile oil. The only disadvantage of this type of emulsion is that it undergoes putrefaction.

3. Soaps and Alkalies

Monovalent soaps form o/w type of emulsion while divalent soaps gives w/o emulsion. These are generally used in emulsion for external use. It is incompatible with acids.

4. Wetting agents (Surface active agents)

Sodium lauryl sulphate, benzalkonium chloride, Tweens, Spans, the sorbitan esters belong to this group.

5. Finely divided solids and colloids

The type of emulsion formation depends on whether these agents are wetted by oil, or water. If the solid is wetted more by water than oil an o/w emulsion will form. A w/o emulsion results, if the solid is wetted by oil. Some agents belonging to this category are magnesium trisilicate given o/w emulsion. Bentonite, a clay is used as an emulsifying agent for both types of emulsions depending on the order of mixing. For o/w emulsion oil should be added last. For w/o type, bentonite is dispersed in water and then gradually added to oil. Bentonite is used in dermatological preparations. It swells to the extent of eight times its own volume in water.

Synthetic emulsifying agents such as carbopols are included in this group.

Preservatives

Simple refrigeration is sufficient for extempore emulsions. Those which are stored for prolong period require inclusion of preservatives.

Preservatives used should be compatible with other ingredients of emulsion, non toxic and tasteless. In acidic medium 2.0 percent benzoic acid may be used. Sodium benzoate (0.5 %) with 0.25% chloroform also gives good result. Chlorocresol 0.1 percent in aqueous cream is preferred to chloroform in the preparation impact little sweet taste. Vanillin and other essential oil may be added for the flavour.

Laboratory Method of Preparation of emulsion

It is very difficult to prepare an emulsion taking the required quantities of water, oil and emulsifying agent and mixing it in one operation. However if part or total quantity of oil with portion of water and emulsifying agent is mixed to form primary emulsion and diluting it either with water or oil to form the required volume is the best method of preparation of an emulsion.

While preparing on emulsion by trituration method copper or porcelain are recommended over glass mortar which are too smooth for the operation. The mortar should have relatively flat bottom. Trituration should be continuous and rapid. Slow trituration will not give effective emulsion formation. There are three methods for preparation of an emulsion.

1. Dry gum method (Continental method)
2. Wet gum method (English method)
3. Bottle method

1. Dry gum or continental method

In this method proportion of the ingredient is four parts of fixed oil, one part of emulgent and two parts of water. Emulgent powder is added in the dry mortar and oil is poured on it. It is mixed to form uniform mixture then required quantity of water is added and mixture is triturated rapidly to form primary emulsion. Primary emulsion is white, creamy, homogeneous and gives characteristic crackling sound when the pestle is moved in it. Then by adding continuous phase with vigorous shaking required volume is prepared.

2. Wet gum method or English method

The proportion of gum, water and fixed oil is one, two, four to form primary emulsion.

In the mortar one part of gum (emulgent) powder is added and two parts of water is poured on it with trituration to form homogeneous mixture. Then oil is added in small succession with continuous trituration to emulsify each portion before addition of the next. If the preparation becomes too thick to triturate then add little quantity of water and then complete the addition of oil with constant trituration. Finally adjust the volume with required quantity of water.

3. Bottle method

Volatile oil get readily emulsified by shaking in bottle with gum and water. As the volatile oil is less viscous the quantity of gum required is more. The proportion of ingredient is two parts of volatile oil, one part of gum and two parts of water while preparing emulsion by bottle method one part of gum is placed in the bottle and two parts of volatile oil is added. It is vigorously shaken to form uniform mixture. Then two parts of water is added and mixture is shaken continuously to form primary emulsion. Shaking at irregular intervals is more effective than regular shaking. Then add remaining water in small portion with agitation to form required quantity of an emulsion.

This emulsion can also be formed in mortar. Water soluble substance (medicament) if present in the formula is dissolved in the water required for the preparation. Resinous tincture is added to the primary emulsion and then the volume is made up. Oil soluble drug present in formula is dissolved in oil of emulsion and then emulsion is prepared by any of the above methods. Insoluble substances in oil and water are incorporated in primary emulsion. If medicinal oily phase is less than ten percent then it is increased by addition of any inert oil such as olive oil suitable to form an emulsion.

In most of laboratory emulsion preparation it is necessary to prepare primary emulsion and then dilute it with dispersion medium. The explanation is simple. If all the oil and water is mixed together the volume of liquid is quite large and the force required to cut the disperse phase into suitable size of globules is difficult to attain. In the preparation of primary emulsion, the volume of liquid to be emulsified is considerably reduced and the force required is also reduced.

In the preparation of acacia emulsions it is better to have gum tears, powder them and then use the powder. It saves the cost of powdering, commercially available powdered acacia is adulterated with fine clay and is dirty coloured.

General method of Preparation, using acacia as emulgent

Measure the oil using dry measuring cylinder and add it to a clean dry mortar and triturate it with corresponding quantity (depending upon the type of oil) of powdered acacia. Add twice as much water as gum and tritutrate the contents until a crackling sound is heard and the mixture assumes a white colour. At this stage primary emulsion is complete. Add the portion of remaining vehicle to complete the required volume with constant trituration. Transfer the emulsion to measure. Rinse the mortar with some more of water and add this to the measure. Finally adjust the volume, stirr the emulsion and bottle it.

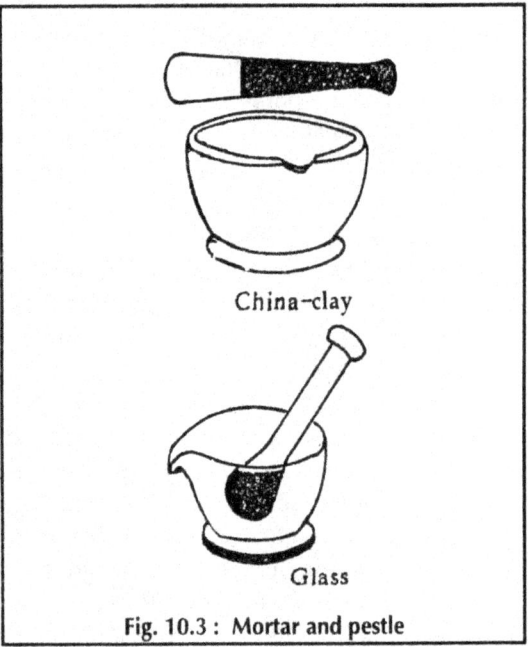

Fig. 10.3 : Mortar and pestle

In Acacia emulsion, the quantity of acacia to be used must be in the following proportions.

For Fixed Oils Castor oil, almond oil, olive oil and liquid paraffin (though not an oil chemically) it is considered under fixed oil for emulgent concentration.	Use one fourth the quantity of gum as the oil.
For Volatile oils Oil of turpentine, Sandal wood oil, oil of cubeb etc.	Use half as much gum as the oil.
For oleo resins Balsam of Tolu, Copaiba etc.	Use an equal amount of gum.

MACHINES USED FOR PREPARATION OF EMULSION

Hand emulsifier is used for small scale work. This is also called as hand homogeniser. It works on the principle that when a jet of coarsely prepared emulsion is forced against a plate the globules are further split in smaller globules to form stable emulsion.

Silverson Emulsifier

For large scale production this emulsifier is used. It consists of a fan shaped blades with a shaft. The shaft is rotated by a motor The blades are surrounded by a sieve with fine mesh. The blades are immersed into the liquid to be emulsified. When rotated the liquid is sucked into the sieve and expelled through the sieve, breaking the dispersed globules into still smaller size. Thus giving stable emulsion.

Simple household mixer can also be used for preparation of stable emulsion.

Formulation of an emulsion.

The various factors affecting the emulsion are :

1. Choice of emulgent
2. Method of emulsification
3. Use of preservative.
4. Use of flavour.
5. Inclusion of other agents such as thickness, Viscosity builders etc.

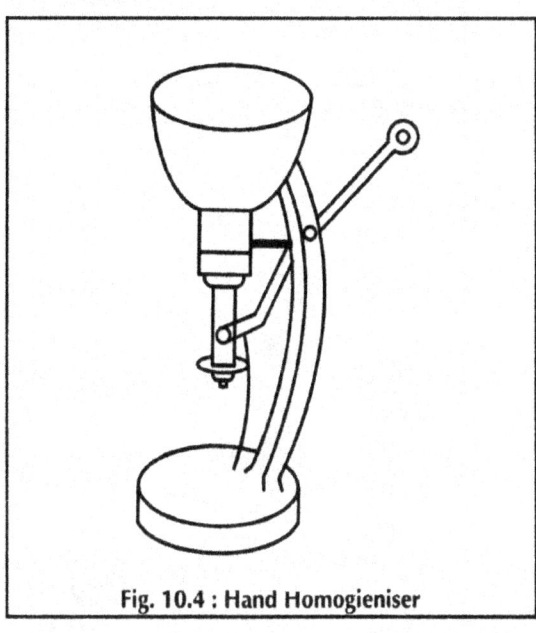

Fig. 10.4 : Hand Homogieniser

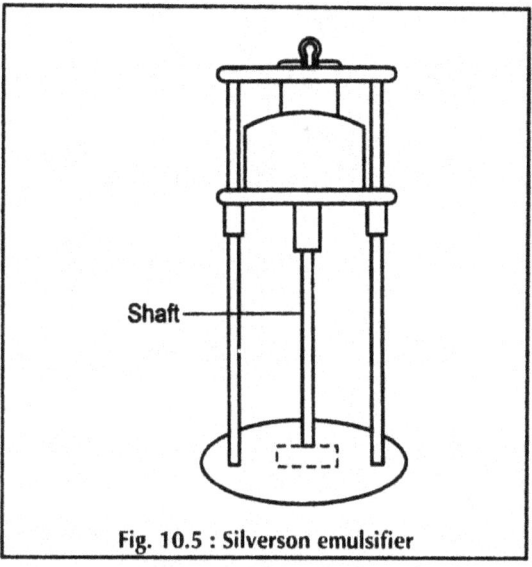

Fig. 10.5 : Silverson emulsifier

For any of the above type of preparation calculate the quantity of gum for any individual type and use the calculated quantity of gum.

Acacia o/w emulsion

Example 1 :

R$_x$

Olive oil	30 ml
Water ad	120 ml

Prepare an emulsion

send 60 ml

Label : Take a tablespoonful twice a day. **Shake well before use.**

Primary Emulsion

Olive oil	30 ml	Fixed oil formula for emulgent
Powdered acacia	7.5 gm	
Water	15 ml	

Prepare as per general method.

Example 2 :

R$_x$

Oil of turpentine	08 ml	volatile oil formula for emulgent

Cinnamon water ad 40 ml

Prepare a draught

Label : Take at once

Primary emulsion

Oil of turpentine	8 ml
Powdered acacia	4 gm
Water	8 ml

Prepare as per general method

Acacia o/w emulsion
Example 3 :

R$_x$

		volatile oil
		Fixed oil
Terbene	06 ml	Take gum
Almond oil	16 ml	quantity 1/2
Tincture of	8 ml	for terbene
Ipecacuanha		and 1/4 for
		almond oil
Water	ad	180 ml

Prepare an emulsion, send 90 ml

Label : Take a tablespoonful every four hours. **Shake well before use.**

Primary emulsion

Terbene	6 ml
Almond oil	16 ml
Powdered acacia (3 + 4)	7 gm
Water	14 ml

Prepare primary emulsion. Dilute the tincture with required quantity of vehicle and add to the primary emulsion and complete the emulsion.

Example 4 :

R$_x$

Terbene		06 ml
Almond oil		16 ml
Tincture of tolu		08 ml
Water	ad	180 ml

Make an emulsion

Label - Use as directed

Primary emulsion

Terbene	06 ml
Almond oil	16 ml
Powdered acacia (3 + 4)	07 g
Water	14 ml

Method of preparations

Prepare primary emulsion. Tincture of tolu is resinous tincture and resins will be precipitated hence it is added after the completion of primary emulsion. Gum in the preparation gives it protection and make it diffusible. After the primary emulsion is prepared, measure the tincture of tolu in a dry measure add it with constant trituration. Then complete as per general procedure.

Acacia emulsion o/w
Example 5 :

R$_x$

Cod liver oil	30 ml
Syrup	12 ml
Ferric ammonium citrate	04 g
Cinnamon water ... ad	90 ml

Prepare an emulsion.

Label - Take a table spoonful twice a day.
Shake well before use.

Primary Emulsion.

Cod liver oil	30 ml
Powdered acacia	7.5 g
Cinnamon wear	15 ml

Prepare primary emulsion. Dilute the syrup to remaining required volume. Dissolve ferric ammonium citrate in it and complete the emulsion as per general procedure.

EMULSION CONTAINING SUBSTANCES INSOLUBLE IN OIL OR WATER
Example 6 :

R$_x$

Liquid Paraffin	30 ml
Phenolphthalein	01 g
Agar	05 g
Syrup	07 ml
Water	90 ml

Prepare an emulsion

Label - Take three teaspoonful twice a day.

Formula for primary emulsion.

Liquid paraffin	30 ml
Phenolphthalein	01 g
Acacia	7.5 g
Water	15 ml

Method

Phenolphthalein is insoluble in water and oil. Hence powder it along with acacia and then add liquid paraffin and prepare primary emulsion in hot mortar.

The volume of primary emulsion is 53.5 ml. Separately heat agar in about 25 ml of water in a tared dish over a small flame until a solution is formed. Add the syrup to agar solution and mix. Gradually add this solution to the warm primary emulsion to measure and make up the volume.

EMULSION CONTAINING OIL SOLUBLE SUBSTANCES

Example 7:

R$_x$

Salol	02 g
Castor oil	10 ml
Peppermint water - to	60 ml

Prepare an emulsion

Lable - Take 15 ml four times a day

Castor oil is fixed oil. Take the proportionate quantity of gums plus 50 per cent additional gum for salol in the formulation.

Formula for Primary emulsion

Castor oil	10 ml
Powdered acacia (2.5 gm + 1.25 gm)	3.75 g
Peppermint water	7.5 ml

Method

Dissolve salol in castor oil by warming the mixture. Triturate the mixture with gum acacia, add the vehicle and continue the trituration until primary emulsion is formed. Then proceed in the manner given is earlier exercise and dispense.

Example 8:

R$_x$

Salol	04 g
Comphorated opium tincture	08 ml
Cinnamon water q.s.	60 ml

Prepare an emulsion.

Label - Take as directed.
Shake well before use.

Here, oil is not included in the prescription. Pharmacist should include sufficient amount of oil such as olive oil and then proceed.

Formula for primary emulsion.

Salol	04 g
Olive oil	08 ml
Powdered acacia (2 + 1)	03 g
Cinnamon water	06 ml

Method

Dissolve salol in warm olive oil and finish the preparation of primary emulsion, calculate the quantity of cinnamon water (cinnamon water minus volume of tincture) and add to it the tincture and complete the emulsion.

IRISH MOSS EMULSION

Example 9:

R$_x$

Cod liver oil		30 ml
Creosote		0.6 ml
Glycerin		16 ml
Mucilage of Irish moss		90 ml
Water	ad	180 ml

Prepare an emulsion send 30 ml.

Label - Take as directed

The mucilage is prepared as follows - Wash the seaweed, (Irish mass) with water. The seaweed is then heated with 40 times of water on a water bath and finally strained. It is done by using cotton wool, in a hot water funnel. It is used in the preparation of cod liver oil emulsion for satisfactory results this emulsifier is essential.

Method

Irish Moss mucilage is placed in a bottle. The creosote is then dissolved in cod liver oil. This mixture is added to the bottle and agitated vigorously. Then glycerine is added. This forms a coarse emulsion. It is then passed through homogeniser. Finally the volume is adjusted and preparation is transferred to a bottle.

METHYL CELLULOSE EMULSION

Example 10 :

℞

Methyl cellulose 20	04 g
Liquid paraffin	50 ml
Vanillin	0.1 g
Syrup	25 ml
Chloroform water ad	200 ml

Prepare an emulsion. Send 100 ml

Label : Take as directed

Shake well before use.

Method

40 ml of boiling water is added to methyl cellulose 20. Then vanillin is dissolved in 65 ml of chloroform water and added to methyl cellulose solution. It is then stirred. Liquid paraffin and syrup is added with vigorous shaking. Pass it through homogeniser. Then make up the required volume and transfer in the bottle and label.

O/W EMULSION CONTAINING AN OLEO RESIN

Example 11 :

℞

Copaiba		08 ml
Infusion of buchu	ad	60 ml

Prepare an emulsion.

Label - Take half tonight and remaining tomorrow night.

Formula for Primary emulsion.

Copaiba	8 ml
Powdered acacia	8 g
Infusion of buchu	16 ml

If infusion is concentrated then dilute one volume with seven volumes of water. Calculate and take required quantity.

Prepare primary emulsion and then finish the emulsion using process described earlier.

O/W EMULSION USING SODIUM ALGINATE AS SECONDARY EMULSIFYING AGENT

Sodium alginate forms viscous solution in water. One per cent solution of sodium alginate is sufficient to produce an emulsion.

Example 12 :

℞

Liquid paraffin		60 ml
Acacia		02 g
Sodium alginate		2.5 g
Water	ad	250 ml

'Liquid Paraffin Emulsion.

'Send 125 ml

Label : Use as directed by physician.

Shake well before use.

Method

Triturate liquid paraffin with acacia dissolve sodium alginate in a portion of water and add it to liquid paraffin-acacia mixture. Make up the volume and pass through an homogeniser.

O/W EMULSION PREPARED WITH EGG YOLK

Yolk of egg has twice the emulsifying property, compared to acacia. An average yolk emulsifies four ounces (120 ml) of fixed oil or two ounces of (60 ml) a volatile oil. It is useful as an emulsifying agent with acid substances. It has also nutritive properties only the yellow portion of egg should be used.

Example 13 :

℞.

Olive oil		60 ml
Egg yolk		08 ml
Water	ad	150 ml

Prepare an emulsion

Send 75 ml.

Shake well before use.

Label - Take one table spoonful after meals.

Method

Separate the egg yolk from the white of the, egg. Place it in a measure and add equal volume of water. Stirr the mixture thoroughly. Take 8 ml of this egg yolk in a mortar and gradually add the oil with constant stirring. When all the oil is added, add little more water with trituration. Then strain through muslin cloth. Transfer to a measure make up the volume and transfer in the bottle. Then label it.

PAEDIATRIC EMULSIONS

Emulsion containing less than 10 % dispersed phase.

Example 14 :

℞

Solution of calciferol	mii
Glycerin	mv
Water ad	℈ i

Make an emulsion.

Label - Give as directed

Shake well before use.

Send two ounces

Calculation

Two ounces = 960 minims

The oily liquid present in two ounces = 32 minims.

32 minims in two ounces of final volume is less than 10 per cent.

10 per cent of 960 minims is 96 minims so 96 – 32 = 64 srunims of fixed oil such as olive oil may be added to raise the percentage to 10 per cent of dispersed phase.

Formula for primary emulsion -

Solution of calciferol	32 minims
Olive oil	64 minims
Acacia (16 + 8)	24 grains
Distilled water	48 minims

Mix calciferol and olive oil and then complete the primary emulsion and proceed as usual after mixing glycerin with water.

Example 15 :

℞

Castor oil		10 ml
Cinnamon oil	ad	25 ml

Prepare an emulsion.

Shake well before use.

Label : Use as directed

This is a preparation for a child. 25 ml is to be dispensed unless other wise directed.

Formula for primary emulsion.

Castor oil	10 ml
Acacia	2.5 g
Cinnamon Water	05 ml

Make a primary emulsion and complete the emulsion as per genera method.

EVALUATION OF SUSPENSIONS

1. Sedimentation method : Sedimentation volume and Redespersibility :

The quality of good suspension depend upon sedimentation volume and redespersibility after shaking.

Keep a measured volume of suspension in a measuring cylinder in an undisturbed state for a certain period of time and note the volume of sediment (H_u). Rate of sedimentation is calculated by using the equation

$$F = \frac{H_u}{H_o}$$

where,

F = Rate of sedimentation

H_u = Ultimate height of sediment

H_o = Initial volume of suspension

It should, however, be noted that rate of sedimentation depends on time and it is likely to vary at different periods of time can be plotted against time to give a curve that indicates the sedimentation pattern on storage. If the curve is horizontal to time axis it indicates a better suspension. However, if it steeps down it indicates poor formulation.

Ease of redespersibility : This can be determined by shaking the suspension with the help of mechanical device which simulates the motion.

2. Viscosity : Rheological method used to determine the settling behaviour and if also gives idea about arrangement of vehicle and particle structural features.

A practical Rheological method involves the use of the Brookfield viscometer mounted on helipath stand. The T-bar spindle is made to descend slowly into the suspension, and the dial reading on the viscometer is then a measure of the resistance the spindle meets at various level in a sediment, T-bar descends as it rotates and the bar is continually entering new and essentially undisturbed material. Dialed reading on viscometer gives useful information regarding stability of suspension.

3. Zeta potential : Measurement of zeta-potential or surface electric charge is useful to determine stability of disperse phase system. It is measured by using micro-electrophoresis apparatus.

4. Micromeretic study : The stability of suspension is related to the size of particles present in a dispersed phase. The change in absolute particle size, particle size distribution and crystal habit are signals towards its instability. Since such an occurrence can ultimately result in the formation of lumps or cake destroying the physical structure of a suspension. Such change can be determined by microscopy, coulter counter method.

EVALUATION OF EMULSION

The most common parameters used to evaluate emulsions include :

1. Phase separation
2. Viscosity
3. Electrophoretic properties
4. Particle size analysis

1. Phase separation : Particularly simple means of determining practical phase separation due to creaming or coalscence, involves withdrawing small samples of emulsion from the top and from the bottom of the preparation after some period of storage and comparing the composition of bottom two samples by appropriate analysis such as water content, oil content, or any other suitable constituent.

2. Viscosity : Emulsions are generally non-Newtonian and hence the viscometer should have universal utility. Viscometers like cone-plate type, viscometer utilizing co-axial cylinder, penetrometer and Brookfield's viscometers are used.

A practical approach for the detection of creaming or sedimentation, before it becomes visibly apparent, utilizes the Helipath attachment of the Brookfield's viscometer. Its dial reading shows higher viscosity at the top means creaming and higher viscosity at the bottom means coalescence. If overall viscosity of emulsion remains constant means emulsion is quite stable.

3. Electrophoretic properties : The zeta potential of emulsion can be measured with the help of the moving boundary method or more quickly and directly, by observing the movement of particles under the influence of electric current. The measurement of electrical conductivity has been claimed to evaluate emulsion stability. The electrical conductivity of o/w or w/o emulsion is determined with the aid of Platinum electrodes, microamperometrically to produce a current of 15 to 50 µA. Measurements are made on emulsions stored for short period of time at room temperature at 37°C. O/w emulsion with fine globules exhibits low resistance; if the resistance increases, it is sign of oil droplet aggregation and instability. A fine emulsion of w/o product does not conduct current until droplet coagulation i.e. instability occurs.

4. Particle size analysis : Particle size analysis may be carried out by using microscope, or coulter counter method. change of the average particle size or the size distribution of oil droplets are important parameters for evaluation of emulsion.

QUESTIONS

1. Define the following :
   (a) Suspensions,
   (b) Flocculated and non-flocculated solutions.
2. What are the requirements of good suspension ? How good suspensions can be prepared, explain with suitable examples ?
3. Write notes on various suspending and thickening agents known to you with their merits and demerits.
4. What are emulsions ? How they are classified and tested ?
5. What are emulsifying agents ? Write a note on each type of emulsifying agents known to you.
6. Describe the various methods of preparing emulsions.
7. What is creaming and cracking of emulsions ? How stable emulsions can be prepared ?
8. Describe the containers for storing the emulsions. How emulsion is to be labelled ?
9. Write notes on :
   (a) HLB value
   (b) Wetting agents
   (c) Diffusible solids
   (d) Preservatives in emulsion
   (e) Emulsifier
   (f) Hectorite
   (g) Paediatric emulsions
   (h) Compound powder of tragacanth.

CHAPTER 11: SUPPOSITORIES AND PESSARIES

INTRODUCTION

Suppositories are solid dosage forms intended for insertion into body cavities such as rectum and vagina.

Those intended for vagina are called **pessaries**.

The medication is carried out through use of a base. The base should melt at the body temperature and release the medicament. Suppositories are meant for local action but some are prepared for systemic action. Suppositiories are prescribed for antiseptic, astringent, local anaesthetic, emmolient or antispasmadic treatments.

Shape

Normally, torpedo shaped suppositories are prepared which facilitate easy insertion in rectum. Vaginal pessaries are spherical or baloon shaped.

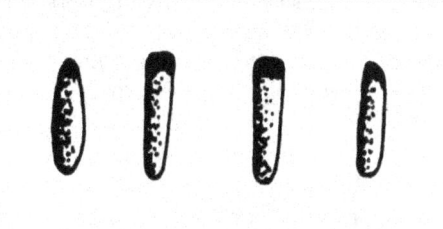

Fig. 11.1: Various shapes of suppositories

Advantages of Suppositories are

1. The drugs absorbed in large intestine from suppositories reach the site of action directly and do not undergo portal circulation and their biotransformation in liver is prevented.
2. Drugs are more rapidly absorbed in rectal mucosa without ionization.
3. Drugs sensitive to acidic pH can be administered safely.
4. Nauseating and bitter drugs can be given in this form without difficulties.

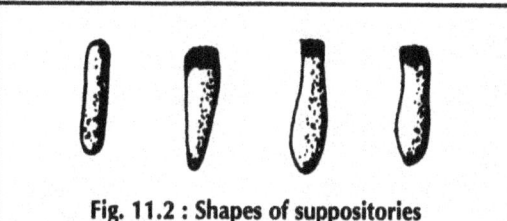

Fig. 11.2 : Shapes of suppositories

Disadvantages

1. Irritant drugs can not be administered by this route
2. Large volume of liquids can not be administered.

Depending upon the method of preparation there are two types of suppositories.

1. Suppositories prepared by cold compression in the moulds.
2. Suppositories prepared by machine.

Suppositories may be prepared by any method

They should

1. have a melting point of not more than 37°C.
2. have a maximum distingration time of. 30 minutes.
3. have uniformity in weight.

Novel Suppository

Although, administration via peroral route is easily acceptable but not always feasible or desirable to patient, such as psychotics, asthmatics, unconscious patients. So, rectal route is desirable one.

To increase the bioavailability of a drug, which are poorly absorbable in water are given by controlled release suppository. The drug release is controlled by various approaches such as addition of adjuvants to the base, preparing double phase suppository in which one phase contains drug. Use of base which having high melting points e.g. suppocire, witepsol H15, Hitepsol W35, preparation of drug, microsphere & incorporated into hollow base, addition of surfactants, preparation of solid reversed micellar solution, preparation of rectal gel. For the drugs which are poorly absorbed in the rectum then the use of absorption enhancer is suggested. Also preparation of liquid suppository is another approach, in this menthol is used for preparation of eutectic mixture. Drugs used for controlled release suppository are mainly of low half life. Means upto 3 hrs.

Packaging of Suppositories

Suppositories are usually packed in shallow, partitioned cardboard boxes which hold the suppositories in upright position & do not allow them to come in contact with each other. If plain boxes are used suppositories should be separately wrapped in waxed paper or in tin foil,

Labelling – " Store in cool place"
" Not to be taken orally"
" For rectal use only"

Pessaries

Similar to suppositories there are two types of pessaries
1. Moulded pessaries
2. Compressed pessaries

Moulded pessaries have a maximum disintegration time of 1 hour while compressed pessaries have a disintegration time of 15 minutes or as stated under the individual monograph of pesssary.

Fig. 11.3 : Various shapes of pessaries

Unless mentioned 10 pessaries are to be dispensed.

Containers

Wide mouth bottles are commonly used for dispensing suppositories. Cardboard boxes with compartments may also be used. Such boxes with compartments are lined with impervious material like wax paper. If the suppository contains volatile ingredients, they should be wrapped in metal foil and the container should be tightly closed.

Unless otherwise directed 1 g mould size suppositories be dispensed.

Storage

An ideal suppositories and pessaries should retain their shape at the room temperature. If the room temperature is high, then they must be stored at 10 to 25° C temperature.

PROPERTIES OF BASES USED

An ideal suppository base should possess the following properties.
1. It must melt at the body temperature with an easy release of medicament;
2. It must be inert and chemically stable;
3. It should be compatible with medicament;
4. It must not turn rancid; and
5. Some bases dissolve or disintegrate in presence of mucous secretion. This property of the base should be retained during aging and in the presence of medicament.

SUPPOSITORY BASES

1. **Cocoa butter or Oil of theobroma :** Cocoa butter almost fulfill the requirements of an ideal suppository base. However, it possess few disadvantages. If it is heated above 60°C its physical properties are temporarily changed and the base melts at room temperature. Certain medicaments such as phenol, lower its melting point while other chemicals may raise the melting point of finished suppositories. This can be avoided by not heating the base above 60°C and by addition of wax when melting point is lowered or by, adding of oil, when melting point is raised.

2. **Glycero gelatin base :** This base is quite satisfactory for preparation of vaginal suppositories and for nasal bougies.

3. **Polyethylene glycol polymers :** Solid polymers of polyethylene glycol are marketed as carbowaxes. These are available in several forms depending on the molecular weight. Although these substances are waxy in nature, the solid forms are soluble in water and their ability to mix in mucous secretion makes them useful as suppository bases. Each base is followed by a number which indicates mean molecular weight; e.g. polyethylene glycol 1000 indicates its mean molecular weight. All polyethylene glycol polymers above the average molecular weight of 1000 are waxy solids.

4. Fractionated **palm kernel oil** or other suitable **hydrogenated vegetable** oil may also be used provided the melting point of suppositories is not more than 37° C.

Moulds :

Moulds are used to prepare suppositories. They are of glass, aluminium, or stainless steel. While cleaning the mould, it should not be scraped, otherwise it gives uneveness to the surface. It must be washed with cleansing solution followed by hot water. Moulds are in two halves and fixed with a tight screw. There are various capacity moulds ranging from 1 g to 8 g. After receiving the new set of mould, it must be calibrated first and then used.

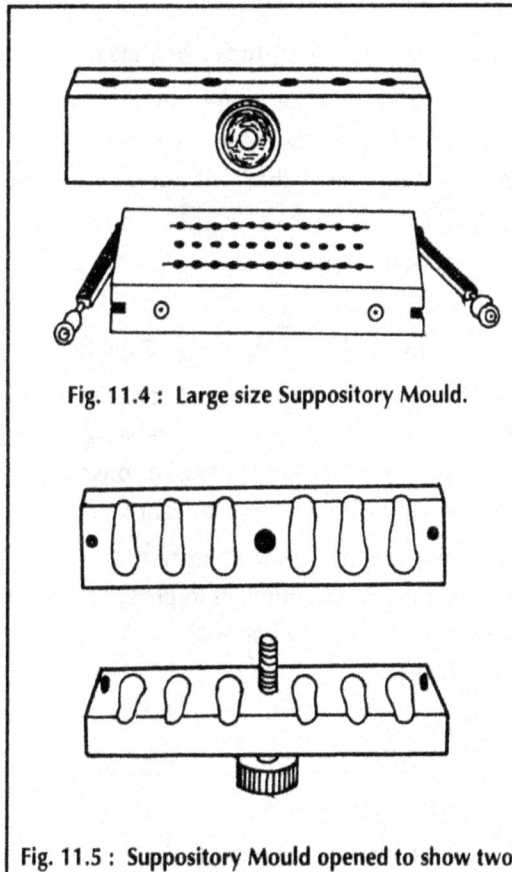

Fig. 11.4 : Large size Suppository Mould.

Fig. 11.5 : Suppository Mould opened to show two halves

Displacement value :

The volume of suppository for a particular mould is fixed and uniform. But the weight of suppositories from one and the same mould differs from substance to substance. This is because of the difference of densities. Hence, it becomes necessary to calculate displacement value of a base for medicament.

The quantity of predicament that displaces one part of cocoa butter or any other base is called the **displacement value** of that medicament with respect to cocoa butter or that base.

The capacity of mould is determined by using the base alone. The capacity and weight of the suppository (with base alone) is permanently recorded. The suppository are weighed and average weight recorded. The approximate volume of liquid base is found out by melting the suppository. Approximate volume is calculated from the weight and density of the medicament.

The displacement value of liquids may be taken as one for practical purposes. When medicament for each suppository is less than 30 mg there is no point in calculating displacement value and making correction, since no serious error occurs.

Table 11.1
Displacement values of some medicaments with respect to cocoa butter

Substance	Displacement value
Alum	2.0
Boric acid	1.5
Chloral hydrate	1.5
Hydrocartisone	1.5
Ichthammol	1.0
Iodoform	4.0
Resorcinol	1.5
Tannic acid	1.0
Zinc oxide	5.0
Zinc sulphate	2.0

Mould may be calibrated in imperial or metric system. 15 grain mould may be considered as equivalent to 1 g mould.

To calculate the quantity of base required, the following procedure is followed :

Suppose ten suppositories of zinc sulphate are to be prepared in a 15 grain mould. The displacement value of zinc sulphate is 2. Each suppository is required to contain 5 grains of zinc sulphate.

i.e. 10×5 = 50 grains of zinc sulphate

$\frac{50}{2}$ = 25 gr Cocoa - butter will be displaced, by zinc sulphate.

The mould capacity is 15 grains for 10 suppositories the total quantity of cocoa butter would be

10×15 = 150 grains

But zinc sulphate displaces 25 grains of cocoa butter.

Therefore, the actual quantity of cocoa butter required would be 150 − 25 = 125 grains.

Actual weight of each suppository will be

125 + 50 = 175 /10 = 17.5 grains

Determination of the displacement value

Prepare and weigh 10 suppositories containing cocoa butter (base) alone.

Let this weight be = 'a'

Prepare and weigh 10 suppositories containing medicament.

Let this weight be = 'b'

b − a = 'c' grains weight of drug

a − c = 'd' will be weight of cocoa butter displaced c grains of drug.

Displacement value = $\frac{c}{d}$

Example

Prepare 10 suppositories each containing 30 per cent of Iodoform.

Let the weight of 10 suppositories of cocoa butter be

= 108 Grains (a)

Let the weight of 10 suppositories containing 30 % iodoform be

= 140 gr (b)

Quantity of cocoa butter in 140 gr

= $70 \times \frac{140}{100}$ = 98 gr (c)

Quantity of Iodoform

= $30 \times \frac{140}{100}$ = 42 gr (d)

Cocoa butter displaced by 42 grains of Idoform

= 108 − 98 = 10 gr

Therefore, the displacement value of Idoform

= $\frac{42}{10}$ = 4.2

Preparation of Suppositories or pessaries :

(1) Lubricate the mould with a liquid or mixture of liquids different from the base i.e. any lubricating fluid that will not be absorbed by the mass, i.e.

Soft soap	14.3 g
Glycerin	14.3 g
Alcohol rectified	71.4 ml

This solution may be used for lubrication of mould. For cocoa butter or gelato-glycerin base suppositories, liquid paraffin, olive oil or arachis oil may be used as lubricant for mould.

While preparing suppository mass, calculate the ingredients sufficient to produce one or two extra number of suppositories.

Example 1 :

℞

    Alum   0.35 g

Send 4 suppositories

Use : One gramme mould

    Quantity for 5 suppositories

    Alum 0.35 × 5 = 1.75 g

The displacement value of Alum is 2.

Thus 1.75 / 2 = 0.875 g of cocoa butter will be displaced.

Total quantity of cocoa butter will be (1 gm mould)

    1 g × 5 = 5 g − 0.875 g = 4.125 g

Method of Preparation

Keep the mould in ice or freezer for cooling.

Lubricate the mould with soap, glycerin and alcohol mixture.

Melt the calculated quantity of cocoa butter in a dish. When 3/4 of base melts, remove the dish from water bath. Pour half of the base on the required alum powder placed on the clean tile. Mix with spatula. Transfer it to dish and stir. If necessary, warm and stir to make the mass pourable. Fill each cavity to over flowing level.

Keep the mould in ice or freezer for half an hour. Remove the mould. Scrape off the excess mass by a sharp razor. Open the mould and remove the suppositories wipe off the excess of lubricant and wrap in butter paper. Keep the suppositories in box, label it.

Example 2 :

R_x

Bisacodyl	10 mg

Send 8 suppositories.

Label : Use one suppository before radiographic examination of the abdomen.

Since bisacodyl is less than 30 mg per suppository there is no need to calculate displacement value. Use 1 gm mould.

Use cocoa butter as base

Calculate for two extra

Amount of bisacodyl for 10 suppositories

$10 \times 10 = 100$ mg

$(10 \times 1g) - 100$ mg $= 9.9$ g of cocoa butter

Method

Follow the method given in exercise 1 above.

Example 3 :

R_x

Indomethacin	100 mg

Send 4 suppositories.

Label : Insert one in morning and night.

Use 2 g mould.

Use combination of Polyethylene glycol 1540 (7 parts) and polyethylene glycol 6000 (3 parts) as a base

Calculate for 5 suppositories

Indomethacin	500 mg
Polyethylene glycol 1540	7 g
Polyethylene glycol 6000	3 g

Method

Melt over a water bath polyethylene glycols in a dish when about 3/4th of base is melted, remove from water bath, add indomethacin and stir to make homogeneous mass. Pour into previously cooled mould. Allow to remain in ice or freezer for half an hour. Remove the suppositories and wipe off lubricant. Wrap in butter paper and keep the suppositories in a box.

Example 4 :

R_x

Eucalyptus oil	0.5 ml

Send five suppositories using cocoa butter as base.

Use 2 gm mould.

Calculate for one extra

$0.5 \times 6 = 3$ ml. Eucalyptus oil

$(6 \times 2) - 3 = 9$ g cocoa butter

Method

Lubricate the mould. Cool it in ice or freezer.

Melt 9 g of cocoa butter over a warm water bath. Remove the cocoa butter from water bath when 3/4th of the base is melted. Cool a little. Add the oil and stir to make homogeneous mass. Fill the cavities of mould and then place in ice for thirty minutes. Remove the suppositories and wipe off lubricant. Wrap in butter prepare and keep in suppository box.

Glycerinated Gelatin

This is used as base for vaginal pessary. The vaginal pessaries weigh from 4 to 8 g. This base dissolves slowly in mucous secretion and releases the medicament.

The following formula is used to prepare glycerinated suppository base :

Purified water	10 g
Gelatin	20 g
Glycerin	70 g

Prepare 25 suppositories

Method

Add, gelatin in water and allow it to soak for ten minutes. Then mix glycerin with the above mass and heat it on a water bath until the gelatin is dissolved. Pour the material in 4 g mould. Cool in ice for thirty minutes. Remove the suppositories and wrap in butter paper. Keep it in suppository box.

Example 5 :

R_x

Tetracycline	100 mg
Amphotericin B	50 mg
Glycerinated base	q.s

Send 8 vaginal suppositories.

Label : Insert one every six hours.

Calculate for ten.

Tetracycline	$100 \times 10 = 1000$ mg
Amphotericin - B	$50 \times 10 = 500$ m g
Purified Water	04 g
Gelatin	08 g
Glycerin	28 g

Method

Mix tetracycline and amphotericin - B and add water to produce 4 gm. Mix gelatin and glycerin to above and heat at 40° C on water bath till the gelatin dissolves. Stirr the mixture and fill the cavities of 4 gm capacity mould. Cool by placing the mould in ice. Remove the suppositories. Wipe off the lubricant and wrap in butter paper. Keep the suppositories in box.

Example 6 :

R_x

Dibucaine hydrochloride	150 mg
Glycerinated gelatin	q.s.

Send 5 pessaries.

Calculate for seven

Dibucaine hydrochloride	1050 mg
Water	3.5 g
Gelatin	07 g
Glycerin	24.5 g

Use 4 gm mould

Method

Dissolve dibucaine hydrochloride in a little water. Add more water to weigh 3.5 g. Mix glycerin and gelatin with the above mixture and heat it on water bath to dissolve gelatin. Then stir the mixture and pour it in the previously cleaned lubricated mould. Keep it on ice for half an hour. Remove, wrap in butter paper. Keep the pessaries in a box. Put a label with a direction 'Use as directed.

Evaluation of Suppositories

1. **Appearance** : The B.P. states that when cut longitudinally and examined with naked eye, the internal and external surfaces of the suppository should be uniform in appearance. Compliance with this standard indicates satisfactory subdivision and dispersion of suspended materials.

2. **Uniformity of weight** : Twenty suppositories are weighed individually and the average weight determined. No suppository should deviate from the average weight by more than 5 per cent, except two may deviate by not more than 7.5 per cent.

3. **Melting range test** : For this test USP tablet disintegration apparatus is used and it measures the melting range of entire suppository. This test is actually a macromelting range test and consist of immersing the suppository in constant

temperature water bath at 37°C. The time required to melt the suppository or time required to disperse the suppository is measured.

4. Softening time test for rectal suppositories : This test is carried by using a special device which consists of a U-tube partially submersed in a electrically operated constant-temperature water bath. A constriction on one side of the tube holds the suppository in place. Temperature variation in water bath should not be more than 0.1 °C and maintained by thermostat.

On the top of the suppository, a glass rod is placed and the time for the rod to pass through the constriction is noted as the **"softening time"**. This can be carried out at temperatures from 35.0 to 37°C. This is regarded as quality control check and as a measure of physical stability of suppositories over time.

5. Breaking test : To measure the fragility or brittleness of suppositories breaking test is specially designed. The test is carried at body temperature i.e. 37°C. The suppository under test is placed in a dry chamber. The chamber is double walled and water of 37°C is passed through the chamber to maintain 37°C temperature. Suppository supports a disc which is attached to a rod. Another end of this rod is connected to other disc to which weights are put. In the beginning a weight of 600 of is applied and after every minute additional weight of 200 g is added and a point at which the suppository collapses is the breaking point of the suppository.

6. Distintegration : In this test suppository is subjected to a temperature of 36 - 38°C in a water bath and by placing in a very special container which has perforated ends. The water bath is stirred slowly to maintain the temperature and container is inverted below the surface every ten minutes.

Suppository is said to be disintegrated, if

(i) except insoluble powders it goes into solution.

(ii) disintegrated parts sink or rise through the perforation.

Unless otherwise specified in the monograph of a suppository, it must disintegrate within thirty minutes.

Glycerol suppositories B. P. take one hour for disintegration.

QUESTIONS

1. What are suppositories ? How do they differ from pessaries ? What are the advantages and disadvantages of suppositories over other dosage forms ?
2. Write a note on various bases and method used for preparation of suppositories.
3. What you know about
   (a) Various shapes of suppositories.
   (b) Displacement values of medicament.
   (c) Lubricants for suppository mould.
   (d) Ideal requirements of suppository bases
4. How suppositories are evaluated ?
5. State the importance of displacement value of suppository base. How it is worked out ?

●●●

CHAPTER 12: INCOMPATIBILITY IN PRESCRIPTIONS

DEFINITION

The undesired change taking place in the physical, chemical or therapeutic properties of the medicament, when two or more ingredients of a prescription are mixed together, is termed as incompatibility.

While handling a prescription containing combinations, many a times, problems associated with therapeutic, physical and chemical properties of the drugs, arise.

Incompatibilities are, therefore, grouped into three classes :

1. Therapeutic Incompatibility.
2. Physical Incompatibility.
3. Chemical Incompatibility.

1. Therapeutic Incompatibility : In this type, problems arise in combining drugs or dosages prescribed. It is the responsibility of a physician. However, it forms a part of the duty of this pharmacist to bring this problem to the notice of the prescriber.

2. Physical Incompatibility : In this type, mixing or combination of drugs produce, a preparation unacceptable in appearance or inaccuracy in dosage or immiscibility problems. For example, combination of oil and water presents a problem of immiscibility and this defect is corrected by emulsification. Eutectic mixture of powders is another example of physical incompatibility.

3. Chemical Incompatibility : In this type, two or more drugs react to give new compounds which may be toxic or inactive. Remedy lies in replacing one or more ingredients of the same medical usefulness, yet inert.

There are mainly two types of incompatibilities viz. Intentional where the prescriber wants that the prescription, be dispensed as it is and the Unintentional where the prescriber has inadvertently combined such drugs as to give unexpected results e. g. precipitation of drug, which is not what the prescriber wanted.

I. THERAPEUTIC INCOMPATIBILITY

Example 1

R_x

Codeine phosphate 0.5 g

Prepare 10 powders.

Label : One to be taken at bed time.

This is an example of over dosage. Probably, the physician intended to write 5 milligrams and yet prescribed 500 mg. of codeine phosphate. This prescription must be referred back to the prescriber.

Example 2

R_x

Tetracycline hydrochloride 250 mg

Send ten capsules.

Label : Take one capsule every six hours with milk.

In this prescription the dose is alright but the direction is wrong. Tetracycline is inactivated by calcium which is present in milk. Water replaces the milk.

Example 3

℞

Amphetamine sulphate	20 mg.
Ephedrine sulphate	100 mg.
Syrup	ad 100 ml

Let a mixture be made.

Label : Take 25 ml every four hours.

In this prescription there is a combination of two sympathomimitic drugs with additive effect and there is a need to reduce the dose of each, Refer back the prescription to the prescriber.

Example 4

℞

Acetyl salicylic acid	1.5 g
Probenecid	1.0 g

This is an example of antagonism between the two drugs. Both help in the treatment of gout being unicosuric agents. However, the combination leads to neutralization. Refer back the prescription to the physician.

Example 5

℞

Acetophenetidin	150 mg
Acetyl salicylic acid	200 mg
Caffeine	30 mg

Label : Take as directed.

Acetophenetidin is an analgesic and so is aspirin. Acetophenetidin depresses the C. N. S. This side effect is undesirable. Caffeine, a central stimulant is included to overcome the side effect of acetophenetidin. Incompatibility is intentional. Dispense as it is.

II. PHYSICAL INCOMPATIBILITY

Example 6

℞

Castor oil	15 ml
Water upto	60 ml

Make an emulsion

Label : Take at once.

This is a case of physical incompatibility. Oil and water do not mix. Emulsification corrects the incompatibility. Dispense as an emulsion.

Example 7

℞

Thymol	250 mg
Menthol	02 mg
Camphor	02 mg

Send five powders.

This is another example of physical incompatibility. The combination forms a eutectic mixture. Refer to the chapter no. 8 'Powders' and granules and dispense accordingly.

III. CHEMICAL INCOMPATIBILITY

All chemical incompatibilities must be corrected before the prescriptions are dispensed unless the prescriber wants that the incompatible combination be dispensed.

Classification of chemical incompatibilities could be done in three ways :

Classification based on chemical nature of reacting substances.

(a) Inorganic incompatibility
(b) Organic incompatibility
(c) Miscellaneous chemical incompatibility.

Chemical interactions between the drugs of prescription lead to chemical incompatibility. These incompatibilities include effervescence, precipitation, colour changes and at times formation of toxic substances. It is the duty of the pharmacist to correct the incompatibilities with, of course, the consent of the prescriber. At times, the incompatibility is immediately apparent and at other times, the changes occur at a slower rate and the incompatibility is not detectable immediately. It is a practice that such a delayed incompatibility be dispensed in such way that the prescription is used up before ten per cent of therapeutic, activity is lost.

1. Incompatibility of metals :

Many metallic salts are used to fill in prescription. Sodium and potassium salts are commonly used. Generally, precipitation occurs by way of incompatibility. Following example will illustrate it.

Example 8

R̥x

Sodium salicylate	10 g
Potassium iodide	02 g
Potassium bicarbonate	04 g
Water	100 ml

Label : Take 25 ml every four hours.

Type : Incompatibility of metals.

Sodium salicylate and potassium bicarbonate react and sodium bicarbonate is formed which is in excess of its solubility (1 in 10) and hence, precipitated. Solution also darkens due to the presence of salicylate in alkaline solution.

Correction : Refer back the prescription to the prescriber for his consent to dispense Potassium bicarbonate separately.

Generally, where a precipitate is expected to be formed, it is convenient to allow it to be formed in as dilute a solution as possible. In order to do this, dissolve the reactant in one portion of the vehicle and the second reacting substance in second portion of the vehicle and then mix the two portions.

When it is expected that an indiffusible precipitate is going to be formed, mix compound powder of tragacanth to one of the reacting substances to one portion of the vehicle and the second reacting substance to the second portion of the vehicle and then mix the two portions.

Example 9

R̥x

Morphine hydrochloride solution I. P.	0.5 ml
Aromatic spirit of ammonia	ad 30 ml

Label : Take 15 ml. before bed time.

Type : Incompatibility of alkaloidal salt with alkaline substances.

In the present prescription there are 20 mg of morphine hydrochloride present in 2 ml of solution. It has been found that as long as the morphine hydrochloride concentration is 8 mg per 30 ml there will be no precipitation of morphine hydrochloride by alkaline substance such as aromatic spirit of ammonia. Hence, the incompatibility is apparent and not real.

Follow the procedure of a simple mixture.

Example 10

R̥x

Tincture opium	10 ml
Aromatic spirit of ammonia	ad 30 ml

Label : Take 15 ml at bed time.

Type : Incompatibility of alkaloidal salts with alkaline substances.

Tincture opium contains equivalent of 20 mg of anhydrous morphine per 2 ml. The solubility of anhydrous morphine is 1 in 18 and therefore, morphine will be precipitated. Secondly, the maximum dose of tincture opium is 2 ml. While each dose contains 5 ml of tincture in the above prescription. The prescription is to be referred back to the prescriber.

However, the student should prepare the mixture as it is, observe the precipitation and then discard it.

Example 11

℞

Quinine hydrochloride		1.2 g
Sodium salicylate		2.4 g
Water	ad	100 ml

Label : Take 25 ml every four hours.

Type : Incompatibility of alkaloidal salt with salicylate and benzoates.

A precipitate of quinine salicylate is formed. Use method for precipitate yielding combinations.

Example 12

℞

Quinine bisulphate		10 g
Dilute sulphuric acid		20 ml
Potassium iodide		3.0 g
Water	ad	200 ml

Label : Take 20 ml every four hours.

Type : Incompatibility of Quinine acid sulphate with soluble iodides.

The quinine bisulphate is dissolved in diluted, (with equal volume of water) sulphuric acid. The potassium iodide is dissolved in the remaining quantity of vehicle and the two portions mixed and the mixture dispensed.

The mixture is quite clear at first and remains so for three days after which it begins to deposit olive green scales which is the outcome of *Herapath reaction for Quinine*. The sequence of events are as follows :

Dilute sulphuric acid liberates hydroiodic acid (HI) from potassium iodide, hydroiodic acid is partly oxidised to give iodine. The free Iodine + Hydroiodic acid and quinine sulphate then combine to form a compound called *Herapathite*. There is no problem if the mixture is given for a period of less than three days. Over 3 days it is better to send potassium iodide in one bottle and other ingredients in another bottle.

2. Incompatibility of Soluble Iodides :

Example 13

℞

Solution of ferric chloride		02 ml
Potassium iodide		03 g
Water	to	120 ml

Label : Take as directed by physician.

Type : Incompatibility of Iodide with ferric salt.

Ferric chloride solution reacts with Potassium iodide to liberate free iodine which is undesirable. The remedy lies in replacing ferric chloride with ferric ammonium citrate. Refer back to prescriber.

Example 14

℞

Solution of ferric chloride		02 ml
Potassium iodide		03 g
Potassium citrate		06 g
Water	ad	120 ml

Label : Take as directed.

Incompatibility as in Example 13 is avoided by inclusion of alkali citrate which helps in converting ferric chloride to an organic compound before addition of potassium iodide. The organic iron compound does not liberate iodine from potassium iodide.

Method

Dissolve potassium citrate in part of the vehicle then add solution of ferric chloride and then potassium iodide. Make up the volume and dispense.

Example 15

℞

Solution of ferric chloride		02 ml.
Sodium salicylate		03 g
Water	ad	150 ml

Label : Take one tablespoon full every four hours.

Type : Incompatibility of soluble salicylate with ferric salt.

Ferric salicylate is formed which is insoluble and indiffusible hence use method for indiffusible precipitate.

3. Incompatbility of soluble salicylates and benzoates with acids :

Example 16

℞

Sodium salicylate		3.0 g
Quinine sulphate		600 mg
Dilute sulphuric acid		2.0 ml
Water	ad	150 ml

Label : Take as directed

Incompatibility (Example of tolerated incompatibility)

The sulphuric acid will precipitate salicylic acid from sod. salicylate.

Remedy; Sulphuric acid is included to dissolve quinine sulphate, omit sulphuric acid and a clear mixture will be formed.

Example 17

℞

Sodium salicylate		03 g
Syrup of lemon		15 ml
Water	ad	60 ml

Label : Take 15 ml every four hours.

Syrup of lemon contains citric acid which will precipitate salicylic acid from sodium salicylate.

Remedy

Replace syrup of lemon with simple syrup and 1 ml of Tincture lemon. This is an example of adjusted incompatibility.

4. Incompatibility concerned with liberation of Carbon di-oxide gas :

Some combinations yield carbon dioxide gas immediately and others very slowly. The combination when yield gas slowly, can break the bottle containing the mixture through explosion due to slowly built up pressure.

General remedy is to prepare the mixture in an open vessel allow the gas to escape and then bottle, the mixture. Where the reaction proceeds very slowly and gas is evolved slowly, methods such as using hot water or heating may be employed to hasten the formation and escape of gas in an open vessel.

Example 18

℞

Sodium bicarbonate		02 g
Borax		01 g
Glycerin		10 ml
Water	ad	50 ml

Type : Evolution of Carbon-dioxide gas
Method :

Mix all the ingredients in an open vessel. Allow carbon di-oxide to escape. Make up the volume and dispense.

5. Incompatibility of soluble barbiturates :

At times sodium salts of barbiturates are used in mixtures. These solutions are alkaline and, therefore, incompatibility occurs with ammonium salts and acids with precipitation of barbiturate.

Example 19

℞

Sodium phenobarbitone		120 mg
Ammonium bromide		01.2 g
Water	ad	100 ml

Label : Take 25 ml. every night.

Incompatibility :

Phenobarbitone is precipitated by ammonium bromide. Prepare as it is and observe indiffusible precipitate. Repeat the exercise by using sodium bromide and observe.

Dispense by using Compound powder of tragacanth.

Example 20

℞

Bismuth sub-nitrate	04 g
Kaolin pectin mixture	ad 50 ml

This combination forms a cake on standing. Refer back to the physician.

6. Incompatibility of Emulsifying agents :

℞

Phenol	0.5 g
Menthol	0.1 g
Tragacanth	0.5 g
Olive oil	50 ml
Lime water	ad 100 ml

Label : Take as directed by physician.

The free acids in olive oil form divalent soap with lime water. The divalent soap promotes w/o emulsion. While tragacanth favours o/w emulsion. Consult the physician and replace lime water with purified water, or omit tragacanth.

Example 21

℞

Chloral hydrate	250 mg
Send ten capsules	

Label : Take one at night

Incompatibility :

Capsules may collapse as the chloral hydrate softens gelatin capsules.

Remedy :

Send chloral hydrate in solution form. Alternatively use magnesium carbonate as a diluent and store in refrigerator.

Example 22

℞

Acriflavine 0.1 %	15 ml
Dakin's Solution	ad 100 ml

Label : Use as directed by physician.

The Dakin's solution is a source of chlorine. The chlorine reacts with acriflavine and changes the colour of the solution. Consult the prescriber and omit Dakin's solution.

EXERCISE

1. Define incompatibility. How incompatibilities are classified ? Describe one example each.
2. Define intentional and un-intentional incompatibility, state the importance of intentional incompatibility by quoting suitable examples.
3. Quote two examples of alkaloidal incompatibility alongwith remedial solutions for both.
4. State the examples of incompatibility forming carbon-dioxide in formulation. Suggest suitable method to overcome the same.

BIBLIOGRAPHY

1. **Aulton Michael E.** Editor, Pharmaceutics - The Science of Dosage Form Design, First ELBS Edition 1990. Longman Group (FE) Ltd. U.K.

2. **Rawlins E. A.** Editor, Bentley's Textbook of Pharmaceutics. First ELBS Edition 1979. Reprint 1984 Bailliere Tindall, Eastbourne, East Sussex, U.K.

3. **Alfonso R. Gennaro**, Editor Remington's Pharmaceutical Sciences, 18th Edition, 1990, Mack Publishing Company, Easton, Pennsylvania, 18042 U.S.A.

4. **Herbert A. Lieberman, Leon Lachman**, Editors, Pharmaceutical Dosage Forms - Tablets Volume I, 1980, Marcel Dekker, Inc., 270, Madison Avenue, New York 10016.

5. **S. J. Carter**, Editor "Cooper and Gunn's Tutorial Pharmacy" Sixth Edition. CBS Publishers and Distributors, Shahdra, Delhi 110032, by arrangement with Pitman London.

6. Pharmacopoeia of India Supplement 1975, Ministry of Health, Government of India, Delhi.

7. Government of India, Ministry of Health and Family Welfare "Pharmacopoeia of India" Volumes I and II, Third Edition 1985, 1996. Controller of Publications, Delhi.

8. Addendum (I) to Pharmacopoeia of India. Third Edition 1989, Ministry of Health and Family Welfare Government of India, Delhi.

9. Addendum (II) to Pharmacopoeia of India. Third Edition of 1991, Ministry of Health and Family Welfare Government of India, Delhi.

10. **Dittert L.W.**, "Sprowl's American Pharmacy"; J.B.Lippincott Co. 1974. Philadelphia.

11. **Ansel H.C.** "Introduction to Pharmaceutical Dosage Forms" 1969, Lea and Febiger, Philadelphia.

12. **Martin E. W.** "Dispensing of Medication", Mack-Publishing Co. 1971, Pennsylvania.

13. **Lawrence C. A., Block SS**, "Disinfection, Sterilisation and Preservation" 1968, Lea Febiger, Philadelphia.

14. **Gunn-C and Carter S. J.** "Dispensing for Pharmaceutical Students", Pitman London.

15. The Standards of Weights, Measures Act, 1976.

16. The Standards of Weights and Measures (Packaged commodities) Rules 1977.

17. The Standards of Weights and Measures (Enforcement) Act 1985.

18. **E. G. Thomesseni** "Modern Cosmetics" Universal Publishing Corporation.

19. **Balsam M. S. and E. Sagarin,** "Cosmetics Science and Technology" Vol. 1, 2, 3, John Wiley and Sons N. Y.

20. **Breuer M. M.** "Cosmetic Science" Vol. 1, 2, Academic Press. London.

21. **"Wilkinson J. B. and.Moor R.** J.Harry's Cosmeticology" ; Longman Scientific and Technical, England, 7th edition.

22. **Badger W. L. , and Banchero J. T.,** Introduction to Chemical Engineering, Mc Graw-Hill Series in Chemical Engineering 1957, Mc Graw Hill Book Company Singapore.

23. **Leon Lachman, Herbert A. Lieberman, Joseph L.Kanig,** Z, The Theory and Practice of Industrial Pharmacy Third Indian Edition,1990, Vargiese Publishing House Dadar, Mumbai 400014.

24. The Ayurvedic Formulary of India, Part I, First Edition, 1978, Department of Health, Ministry of Health and Family Planning, Delhi.

25. The Indian Pharmacopoeial List - 1946, Department of Health, Govt. of India, Delhi Published by Manager of Publications, Delhi.

26. **E.A. Rawlins Bentley's** Text Book of Pharmaceutics, 1977, 8th Edition, ELBS &Bailliere Tindall, Cassell & Collier, Macmillan Publishers Ltd. London,WCIR 4SG.

27. **Arthur Owen Bentley** A Text book of Pharmaceutics, Third Edition, Reprint 1934 Bailliere Tindall & Cox. London W.C. 2

28. Pharmacopoeia of India Supplement, 1975, Ministry of Health, Govt. of India, Delhi.

29. European Pharmacopoeia, Volume I, 1969, Council of Europe Maisonneuve S.A. 57 Sainte-Ruffiene-France.

30. European Pharmacopoeia, Volume II, 1971, Council of Europe Maisonneuve S.A. 57 Sainte-Ruffiene-France.

31. European Pharmacopoeia Supplement to Volume II, 1973, Maisonneuve S.A. 57 Sainte-Ruffiene-France.

32. The International Pharmacopoeia, Third Edition,Volume I 1979, WHO Geneva.

33. The International Pharmacopoeia, Third Edition,Volume II, 1981, WHO Geneva.

34. **Martin A. N.** 'Physical Pharmacy' Lea Febiger Philadelphia.

35. **Dr. P. K. Sanyal** A Story of Medicine and Pharmacy in India., 1964; 34/1 G Ballygauge circular Road Kolkota 19.

36. Govt. of India, Ministry of Heath, New Delhi, Pharmacopoeia of India" 1955, 1966, 1985 and 1996 editions.

37. British Pharmacopoeia Veterinary 1977, first edition. Her majesty's stationary office London.

38. British Pharmacopoeia 1993. Her Majesty's stationary office. London.

39. United States Pharmacopoeia USP XV

    United States Pharmacopoeial Convention Inc.

    12601 Twinbrook Parkway rockvilfe Md 20852.

40. British National Formulary.

    Pharmaceutical Society of Great Britain and British Medical Association London.

41. **Brians Furniss Vogel's** Text book of Organic Chemistry, Fifth ELBS Edition 1989. Longman group (FE) Ltd. U.K.

42. Addendum (I) to Pharmacopoeia of India, Fourth Edition, 1996, Ministry of Health and Family Welfare Government of India, Delhi.

43. **James E. F. Reynolds**, Editor Martindale Extra Pharmacopoeia, 30th Edition, 1993 published by The pharmaceutical Press London.

44. **W. A. Poucher**, Editor Poucher's perfumes, cosmetics and soaps. Volume 3, 9th edition, 1993 published by Blackie Academic and Professional, an imprint of Chapman and Hall London, U.K.

45. **M. L. Schroff**, Editor Principles of Pharmacy part I, Published by Five Star Enterprises, Kolkota.

46. **Leon Lachman**, Editor, The Theory and Practice of Industrial Pharmacy, Third Edition, 1987, published by Vargese Publishing House, Mumbai.

47. **Harkishan Singh** : Editor, Pharmaceutical Education, Vol. II, 1998. published by Vallabh Prakashan Delhi.

48. **S. J. Carter**, Editor, Copper and Gunns Dispensing for Pharmaceutical students, 12th edition, 1987 published by CBS Publisher and Distributor, Delhi.

49. **B. M. Mithal** Editor, A Text Book of Pharmaceutical Formulation, 5th edition, reprint, 1996, published by Vallabh Prakashan, Delhi.

INDEX

A
Abrasive action, 91
Abrasive, 90
Agnivesa, 1
Alligation, 45
Antioxidants, 114
Apothecaries system, 43
Aristotle, 1
Avoirdupoise system, 43
Ayurveda, 1
Ayurvedic pharmacopoeia, 13

B
B.P.C., 6
Bandages, 79
Bases for suppositories, 128
Bentonite, 106
Bhardwaj, 1
Bibliography, 141
Breaking test, 133
British natural formulary, 7
British pharmacopoeia, 5

C
Cachets, 18, 19, 83
Calandria evaporator, 62
Calcination, 55
Capsules, 18, 19
Carbomer, 107
Catgut sterilization, 82
Catgut, 81
Charaka samhita, 1
Charaka, 2
Chemical incompatibility, 136
Clark's rule, 31
Collodions, 103
Colorants, 94
Community prescriptions, 28
Cowling's rule, 31
Cracking, 113
Creaming, 113
Creams, 18, 20
Crenutation, 48
Crepe bandage, 80

D
Decoction, 72
Desication, 56
Development of pharmacy, 2
Dhanwantari, 1
Digestion, 72
Dilling's rule, 31
Dioscorides, 1
Dispensing balance, 25
Dispensing of medication, 17
Displacement value, 129
Distillation destructive, 57
Distillation fractional, 59
Distillation molecular, 58
Distillation steam, 58
Distillation vacuum, 59
Distillation, 56
Domette, 80
Dosage forms, 17, 18
Doses veterinary, 39
Doses, 32, 38
Dryer fluidized bed, 65
Dryer tray, 64
Dryer vacuum, 66
Dryers, 62
Drying equipments, 64
Drying theory, 63
Drying, 62
Dusting powders, 18, 19

E
Ear cones, 18, 20
Ear drops, 18, 19
Egg yolk, 122
Elegance, 114
Elixers, 18, 93
Emulgents, 111
Emulsifying agents, 111, 115
Emulsion types, 111
Emulsions, 18, 111
Enemas, 103
European pharmacopoeia, 8
Eutectic mixtures, 84
Evaluation of emulsions, 123
Evaluation of gelanicals, 71
Evaluation of suppositories, 132
Evaporation, 60
Evaporator calandria, 62
Evaporator multiple effect, 61
Evaporator types, 61
Evaporators, 61

Explosive mixtures, 85
Exsiccation, 55
Extra pharmacopoeia, 12
Eye drops, 18, 19

F
Fabric, 79
Fibres, 79
Film evaporator, 62
Flannel, 80
Flaroons, 94
Flocculation degree, 110
Flocculation, 109
Fluidised bed dryers, 65
Fractional distillation, 59
Freeze drying, 67
Fried's rule, 31
Fusion, 55

G
Galen, 1
Galenical pharmacy, 2
Galenicals evaluation, 78
Galenicals, 71
Gargles, 18, 19, 95
Gelatin, 116
Glycero-gelatin base, 128
Granules, 18, 19, 83
Gums, 116

H
Hand homogieniser,
Heat processes, 55
Heating baths, 68
Herbal powders, 90
Hippocrates, 1
History of pharmacy, 1
HLB values, 116
HLB, 115
Hospital prescriptions, 29
Hygroscopic sub, 85
Hypertonic solutions, 48
Hypotonic solutions, 48

I
Ignition, 55
Imperial system, 43
Implants, 18, 20
Imports of drugs, 4
Incompatibility alkaloids, 137
Incompatibility iodides, 138
Incompatibility metals, 137

(145)

Incompatibility types, 135
Incompatibility, 135
Indian addendum, 11
Indian pharma codex, 14
Indian pharmacopoeia, 9
Indian pharmacopoeial list, 9
Infusion, 71
Injectables, 21
Inscriptions, 22
Insufflation, 89
International pharmacopoeia, 8
Ionising sub, 116
Irish moss emulsion, 121
Isotonic solutions, 47

Jellies, 18, 20

Latin terms, 25, 28
Ligatures, 81
Linctus, 93
Liniments, 97
Liquids, 21
Lotions eye, 102
Lotions, 18, 19, 100

M

Maceration double, 72
Maceration triple, 72
Maceration, 72
Measures capacity, 44
Measures of weight, 44
Melting range test, 132
Methyl cellulose, 106, 122
Metric system, 44
Mixtures, 18
Mortar pestle, 118
Moulds, 129
Mouth washes, 18, 94

N

Nasal bougies, 18, 20
Nasal drops, 18, 19, 97
NF, 14
Non-ionizing sub, 116

O

Ointments, 18, 20
Oleo resins, 118, 122

P

Paraselsus, 2
Paratonic solutions, 48

Parenterals, 18
Pastes, 18, 20
Percentage solutions, 49
Percolation reserved, 75
Percolation vol. liquids, 76
Percolation, 74
Pessaries, 18, 20, 127
Pharmacopoeia British, 5
Pharmacopoeia dublin, 5
Pharmacopoeia edinburgh, 5
Pharmacopoeia, 5
Pharmacopoeial codex, 6
Phase inversions, 112
Phase separation, 114
Pills, 18, 19
Plasters, 18, 20
Posology, 29
Powder types of, 84
Powders bulk, 86
Powders dusting, 89
Powders effervescent, 88
Powders efflorescent, 84
Powders hygroscopic, 84
Powders tooth, 90
Powders wrapping, 85
Powders, 18, 19, 83
Prescribing, 28
Prescription checking, 25
Prescription handling, 25
Prescriptions, 22
Preservatives, 114, 117
Proof spirit, 51

Reserve percolation, 95

S

Sedimentation, 123
Semisolids, 21
Sifting, 84
Signature, 23
Silversion emulsifier, 119
Snuffs, 18, 19
Snuffs, 89
Solids, 21
Sox-helation, 76
Spatuation, 83
Spirits, 77
Stabilizers, 94
Stoke's law, 113
Sublimation, 56
Superscription, 22
Suppositories bases, 128
Suppositories, 18, 20, 127

Surfactants, 90
Surgical aids, 79
Surgical dressings, 79
Sushrutha samhita, 1
Sushrutha, 1
Suspensions, 18, 105
Sutures absorbable, 81
Sutures non-absorbable, 81
Sutures, 80
Syrup diabetic, 93
Syrup, 93

Tablet triturates, 83
Tablets, 18, 19
Theobroma oil, 128
Therapeutic incompatibility, 135
Thickening agents, 106, 114
Throat paints, 18, 95
Tooth powders, 18, 19
Tragacanth, 106
Trituration, 83
Tumbling, 84

Uniformity of weight, 132
Unorganised drugs, 73
USP NF, 7
USP, 7

Vehicles, 93
Veterinary doses, 39
Viscosity, 123, 124
Volatile oils, 85, 118

Water aromatic, 93
Water, 93
Wedge theory, 115
Weights and measures, 43
Wet gum method, 117
Wetting agents, 107, 117
Wrapping of powders, 85
Wrapping suppositories, 128

Young's rule, 31

Zeta potential, 124

●●●

www.ingramcontent.com/pod-product-compliance
Lightning Source LLC
Chambersburg PA
CBHW080342170426
43194CB00014B/2660